AF804860

Building a Human-Centred Infrastructure for Sustainable Industry 5.0 in Asia

Priyanka Agarwal · Nitendra Kumar ·
Sanjeev Bansal · Yeliz Karaca
Editors

Building a Human-Centred Infrastructure for Sustainable Industry 5.0 in Asia

palgrave
macmillan

Editors
Priyanka Agarwal
Department of HR, OB
& Psychology
Amity University
Noida, Uttar Pradesh, India

Sanjeev Bansal
Department of Decision Sciences
Amity University
Noida, Uttar Pradesh, India

Nitendra Kumar
Department of Decision Sciences
Amity University
Noida, Uttar Pradesh, India

Yeliz Karaca
Department of Mathematics
and Department of Neurology
University of Massachusetts (UMass)
Worcester, MA, USA

ISBN 978-981-95-0416-9 ISBN 978-981-95-0417-6 (eBook)
https://doi.org/10.1007/978-981-95-0417-6

© The Editor(s) (if applicable) and The Author(s), under exclusive license to Springer Nature Singapore Pte Ltd. 2025

This work is subject to copyright. All rights are solely and exclusively licensed by the Publisher, whether the whole or part of the material is concerned, specifically the rights of translation, reprinting, reuse of illustrations, recitation, broadcasting, reproduction on microfilms or in any other physical way, and transmission or information storage and retrieval, electronic adaptation, computer software, or by similar or dissimilar methodology now known or hereafter developed.
The use of general descriptive names, registered names, trademarks, service marks, etc. in this publication does not imply, even in the absence of a specific statement, that such names are exempt from the relevant protective laws and regulations and therefore free for general use.
The publisher, the authors and the editors are safe to assume that the advice and information in this book are believed to be true and accurate at the date of publication. Neither the publisher nor the authors or the editors give a warranty, expressed or implied, with respect to the material contained herein or for any errors or omissions that may have been made. The publisher remains neutral with regard to jurisdictional claims in published maps and institutional affiliations.

Cover illustration: Maram_shutterstock

This Palgrave Macmillan imprint is published by the registered company Springer Nature Singapore Pte Ltd.
The registered company address is: 152 Beach Road, #21-01/04 Gateway East, Singapore 189721, Singapore

If disposing of this product, please recycle the paper.

Preface

The dawn of Industry 5.0 leads to a transformative shift in the way societies and industries evolve—putting humans at the heart of innovation. *Building a Human-Centred Infrastructure for Sustainable Industry 5.0 in Asia* brings together interdisciplinary perspectives to understand fundamental shifts required in governance, education, digital infrastructure, and ethical innovation.

The chapters in the book reflect collaborative insights from researchers, practitioners, and academicians. Together, they offer case studies, frameworks, and policy recommendations to chart out a roadmap for sustainable Industry 5.0 infrastructure in Asia.

Chapter Advancements and Enhancements in the Era of Industry 5.0 talks about Advancements and Enhancements in the Era of Industry 5.0 especially in the context of rapidly changing economies like those in the Asia-Pacific region and aims to offer insights into creating a future where innovation benefits both industry and society as a whole.

Chapter PV Glasses in Human-Centred Infrastructure for Sustainable Development Fostering SDG 11 Supporting Industry 5.0 aims to be a pioneering step to future sustainable infrastructure meeting the demands of SDG 11—Sustainable Cities and Communities. It talks about Smart energy management systems with special reference to PV Glass Technology as Human-Centred Infrastructure—A Paradigm for Industry 5.0.

Chapter Empowering the Workforce for Industry 5.0: Skills, Training, and Human-Centric Transformation explores the critical dimensions of workforce empowerment of Industrial 5.0. The chapter addresses the uniqueness of Industry 5.0 compared to Industry 4.0 by signalling its importance in sustainability, personalization, and inclusivity. This chapter also identifies real gaps to be filled through skills development, focusing on reskilling, upskilling, and the need for lifelong learning.

Chapter Human-Centric Pedagogies in the Age of Intelligent Systems: Envisioning the Future with Industry 5.0 explores how educational systems might use human–machine collaboration to foster empathy, adaptability in addition to improving learning results. In an era increasingly influenced by intelligent systems like artificial intelligence, robotics, and data analytics, this chapter examines the rise of human-centric pedagogies that prioritize emotional intelligence, creativity, ethical reasoning, and critical thinking.

Chapter Digital Banking Transformation in Asia: Fintech, Inclusion, and Future of Industry 5.0 delves into the adoption of innovative fintech practices like artificial intelligence (AI), blockchain, etc., which are the key driver towards building a human-centred infrastructure aligned with the goals of Industry 5.0 in Asia.

Chapter Banking Outreach and Usage Pattern of Banking Services in Bihar examines the banking outreach and evaluates the status of financial inclusion to measure its progress. It also tries to identify the reasons behind financial exclusion and finally aims to evaluate the impact of banking outreach on other economic indicators.

Chapter Indian Rupee: An Emerging Trading Currency of Asia and Across in Industry 5.0 investigates the globalization of the Indian Rupee and the resultant consequences on Asia and the global economy. It aims to analyse issues of the historical context of the internationalization of the Rupee, undertake a comparative approach to India and other countries' policies, examine its impact on developing economies in Asia and the rest of the world, study its role in the flows of trade and investments, and understand the dynamics behind the currency's upsurge.

Chapter Role of the Finance Sector in Building a Human-Centered Infrastructure for Sustainable Industry 5.0 in Asia explores the critical role of the finance sector in facilitating the transition to Industry 5.0 in Asia, which prioritizes human-centred, sustainable, and resilient infrastructure. The chapter highlights practical examples and case studies from across Asia, underscoring the interplay between finance and technology in achieving sustainable growth. Key theoretical and managerial implications are presented to inform policymakers, industry leaders, and researchers about the strategic alignment of finance with human-centric industrial transformation.

Chapter Can Green Technologies, Renewable Energy Sources and Circular Economy for Sustainable Industry 5.0? An Explorative Study using Cross-Case Analysis investigates the integration of green technologies, renewable energy sources, and the circular economy within the framework of Sustainable Industry 5.0 through a cross-case analysis methodology. The objective of this chapter is to examine how these elements can synergistically contribute to sustainable industrial practices, addressing critical challenges such as climate change and resource depletion.

Chapter Green Accounting and its Role in Industry 5.0 Sustainability Framework examines the prospect of artificial intelligence in optimizing DeFi protocols, risk management, and process of decision-making based on present research and industry practices. It investigates means to enhance the efficiency, security, and accessibility of decentralized financial systems.

Chapter Enhancing Employee Wellbeing in Industry 5.0: A Comprehensive Literature Review emphasizes the need for flexible, ethical, and inclusive aligned work models. The chapter further discussed the evolving role of employee wellbeing within the context of Industry 5.0, examining the key themes such as emotional intelligence, personalized work experiences, machine collaboration, and sustainable and ethical work practices.

Chapter Women-Led Social Enterprises in Industry 5.0: Pioneering Sustainable and Inclusive Growth in South Asia discusses women's entrepreneurship which has become a key factor in the growth of South Asian Countries. It identifies the association between social entrepreneurship and women-empowered development projects to solve social challenges. It outlines recommendations for increasing and supporting women's social entrepreneurial initiatives, thereby increasing the positive effects of such enterprises on women's communities in South Asia. The chapter goes further and explores how these businesses try to encourage social and economic integration by relevant examples.

Chapter Human-Centered Infrastructure for Sustainable Smart Cities in Industry 5.0 incorporates cutting-edge technologies to improve urban living and environmental sustainability, human-centred infrastructure for sustainable smart cities. The chapter aims to facilitate sophisticated technology and human collaboration by integrating a robust infrastructure that blends digital and physical elements.

The book presented here is not merely an academic or technical exercise; it is a call to action. As we navigate the complexities of climate change, automation, demographic shifts, and ethical governance, the choices we make today will define the sustainability and inclusivity of tomorrow's industrial systems.

We hope that the insights serve as a compass and a source of inspiration for governments, industries, academic institutions, and organizations across Asia. By embracing the ethos of Industry 5.0, Asia can lead not only in technological innovation but in building a future that is truly sustainable, inclusive, and profoundly human.

Let us commit ourselves not just to smarter industries, but to better societies!

Noida, India
Noida, India
Noida, India
Worcester, USA

Dr. Priyanka Agarwal
Associate Professor—HR, OB & Psychology

Dr. Nitendra Kumar
Assistant Professor—Decision Sciences

Dr. Sanjeev Bansal
Addl. Pro Vice-Chancellor, Dean—Faculty of Management Studies, Director—Amity Business School, Professor—Decision Sciences

Dr. Yeliz Karaca
Associate Professor, Department of Mathematics and Department of Neurology

Acknowledgements

The Book *Building a Human-Centred Infrastructure for Sustainable Industry 5.0 in Asia*, represents not merely an academic endeavour, but a collaborative journey shaped by the insight, encouragement, and generosity of many individuals and institutions to whom we owe a profound debt of gratitude.

We extend heartfelt gratitude to Amity Business School, Amity University Uttar Pradesh for providing an enabling research environment, access to key academic resources and continuous institutional support.

We acknowledge the diligent work of all the reviewers whose constructive feedback ensured the quality and rigour of the chapters.

Our Special thanks to entire team of Springer Nature team specially Ms. Aparajita Singh and Ms. Madhu Bala Vindan, for giving us the opportunity to collaborate.

We extend our thanks to the contributors for active participation, sharing their deep expertise and commitment to academic excellence. Their perspectives are embedded in each page of the book.

Last but certainly not least, we would like to provide extended thanks for all the fellow members who made a difference in this Journey.

What is presented here is a moment in a larger conversation, one that we hope will continue to evolve, challenge, and inspire. Wishing all the readers an interesting reading!

Contents

List of Contributors

Garima Agarwal ACED, Amity University Uttar Pradesh, Noida, India

Priyanka Agarwal Department of Human Resource Management, Amity Business School, Amity University, Noida, Uttar Pradesh, India

Shweta Anand School of Management, Gautam Buddha University, Greater Noida, UP, India

Vikas Batra Department of Economics, Indira Gandhi University, Meerpur, Rewari, Haryana, India

Jayanta Chakraborti Global Institute of Business Studies, Bangalore, India

Alka Chaudhary Amity Business School, Amity University Uttar Pradesh, Noida Campus, India

Rashi Chaudhary G L Bajaj Institute of Management and Research, Greater Noida, India

Mouripa Deb Symbiosis Institute of Business Management, Noida, Symbiosis International (Deemed University), Pune, India

Lakhwinder Kaur Dhillon Department of Accounting &Finance, Amity Business School, Amity University, Noida, Uttar Pradesh, India

Kiran Jindal Mehr Chand Mahajan DAV College for Women, Chandigarh, India

Malla Jogarao School of Maritime Management, Indian Maritime University, Visakhapatnam, India

Nitendra Kumar Amity Business School, Amity University, Noida, UP, India

Vandana Kumari Department of LSW and PMIR, A N College, Patna, Bihar, India

Sushil Kumar Maurya GNIOT MBA Institute Greater Noida, Greater Noida, India

Annu Mishra Department of Computer Science and Engineering, Sharda School of Computing Science and Engineering, Sharda University, Greater Noida, India

Reeta Mishra IILM University, Greater Noida, UP, India

Vivekanand Pandey Amity University, Patna, Bihar, India

Ritesh Ravi Bihar Institute of Public Administration and Rural Development, Gaya, Bihar, India

P. Sanjeevi School of Maritime Management, Indian Maritime University, Visakhapatnam, India

Neeraj Kumar Sharma Greater Noida Institute of Technology, Greater Noida, India

Sandeep Sharma Swiss School of Applied Sciences for Economics and Management at Lausanne, Lausanne, Switzerland

Bhupinder Singh Department of Computer Science and Engineering, Sharda School of Computing Science and Engineering, Sharda University, Greater Noida, India

Pooja Singh G L Bajaj Institute of Management and Research, Greater Noida, India

Preeti Singh Daulat Ram College, University of Delhi, New Delhi, India

Rushina Singhi Nilkamal School of Mathematics, Applied Statistics and Analytics, SVKMs NMIMS, Mumbai, India

J. Siva Durga Prasad School of Maritime Management, Indian Maritime University, Visakhapatnam, India

Purwa Srivastava Jaypee Institute of Information Technology, Uttar Pradesh, Noida, India

Sadhana Tiwari Department of Operations and Supply Chain Management, GNIOT Institute of Management Studies, Greater Noida, Uttar Pradesh, India

Padmesh Tripathi Delhi Technical Campus, Greater Noida, UP, India

Ritu Wadhwa Amity Business School, Amity University, Uttar Pradesh, Noida, India

List of Figures

List of Tables

Banking Outreach and Usage Pattern of Banking Services in Bihar

Can Green Technologies, Renewable Energy Sources and Circular Economy for Sustainable Industry 5.0? An Explorative Study using Cross-Case Analysis

Women-Led Social Enterprises in Industry 5.0: Pioneering Sustainable and Inclusive Growth in South Asia

Advancements and Enhancements in the Era of Industry 5.0

Neeraj Kumar Sharma, Sushil Kumar Maurya, and Sandeep Sharma

1 Introduction

Before the inception of the Industrial Revolution, production was governed by customary practices that were aligned to mass production but inefficient at mass reduction, causing production to multiply possibly by eight times. The Second Industrial Revolution was the dawning of technological developments in the areas of electricity, mechanics or machine and mechanics, and other electronics already in place. Frederick Taylor's book 'Principles of Scientific Management' was instrumental to the development of Industry 2.0. The shift to partial automation started

N. K. Sharma
Greater Noida Institute of Technology, Greater Noida, India
e-mail: sneeraj@yahoo.com

S. K. Maurya (✉)
GNIOT MBA Institute, Greater Noida, India
e-mail: maurya.k.sushil@gmail.com

S. Sharma
Swiss School of Applied Sciences for Economics and Management, Lausanne, Switzerland
e-mail: saneeps@yahoo.com

© The Author(s), under exclusive license to Springer Nature Singapore Pte Ltd. 2025

P. Agarwal et al. (eds.), *Building a Human-Centred Infrastructure for Sustainable Industry 5.0 in Asia*,
https://doi.org/10.1007/978-981-95-0417-6_1

the beginning of Industry 3.0, enhancing the dependability of the process and, of course, the efficiency of the production. CNC technology, which created further technological switch and opportunities for further volume changes in both practical applications, of machining processes increased.

The advances in Industry 3.0, which involved modernizing manufacturing systems and upgrading existing solutions, was the basis for Industry 4.0 [04]. With Industry 4.0, Information and Communication Technology (ICT) began to be integrated into manufacturing processes allowing for real time data analysis and improving strategic decision making. This use of ICT has allowed for improved efficiencies, increased flexibility, and improved resilience to market changes, ushering in a new era of digital manufacturing [1].

Industry 5.0 merges human intellectual capacity with machine capacity and productivity, melding artificial intelligence into humans' ways of work in a factory. Designed with Industry 4.0 issues in mind, Industry 5.0 is a people-focused approach and aims to make human beings met's the societal issues. There are enabled advanced systems that include interoperable sensor network, intelligent home automation, co-bots, and other smart technologies. Co-bots rehabilitate human operator efficiency and precision by placing humans at the center of the manufacturing and industrial process and empowering humanity's role with those that are more meaningful and purposeful.

2 Need for the Study

The promises of emerging can be hopeful for progress but equally stressful for the sustainability of todays industries. The advancement of Industry 4.0 technologies is parallel to increased resources, environmental harm, and greater need for energy. The continual automation and industry developed by Industry 4.0 has also raised concerns about falling safety standards. While sustainability has the potential to be regarded as significant within Industry 4.0, there are still concerns regarding limited benefits for African countries, indicating that the industrial revolution might not be any beneficial in low- and middle-income countries. There are examples showing that Industry 4.0 can provide such energy efficiency opportunities but we still want to make judiciousness to follow sustainable development goals.

The combination of machinery and resources in Industry 4.0 facilitates the generation of large amounts of data and raises new challenges, especially in quality control. Quality management sectors can use the data to manage the quality of products coming from manufacturing processes. Besides the data coming from processes, the data can support better virtual quality management and operational virtual supply chains.

Industry 5.0 is developing to overcome some limitations of Industry 4.0 in the 4th industrial revolution. Industry 4.0 has made advances, but it lacks the comprehensive framework in order to meet specific European goals, causing a technological monopoly. Industry 5.0, is to consider anticipated disruptions like the COVID-19 pandemic, and is implementing sustainability in a much more holistic way. Industry 4.0 highlighted sustainability, but faced challenges and inefficiencies. Industry 5.0 focuses mostly on and also individual participation (to other areas of interaction and sustain well-being). Industry 5.0 focuses on creating a harmonious balance between technology and the human being's creative and ethical side.

3 Research Objective

Industry 4.0 has greatly enhanced supply chain management, automated manufacturing processes, and increased the use of cyber-physical systems, via intelligent manufacturing systems, intelligent products, IoT, AI, cloud computing, sophisticated supply chain solutions. However, while these technologies are valuable, human workers are often overlooked and that creates a wide variety of issues. Furthermore, additional cybersecurity and privacy security challenges are created as the pace of digital technology accelerates, which exposes companies to a larger array of data security threats. In addition, the added complexity of connecting technical systems and potential functional disruption to supply chain operations all requires dedicated management focus.

This study adopts a review-based approach to investigate the role of Industry 5.0 with innovative technologies including; Industry 5.0 both does provide a number of technologies to help overcome the limitations and to better examine obstacles found in Industry 4.0. Industry 5.0 offers opportunities for new technological advancements to be implemented to overcome the barriers found in Industry 4.0 and the focus will be on the array of technologies in Industry 5.0, to be examined for opportunities for coexistence and collaboration with human operators. This study hopes to identify how Industry 5.0 technologies can mitigate the complexity and instability that arose during the Industry 4.0 epoch.

With the rise of digital technologies in use across virtually all industries, the ability for organizations to manage security threats—data breaches, privacy issues etc.—is compounded due to the nature of integration complexities as it relates to tech systems and managing supply chains. It is evident, that organizations require a greater level of cybersecurity and a strengthened chain supply approach.

This research utilizes a review perspective to examine the aforementioned challenges that accompanies Industry 4.0, as Industry 5.0 highlights its technological advances. Industry 5.0 not only exposes numerous cutting-edge technologies, but can be either part of, or help overcome the challenges of Industry 4.0. Therefore, the main goal of this study is twofold, to identify and analyze the challenges of Industry 4.0, and to then explore the broad range of technologies for Industry 5.0 and assess their possibilities for application and integration with physical labor. Ultimately for this study, it is about exploring Industry 5.0 technologies to see how they could potentially overcome the challenges faced in Industry 4.0.

4 Research Methodology

This study takes a review-based approach and uses seventy-four literature reviews to thoroughly analyze the required methodologies and data.

5 Industry 4.0

Merging industries have become a prominent topic of discussion for new academics focused on cutting costs, managing resources and assets, and improving production efficiency and product quality—which coincide with the core objectives of Industry 4.0. Manufacturing more than ever has been slow to modify its decline; however, AI enables options for combining the uses of AI with the principles of Industry 4.0 so that manufacturing can be enhanced. The extent to which AI can be integrated into manufacturing operations has been shown to reduce costs in production and other product-related problems as evidenced in multiple research projects.

Artificial intelligence (AI) refers to a variety of applications across but not limited to safety automation, strategic planning, operational control and monitoring, predictive analytics and diagnostics, informed decision-making, and data-driven algorithm development. These applications are essential to achieving the industry goals to replicate product processes, improve factor efficiency, error, and change management, and increase product efficiency. Imaging for AI also allows for machine learning, data analysis, problem identification, and solution development. AI has a tremendous impact on the improvement of meeting high customer expectations.

Technology driven by artificial intelligence (AI) alters industry practices, enhancing maintenance and inspection procedures, monitoring operating activities, improving industrial processes, controlling services and process, and helping to implement changes.

In the area of Industry 4.0, AI-powered methods have at least the following benefits:

Predictive Maintenance: The predictive algorithms powered by artificial intelligence can help prevent machinery failures before they occur, which can reduce downtime for the plant as well as repair and maintenance costs. By checking and analyzing trends and anomalies in the data it collects from the equipment sensors, predictive algorithms allow for early notifications for maintenance to be completed before losing productivity and economic costs of unforeseen interruptions. These predictive maintenance technologies also increase equipment longevity and lifespan.

Quality Control Improvements: AI supports the real-time monitoring and assessment of company's production standards, therefore enhancing the ability to determine defects and deviations from set standards. AI uses advanced data analytics and machine learning algorithms to detect patterns and anomalies very rapidly in the manufacturing process so that deviations may be identified and fixed to maintain the production process within accepted standards and therefore yield lower defect rates—better product quality, increase operational productivity, increase customer satisfaction.

Supply Chain Management: AI applications can recommend sales forecasts, optimize inventory levels, and help manage production logistics to deliver goods on time while reducing waste. These applications are able analyze past performance and current trends to help organizations make more efficient supply chain decisions.

Operational Efficiencies: AI is capable of analyzing data that has been collected from many sources to identify constraints and inefficiencies in manufacturing processes and activities and to suggest opportunities for improvements.

Efficiency Reductions in Energy Usage: AI can increase the amount of energy used by manufacturing processes, leading to major cost and environmental savings.

Customization and Flexibility: AI can allow for customization of products during manufacturing and more flexibility to meet specific needs of customers.

Enhancement of Safety and Security: AI can enhance safety by monitoring conditions in workplaces to identify potential hazards, and can enhance cyber security.

Data Driven Decision Making: AI collates and interrogates vast amounts of data, leading to data-driven insights and informed strategic decision making.

Management of various branches using intelligent systems; coordination of activities using monitoring capabilities. Notifications about errors or issues, and creating virtual experiences to observe branches in a variety of locations. (incl measures for control of branches).

Constant analysis and integrated monitoring can lead to identifying issues before errors are made, meaning potential management costs are reduced.

Scenarios can now be replicated by AI, thus optimizing the conditions to improve system performance.

Quickly able to identify patterns, and predict the future, AI can enhance management of systems and reduces costs, while optimizing use of human resources and system characteristics.

This comprehensive review paper outlines the technologies and approaches to formulate AI strategies in the scope of Industry 4.0, considering the salient role of AI and the challenges surrounding the implementation of AI in Industry 4.0. As the global society awaits the impacts from the Fourth Industrial Revolution (4IR) primarily driven by technology innovation, the interactions of artificial intelligence and Industry 4.0 are receiving increasing scrutiny. Growing research is exploring how can this revolution help us decrease poverty, positively impact infrastructure, and achieve the Goals for Sustainable Development [2].

The partnership of artificial intelligence and its technologies within the industry sector produces efficiencies in both manufacturing and supply chain management. There is a range of research by Rezazadegan and Sharifzadeh [3] and Corti et al. [4] which focuses on aspects of data management, application of big data, and quality control in specific aspects of Industry 4.0. Yet, there is still a demand for a broader rationale which incorporates aspects such as design aspects, a more holistic perspective of quality management at the manufacturing phase, and the challenge of data and systems management on a national or national scale.

This research is important because it provides a brief guide and a complete architectural viewpoint of the role of AI in Industry 4.0. In addition, it provides a taxonomy on the application of AI in Industry 4.0. It categorized integration modes, instruments, evaluation methods, and criteria for Industry 4.0. This approach was intended to improve the understanding and structured implementation of AI technology in industry, resulting in greater efficiency, innovation, and competitiveness.

6 Challenges of Industry 4.0

Industry 4.0 is often called the fourth phase of industrial evolution; this phase has many newly invented technologies within manufacturing and industrial sectors. While providing many opportunities, it also has a number of challenges that organizations must address. Below are the main challenges associated with Industry 4.0.

Security Issues:

Cyber Security Risks: Industry 4.0 has increased connectivity and reliance on digital systems, increasing organizations vulnerability to cyber threats. It will be a challenge to protect their networks, data, and ways of communicating.

Data Privacy: Industry 4.0 has increased organizations reliance on data which raises important issues concerning the protection of sensitive data and compliance with data privacy laws. The industries collect, store, and analyze large amounts of data to make better decisions and improve efficiencies; by protecting the confidentiality, integrity, and availability of the data, organizations have to employ alternative cybersecurity controls to comply with legislation and protect the trust of stakeholder stakeholders.

Interoperability:

Integration of Technologies: Industry 4.0 involves the integration of many technologies from various technologies that include IoT devices, AI, and robotics. Different technologies from different vendors have a large risk that they may not work together.

Skilled Workforce Shortage:

Skill Gap: Surrounding the adoption of some cutting-edge technologies is a technological skill gap. Companies are often put in the position of trying to improve the skills of qualified employees to adopt these advanced technologies because of the small number of currently-skilled professionals.

High Implementation Costs:

Huge Cost: Implementation of Industry 4.0 technologies relies heavily on up-front foundation costs (infrastructure, technology, and education of staff). It is a significant issue for many businesses, especially SMEs.

Change Management:

Cultural Change: Industry 4.0 is a cultural change that organizations will adopt; the change is towards a more data-based and technology-based organization. Employee and management resistance to this process often hinders the successful adoption of 4.0 practices.

Reliability & Downtime:

System Reliability: Reliability of interconnected systems is of the utmost importance; unexpected system downtime or failure can have a negative impact. Sustaining industry 4.0 systems' reliability and robustness is a constant challenge.

Regulatory Compliance:

Compliance to Standards: Keeping up with industry standards and regulatory requirements as technology changes quickly is a challenge. Organizations are tasked with knowing the latest industry regulations on data, cybersecurity, and other technologies.

Ethical Considerations: The use of AI automation also has ethical implications, including impacts on jobs, decision making processes, and use of technology responsibly. Organizations must carefully consider these ethical implications.

Data Management:

Data Tsunami: The sheer volume of data produced by Industry 4.0 makes it challenging to manage, analyze, and act on. Making sure that the quality and accuracy of data is a priority.

Environmental Considerations:

Sustainability: The increased use of technology and creation of electronic components raises environmental challenges. Finding the balance between digital communication and sustainability continues to be a challenge.

Solutions to these challenges require a holistic approach that embraces technology disruption, reskilling the workforce and that has a sound strategic plan. Organizations that navigate these challenges will benefit immensely from the opportunities presented by Industry 4.0.

7 Industry 5.0 Industry

Industry 5.0 marks a shift to bring human knowledge and experience back into industry and develop a collaborative relationship between human workers and machines to improve productivity through human innovation. The goal of Industry 5.0 is to improve waste management through Industry Upcycling building upon the technology of Industry 4.0 with added benefits including network sensor data analytics. Some of the key features of Industry 5.0 include Smart Additive Manufacturing to improve flexible manufacturing, **Predictive Maintenance** as a means of maintaining equipment, Hyper Customization that provides customers with product options to fulfill their own specific needs, Cyber-Physical Cognitive Systems that combine digital and physical areas for improved intelligent operations, and system of collaborative robots (COBOTs) that can successfully work adjacent to and with humans in a means of improving workflows and safety.

Intelligent Additive Manufacturing

The incorporation of Artificial Intelligence (AI) into the Additive Manufacturing field has enhanced its performance. Smart Additive Manufacturing encompasses three different levels [5].

Market Level The combination of cloud computing with Additive Manufacturing has allowed companies to provide 3D printing services over the internet. Customers can now access AM resources directly from the computer so they must carefully make decisions to ensure the accuracy of their printed component part [6].

System Level Cyber-Physical Systems (CPS) have a huge potential. CPS is available to develop a range of applications for different 3D printers target to process the data and optimize in real-time, providing a more efficient printing process. When confronted with issues, previous data is used to automatically tune and generate results [7]. Technology Level Developments in Information and Communication Technology (ICT), such as cloud computing, 5G networks, the Internet of things (IoT) and edge computing, support the ability to collect huge amounts of data, inclusively on an extreme scale. AI agents using efficient algorithms to analyse data, make decisions, plan and store huge volumes of data including data collection and data organisation. These developments expand the opportunities to look at and understand data in real-time, increasing decision making and operational efficiencies in various contexts.

Predictive Maintenance

Maintenance is a significant contributor to operating costs (15–60%) in production contexts. Predictive maintenance utilizes data collected from multiple sensors to estimate the life of an asset and schedule maintenance based on the condition of the equipment being maintained. This means that there would be a reduction in maintenance costs as well as a greater consideration of the human dimension, recognizing the importance of human consent to decisions made from predictive maintenance systems. Predictive maintenance is a multi-step process that includes signal processing, fault detection, prognosis, maintenance scheduling, decision-making, and actions.

Collaborative Robots

Collaborative robots or COBOTs are designed to work with human workers to perform repetitive or dangerous work. This enables human workers to focus on more complex and higher value work. Collaborative robots were developed to support the human worker, rather than replace them, executing the more monotonous and tiresome parts of the work process, and improve workplace safety and production. However, there are still many challenges to implementing COBOTs, including employee acceptance, design challenges that would allow humans and robots to work together, new software frameworks to support human–robot collaboration, and designing user interfaces.

Cyber-Physical Cognitive Systems

Cyber-Physical Cognitive Systems the broader trust autonomy many ethnic systems applied to provide digital, cognitive, and physical dimensions to contribute to a variety of applications. Cyber-Physical Cognitive Systems better inform decision-making, clarify placement of common products, and are used in highly regulated environments such as defense. The use of trusted autonomous systems has a socially constructive impact (i.e., helping the elderly; cultivating human assurance in robotic systems; improved performance during complex interaction; etc.) to those in their work setting and to their clients. In addition, cognitive cyber symbiosis enhances manufacturing reliability by empowering enhanced collaboration between humans and machines, using collaborative smart interfaces to establish connection to cognate effecting both human cognitive and human physical short- and long-term needs. The dual capability of human reasoning, and machine efficiency, also generate technological perspectives and solutions that are more effective and scalable.

Hyper Customization

Hyper Customization addresses the emerging need of consumers who want personalized, one-off products on demand using big data analytics and AI. Hyper customization takes advantage of robotic efficiency in production, combined with people's creative capacity to make mass-customized products. The evolution towards adaptive manufacturing capabilities is essential to hyper-customization and requires agile manufacturing. The concept of "Mass Individualization" relates to producing many personalized products for users with specific coherence to meet [discrete] needs of the users. This strategy would require modular product designs, open architecture systems, and developed manufacturing systems to maximize flexibility [8–14].

Industry 5.0 Mitigating Industry 4.0 Obstacles

Industry 5.0, appropriately addresses many of the problems posed by Industry 4.0. Some of these problems include.

Supply Chain Issues

Supply Chain 4.0 is about utilizing the cutting-edge strategies and technologies to optimize supply chain functions, focusing on personalized production, increased transparency, an increase in adaptability, waste reduction, and more agile. In contrast, Supply Chain 5.0 aims to combine human intuition with technology, utilizing the improvements offered by Supply Chain 4.0 and adding another tier to the system with customized development. Supply Chain 4.0 and 5.0 rely on similar types of technologies like the Internet of Things (IoT), artificial intelligence (AI), and blockchain technologies, Supply Chain 5.0 is approached as a more sophisticated manner by layering on enhancements on top of these technologies, particularly in terms of AI deployment and the usage of Collaborative Robots (COBOTs), which support a more interested and cooperative work environment. Lastly, an integral part Supply Chain 5.0's development is sustainability in supply chain operations, creating a supply chain that is a more efficient system but also environmentally friendly and socially responsible.

Data Security Challenges

The advancement of Industry 4.0 and increased use of the Internet of Things (IoT) has resulted in unprecedented levels of data theft, cyber-attacks, and security vulnerabilities, and the importance of data protection and authenticity cannot be overstated. Consequently, Industry 5.0 tackles these problems by providing blockchain technology as an additional decentralized layer to the Industrial Internet of Things (IoT).

This provides a seamless manner to combine data from veritable sources together in a Smart Manufacturing context, in addition, the decentralized feature of blockchain can play a role in reducing inconsistences within the network, making it easier to resolve errors through these interactions, and, as a result, improve reliability and integrity of the network.

Along with providing an improved level of data integrity and trust, the introduction of Smart Contracts using blockchain technology, scales the autonomy of Industry 5.0 systems. This reduces the amount of intermediary (middlemen) contact in transactions, as well as the need to retain extensive manual documentation (which increases recordkeeping costs). That means the addition of the Smart Contracts will minimize cost of transactions from the intermediary parties and cost of recordkeeping. Also, the implementation of resilient manufacturing strategies can improve data security in Industry 5.0 context since sensitive and confidential IoT data is a serious concern. Resilient strategies could improve the security requirements of the manufacturing systems to respond better to threats and vulnerabilities, in-stead of waiting for the rights to try and respond [15–17].

Technical Integration Challenges

Industry 4.0 presented challenges with the ongoing digitization of technologies. In comparison, Industry 5.0 has a human orientation, where human creativity is coupled with machine precision to enhance productivity and performance. It contributes to enhanced product quality by using robots to complete repetitive tasks [8].

Human Resource Challenges

Industry 4.0 began the automation of traditional production processes. Now Industry 5.0 highlights the importance of making humans the center of everything, especially with improving human–machine interactions. Forming this relationship is important, especially when using collaborative robots or COBOTs employed besides human workers to achieve certain tasks. By maintaining this relationship, worker enhanced efficiency occurs and pushes for more strategic and value-added tasks, along with predictive maintenance with the goal of preventing equipment failure on a proactive basis to sustain operational effectiveness [02].

Technology Improvements Under the Umbrella of Industry 4.0 and Applications

In Industry 4.0, Industry 5.0 connected to several technological improvements to are beneficial in manufacturing processes to increase efficiencies and allow for more smart decision making. Technology is listed here is the major improvements in Industry 4.0 and its applications:

1. **Internet of Things (IoT):**

   The Internet of Things (IoT) connects devices to the internet, allowing them to collect and share data. In manufacturing, IoT leverages connectivity to monitor equipment and production processes in real time.
2. **Big Data and Analytics:**

   Big data analytics can process large amounts of data from IoT devices and provide valuable insights, predict when things will need maintenance, and improve manufacturing processes.
3. **Artificial Intelligence and Machine Learning:**

   Artificial Intelligence (AI) and Machine Learning (ML) provide machines the ability to learn from the data they are processing, thus improving their ability to predict and make decisions. Inside of manufacturing, AI can be used for a variety of tasks. For example, to ensure products are correct quickly, AI is used in quality control to find and fix problems and ensure product quality. AI uses data from sensors and machines for predictive maintenance to help manufacturers predict when a breakdown may happen so it helps reduce downtime while minimizing repair costs. AI can also be used to improve manufacturing efficiency and productivity, as it analyzes performance data for inefficiencies and helps users provide recommendations to improve the process.
4. **Robotics and Automation:**

   Robots and advanced automation systems perform tasks humans would typically do, increasing efficiency, reducing mistakes, and improving production speed.
5. **Cyber-Physical Systems (CPS):**

   Cyber-Physical System (CPS) integrates computer-based algorithms with physical components to create “smart” systems. In manufacturing, CPS allows production processes to be monitored, managed, and synchronized in near real-time for efficiency and increased productivity.

6. **Augmented Reality (AR) and Virtual Reality (VR):**

   Applications: AR and VR are immersive technologies used in manufacturing applications for training, maintenance, and simulating complex processes.

7. **3D Printing (Additive Manufacturing):**

   Uses: 3D printing refers to a process for creating three-dimensional objects via the printing of successive layers of materials. 3D Printing assists with rapid prototyping, customized manufacturing of products, and minimization of material waste.

8. **Blockchain Technology:**

   Application: Blockchain ensures secure, transparent and auditable transactions. Supply chain management can benefit from blockchain to provide increased transparency and trust for stakeholders.

9. **Cloud Computing:**

   Cloud computing encompasses a scalable, flexible computing infrastructure, enabling data storage, processing, and analysis capabilities to more easily support collaboration and provide access to resources from almost anywhere. Cloud computing allows organizations and/or individuals to utilize applications and services that are hosted on shared and remote servers, rather than utilizing large hardware and software platforms in-house. The cloud provides elasticity, as the data storage, processing, and other computing functions can alter based on fluctuating workloads, and provide variable amounts of compute resources on demand. The ability to scale and minimize costs can enhance organizational productivity and improve operations.

10. **Edge Computing:**

    Edge computing processes data close to its point of origin—such as IoT devices—reducing latency and improving real-time decision-making ability. This method simplifies the handling of data because it reduces the requirement for data to be transferred back and forth to centralized data centers, and therefore delivers faster outcomes and results.

11. **5G Technology:**

    5G technology allows for faster, more reliable communications between devices, providing access to low-latency use cases in manufacturing, like robotics and real-time data monitoring.

12 **Digital Twin Technology:**

    Digital twins act exists as virtual counterparts of real-to-life systems or products, allowing the ability to simulate, observe, and predict the performance of the physical asset.

The technologies mentioned here are all part of a movement towards Industry 4.0 pointing to the smart handshake between advanced digital technology and smart manufacturing to establish new avenues to identify, meet, and adapt to customer and market requirements, increase productivity, and support competitive rationale in the global economy.

8 Results and Discussion

The transformation of the industrial sector has gone from generating electricity by steam to fully automated electricity generators with the introduction of Industry 4.0. It has overcome many obstacles particularly in logistics and supply chain issues because it is now possible to track products to an exact location and predict market trends accurately. Industry 4.0 has improved efficiency in production, created opportunities for customization, and improved flexibility in operations. Despite the benefits of Industry 4.0, the obstacles and challenges to adoption and implementation remain with the complexities associated with various technologies, concerns about data and cybersecurity, management issues, and the need for the workforce to adapt to a new and more digital workplace. There remains a need for continual innovation and advancement in the industry to be able to fully utilize and capitalize on the advancements and capabilities of industry 4.0.

Industry 5.0 is a future advancement that will represent an important change with a focus on human-centric system and new advanced technologies like predictive maintenance, extreme personalization, cyber-physical cognitive systems, and collaborative robots (COBOTs) are a few of the advances which will overcome the restrictions of industry 4.0 in combinations of human ingenuity with machine accuracy. COBOT collaboration is important, and will enable humans to work seamlessly with machines.

Although there are benefits associated with Industry 5.0, it also introduces challenges for industries while implementing COBOTs. These COBOTs need to be integrated as early as possible in the production system design, as there are challenges associated with design (considering COBOTs will need to work with humans while ensuring safety, efficiency and collaboration) and there is added complexity involved with the design, as well as making necessary changes to improve the production system designs based on the COBOTs' capabilities as well as limitations. It is important to recognize and consider above mentioned challenges as Industry 5.0 is responsible for advancing productivity, innovation and people (increased human participation as automation streams across industry) within industry as they evolve beyond robots and mass production.

This research acts as an important reference within the industrial sector and academia to provide awareness of the challenges associated with Industry 4.0 and importantly, the potential that Industry 5.0 presents to counter such challenges. Understanding the specifics of Industry 4.0 technologies, their limitations, in particular to the advancements Industry 5.0 provides show opportunities for continual research and possible applications. This study recognizes that Industry 4.0 has resulted in industry facing the challenges, yet significant advancements in associated areas will lead to continued improvements in technology going forward, rather than design dead ends.

Industry 5.0 builds on the foundation that Industry 4.0 established and emphasizes human-centric approaches more heavily. Within the scope of supply chain management, Industry 5.0 maintains the benefits established by Industry 4.0, such as mass customization at its most extensive, while also embracing the use of collaborative robots (COBOTs). This ensures human input will remain important and viable in operations.

One prominent issue that was mentioned in Industry 4.0 was the issue of safety as it pertained to data breaches. Some research says the adoption of blockchain middleware could provide a means to mitigate vulnerabilities stemming from poor user data protection by employing a secure, decentralized method of conducting data transactions.

As previously shown, there is a systematic list of technologies that help make Industry 4.0 possible and each of its challenges that could work towards building on those technologies. Findings from the adoption of Industry 5.0 strategies may provide insight into how to develop pathways to overcome challenges posed in Industry 4.0, that could put us in a better position moving forward in developing more integrated, human-centered approaches to supply chain management and industrial development. This approach endeavors to retain the safety and processes associated with the technological advancements introduced in Industry 4.0 while enhancing degree of sustainability, innovation and collaboration in industrial development moving forward.

Future research projects in this area could look to solve security issues to support transition to an industry 5.0 approach. Better automation and deeper trust in automation that incorporates human behavior and needs could contribute to better collaboration between humans and human–robot collaboration as well. Also, the integration of 4D printing technology could be explored to improve printability, especially in terms of the prosthetics field. The growth of human–machine interactions and the development of intelligent control, such as enhancing pattern recognition algorithms, may also serve as productive channels for future research.

9 Limitations

With the emerging status of Industry 5.0 and the lack of widespread literature on the topic, exhaustively covering every aspect of its technology, implications, and data limitations represented a challenge, and these areas have not been covered thoroughly in this piece.

Moreover, because the technologies promoted in industry 5.0 have not been adopted yet and related systems are still being developed, the enhancements to the technologies can mostly only be assumed as a progression based on the literature we have to this point. Continuation of our research and documenting will be critical as we move forward with Industry 5.0 and its deployable technologies. It will provide a clearer understanding of the contributions to Industry 5.0 that will impact the industrial environment.

The unpredictability of future challenges and obstructions that Industry 5.0 technologies may have complicates the task of assessing their potential disadvantages and challenges. Consequently, there is an urgent need for future research initiatives to focus on the identification and understanding of future challenges related to the adoption and implementation of Industry 5.0 technologies. This would allow researchers and practitioners to make an important contribution to the continued development of Industry 5.0 through developing appropriate measures and actions to tackle challenges. This would facilitate the potential integration of these technologies into current industrial following efforts that suggest Industry 5.0 achieves its goal of a human-centric, productive, and sustainable future for industry.

10 Influence of Industry 5.0 on the Asia-Rim Region

The Asian region, has variants of industrial composition from those with more advanced economies to others with manufacturing potential, these countries will experience some, significant changes from Industry 5.0. While Industry 4.0 has attempted to introduce the automation and digitization, Industry 5.0 is focusing on the collaboration of human intelligence and emphasizing sustainability while taking into consideration humanity and technology working together. This will be important for Asia with their driving economies and socio-economic characteristics ....

1. **Human-Machine Collaboration (Labor-Intensive Economies)**

Countries such as, India, Bangladesh and Indonesia will still be largely dependent on labor-intensive economies. With collaborative robots (COBOTs), a key part of Industry 5.0 that promotes the efficiency of humans with machines and enhances productivity rather than taking it away, and of preserving jobs particularly in labor-intensive industries such as textiles, electronics, automotive etc. [18].

2. **Hyper-Customization and Export Agility**

Asia has become the predominant manufacturing container for the world, especially China and Vietnam, can provide organizations with cost-effective, customized, on-demand products before they have truly established an effective and timely system to get products to sites and transport to markets. Smart manufacturing technologies using AI, AR, and data analytics combined with customization and the "must-have" concept, can increase mass individualization with the ability to accelerate product throughputs in line with market demand [14].

3. **Workforce Development and Upskilling**

The human-centric vision that underpins Industry 5.0 can advance the challenge of a workforce that is digitally underprepared and anxious in many emerging Asian economies. By recognizing that human–machine collaboration will be an essential future focus, Nations can focus on reskilling to help workers perform tasks that require strategic thinking, ethical thought, creativity, and technical literacy [19, 20].

4. **Resilient and Sustainable Manufacturing**

The COVID-19 pandemic highlighted vulnerabilities and weaknesses in Asian supply chains. Industry 5.0 can offer predictive maintenance solutions, blockchain capabilities for secure tracking of supply chains, and smart contracts to strengthen resilience, and minimize environmental impacts within sustainability goals [17, 21].

5. **Leapfrogging Opportunities for Emerging Economies**

Despite having historically struggled to have modern and effective manufacturing infrastructure, Individuals and nations such as Nepal, Laos, and Cambodia have immunity to have the leapfrogging notion enabled by Industry 5.0, where they can bypass legacy infrastructure and immediately integrate advanced, decentralized, intelligent manufacturing on a level playing field. Edge computing capabilities integrated with cloud-based AI capabilities can facilitate a low barrier entry for recently emerged economies into competitive manufacturing frameworks [22, 23].

11 Conclusion

The above paper has taken a thorough look at the shortcomings of Industry 4.0, and shown how Industry 5.0 offers human-centric, resilient, and sustainable approaches to overcome these issues. Using advanced technologies, such as predictive maintenance, hyper-customization, cyber-physical cognitive systems, and collaborative robots (COBOTs), Industry 5.0 is not only about operational efficiency; it is also focused on enabling a talented workforce and sustainability practices [19, 24].

An interesting aspect of Industry 5.0 is the applicability to the Asia Continental Zone, where the marriage of human creativity with intelligent automation holds much potential. From labour-heavy economies such as India and Bangladesh, to advanced technology countries like Japan and South Korea, Industry 5.0 offers the capacity to meet workforce challenges [19, 20], produce for export-customized manufacturing [14], and build more sustainable and resilient supply chains [17, 21]. Furthermore, it offers leapfrogging opportunities for emerging Asian economies such that they can adopt new solutions without being anchored heavily to legacy systems [22].

While still in its infancy, Industry 5.0 provides a steppingstone towards a more inclusive industrial future—with it sustaining the benefits of Industry 4.0 but shifting focus back to human-centric values, agility, and the environment. Ongoing research is required to deepen understanding of technologies, address implementation approaches and contextualize the impact in any region, particularly in underrepresented locations. As part of the transition to Industry 5.0 in Asia, it will be necessary for preserving industrial competitiveness while at the same time advancing a sustainable people-centric agenda.

References

1. Dalenogare L.S., Benitez G.B., Ayala N.F., Frank A.G. The expected contribution of industry 4.0 technologies for industrial performance Int. J. Prod. Econ., 204 (2018), pp. 383–394
2. Mhlanga, D. Artificial intelligence in the industry 4.0 and its impact on poverty innovation infrastructure development and the sustainable development goals: Lessons from emerging economies?. Sustainability, 13 (11), (2021), pp. 5788. https://doi.org/10.3390/su13115788
3. Rezazadegan, R., & Sharifzadeh, M. Applications of artificial intelligence and big data in industry 4.0 technologies. Industry 4.0 vision for energy and materials: Enabling technologies and case studies, (2022), pp. 121–158
4. Corti, D., Purcell, L. A., Snell, G., & Veesler, D. Tackling COVID-19 with neutralizing monoclonal antibodies. Cell, 184 (12) (2021), pp. 3086–3108. https://doi.org/10.1016/j.cell.2021.05.005
5. Wang Y., Zheng P., Peng T., Yang H., Zou J. Smart additive manufacturing:

current artificial intelligence-enabled methods and future perspectives Sci. China Technol. Sci., 63 (9) (2020), pp. 1600–1611
6. Luo X., Zhang L., Ren L., et al. A dynamic and static data-based matching method for cloud 3d printing Robot. Comput. Integr. Manuf., 61 (2020), p. 101858
7. Tao F., Zhang H., Liu A., et al. Digital twin in industry: State-of-the-art IEEE Trans. Ind. Inf., 15 (2018), pp. 2405–2415
8. Maddikunta P.K.R., Pham Q.V., Prabadevi B., Deepa N., Dev K., Gadekallu ... T.R., Liyanage M. Industry 5.0: A survey on enabling technologies and potential applications J. Ind. Inf. Integr., 26 (2022), Article 100257
9. Koren Y., Shpitalni M., Gu P., Hu S.J. Product design for mass-individualization Procedia CIRP, 36 (2015), pp. 64–71
10. Leng J., Chen Z., Sha W., Ye S., Liu Q., Chen X. Cloud-edge orchestration-based bi-level autonomous process control for mass individualization of rapid printed circuit boards prototyping services J. Manuf. Syst., 63 (2022), pp. 143–161
11. Leng J., Chen Z., Sha W., Lin Z., Lin J., Liu Q. Digital twins-based flexible operating of open architecture production line for individualized manufacturing Adv. Eng. Inform., 53 (2022), Article 101676
12. Leng J., Zhou M., Xiao Y., Zhang H., Liu Q., Shen ... W., Li L. Digital twins-based remote semi-physical commissioning of flow-type smart manufacturing systems J. Clean. Prod., 306 (2021), Article 127278
13. Leng J., Liu Q., Ye S., Jing J., Wang Y., Zhang ... C., Chen X. Digital twin-driven rapid reconfiguration of the automated manufacturing system via an open architecture model Robot. Comput.-Integr. Manuf., 63 (2020), Article 101895
14. Jiang P., Leng J., Ding K., Gu P., Koren Y. Social manufacturing as a sustainable paradigm for mass individualization Proc. Inst. Mech. Eng. B, 230 (10) (2016), pp. 1961-1968
15. Leng J., Chen Z., Huang Z., Zhu X., Su H., Lin Z., Zhang D. Secure blockchain middleware for decentralised IIoT towards industry 5.0: A review of architecture, enablers, challenges, and directions Machines, 10 (10) (2022), p. 858
16. Leng J., Sha W., Lin Z., Jing J., Liu Q., Chen X. Blockchained smart contract pyramid-driven multi-agent autonomous process control for resilient individualised manufacturing towards industry 5.0 Int. J. Prod. Res. (2022), pp. 1–20
17. Leng J., Jiang P., Xu K., Liu Q., Zhao J.L., Bian Y., Shi R. Makerchain: A blockchain with chemical signature for self-organizing process in social manufacturing J. Clean. Prod., 234 (2019), pp. 767–778

18. Jamwal A., Agrawal R., Sharma M., Giallanza A., Javaid M., Haleem A., Singh R.P., Haq M.I.U., Raina A., Suman R. Industry 5.0: Potential applications in COVID-19J. Ind. Integr. Manag., 5 (04) (2020), pp. 507–530
19. Romero D., Bernus P., Noran O., Stahre J., Fast-Berglund Å. The operator 4.0: Human cyber–physical systems & adaptive automation towards human-automation symbiosis work systemsn IFIP International Conference on Advances in Production Management Systems, Springer, Cham (2016), pp. 677–686
20. Shamim S., Cang S., Yu H., Li Y. Management approaches for industry 4.0: A human resource management perspective 2016 IEEE Congress on Evolutionary Computation (CEC), IEEE (2016), pp. 5309–5316
21. Frederico G.F. From supply chain 4.0 to supply chain 5.0: Findings from a systematic literature review and research directions
22. Abbass H.A., Petraki E., Merrick K., Harvey J., Barlow M. Trusted autonomy and cognitive cyber symbiosis: Open challenges Cogn. Comput., 8 (3) (2016), pp. 385–408
23. Nahavandi S. Industry 5.0—A human-centric solution Sustainability, 11 (16) (2019), p. 4371
24. Jamwal A., Agrawal R., Sharma M., Giallanza A. Industry 4.0 technologies for manufacturing sustainability: A systematic review and future research directions

PV Glasses in Human-Centred Infrastructure for Sustainable Development Fostering SDG 11 Supporting Industry 5.0

Bhupinder Singh and Annu Mishra

1 Introduction

The photovoltaic (PV) glass technology integrated into human-centered infrastructure is a major milestone for sustainable urban development under the United Nations' 11th Sustainable Development Goal (SDG). This goal puts a spin on previous sustainable urban development, focusing on building inclusive, safe and resilient cities where technological innovation and energy efficiency are important triggers. Light glass, commonly known as a photovoltaic glass, integrates renewable-energy production into architectural design. This allows buildings to supply electricity while preserving their individual beauty as well as function. Industry 5.0 backs up these moves with a focus on human–machine collaboration, advanced manufacturing and sustainable development [1]. Yet, for all of this to be a reality, the widespread advance of light glass technology means strong

B. Singh (✉) · A. Mishra
Department of Computer Science and Engineering, Sharda School of Computing Science and Engineering, Sharda University, Greater Noida, India
e-mail: bhupindersinghlaw19@gmail.com

© The Author(s), under exclusive license to Springer Nature Singapore Pte Ltd. 2025

P. Agarwal et al. (eds.), *Building a Human-Centred Infrastructure for Sustainable Industry 5.0 in Asia*,
https://doi.org/10.1007/978-981-95-0417-6_2

regulatory and policy frameworks must ensure good publicity, capital turnover and standardization.

The application of PV glass in urban infrastructure has brought a creative approach to meeting energy needs while remaining sensitive to environmental protection. As people's built environments increasingly concentrate in cities, problems arise in their wake. These include issues concerning carbon emissions, natural resources and energy use inefficiencies which become unbearable. PV glass is a twin-purpose solution: creating clean energy as well as being used not only a structural component of windows, facades and roofs but also part carriage for the sunlight. Light glass allows natural daylight to wash indoor spaces, doing away with the need for artificial lighting. Light glass also picks up sunshine in between times and thus is a kind of power plant in miniature. This kind of synergy squares with the targets of SDG 11. It means making resources more efficient, slashing greenhouse gases while at the same time boosting cities' ability to remain resilient.

Urban infrastructure's bringing in of operationization of PV glass technology is not purely a technological problem but also a matter of governance. Appropriate regulations and policy framework not only act as a catalyst for it to be taken up and as gurantees of quality but also provide favorable financial returns to its stakeholders. Governments and regulatory bodies should provide clear guidelines on building codes, energy performance standards and architectural design standards that encourage the use of PV glass. For example, the European Union?'s Energy Performance of Buildings Directive (EPBD) stipulates energy efficiency standards for all new buildings, thus facilitates new technologies such as PV glass. Similar rules also apply in places like Japan, where the Building Energy Efficiency Standard embeds renewable energy generation in urban design. Governments set up financial incentives areimportant in overcoming the high cost of initial investment when it comes to PV glass technology. Policymakers should give reduced taxes, subsidies and low interest loans in order to make it easier for real estate developers, architects and developers to use PV glass systems [2]. In addition, governments can introduce feed-in tariffs and net metering policies allowing excess electricity produced by PV glass installations to be sold back to the grid. Such systems have been effective in promoting renewable energy in German and Chinese regions. Furthermore, public–private partnerships (PPPs) can play a key role in expanding PV glass projects, bringing together public sector resources with private-sector expertise and capital.

The other essential element of macroeconomic regulation is standardization. PV glass manufacturing, installation, and maintenance were all subject to the same technical standards across the board, so the product was stable, level is safe and efficient. International authorities have come up with rules for photovoltaic economies in their entirety on such aspects as performance targets and safety precautions. In order to facilitate exchange of technology as well as cross-border trade, national governments should take heed of these global standards in their own regulations. Certification systems and third-party audits can also help to increase consumer trust in PV glass products, by guaranteeing adherence to requirements for quality and performance.

In smart city projects, urban-planning policies must also place a strong emphasis on PV glass integration. Smart cities use technology, data modeling and sustainable design to create environments with every conceivable convenience but which still minimize their environmental footprints. PV glass is an integral part of this environment: it forms the backbone of smart buildings, self-generating electricity and giving relief from dependence on centralized power grids. Government regulators must require public infrastructure projects of the type commonly found in schools, hospitals and government buildings to include PV glass technology in order to set a model for private developers [3].

In the context of Industry 5.0, regulatory frameworks should pay attention to the integration of PV glazing technology with other advanced technologies such as Artificial Intelligence (AI), the Internet of Things (IoT), and machine learning. Smart energy management systems can reach the best performance from PV glass if they predict energy demand, monitor real-time production trends and match available energy storage solutions. Policy must encourage the integration of these types of technologies into PV glass systems and also guarantee that in the process data privacy is upheld, cybersecurity should be secure, and inter-operability exists among different technological platforms [4]. Sustainability reports and accountability are also important. For all urban development projects which involve PV glass technology, the government and regulatory bodies have to require that they provide a report on any sustainability factors applicable. Such reports would break down their lifecycle data, following the life of construction materials from extraction to final disposal. Publicizing the performance of policy-relevant indicators helps ensure accountability and make infrastructure project more consistent with global sustainability objectives.

Education for personnel and intro to PV glass technology are essential parts of successful policy implementation. The aspects include that a sound regulatory structure should also include such things as worker training, capacity building and publicizing knowledge about PV glass technology. Engineers, architects and city planners ought to have a profound understanding of the workings of PVB glass together with the design options and codes for such buildings. All stakeholders and users of these facilities can also have a stake in durable urban development projects [5].

Although the prospects appear encouraging, there are challenges to obtaining the widespread adoption of PV glass technology. Among these cost support and technological limitations must be considered; social disparities also have their weight (and should be taken into account). When a country is poor and runs short of resources, such problems become crucial. International cooperation can in fact serve to overcome these difficulties. To adapt PV glass technology for use in low-income areas it would help if international organisations like the United Nations Framework Convention on Climate Change (UNFCCC) and the Green Climate Fund (GCF) could extend their financial support and full technical aid.

Integrating PV glass technology into human-centred infrastructure is not only an important step towards achieving SDG 11, it supports Industry 5.0 as well. All the accompanying institutional and policy frameworks represent a supportive force ensuring both promotion of technology and financial feasibility, preservation of the environment [6]. By coordinating national policies with international standards and offering financial support, promoting extensive public–private partnerships, providing an education infrastructure and ways of increasing public awareness, governments can create an environment conducive for the adoption of PV glass building materials. PV glass technology will have the decisive role in the future of smart cities and resilient, energy-efficient urban areas supported by strict regulations. To solve the future energy crisis and make human settlement possible, it is the intersection of policy, technology, and human-centric design that holds the key. Ongoing appraisals are essential if infrastructure policies are to keep up with technological advances and evolving urban life. Governments need to set up a system for monitoring and evaluating current policies. That way they can see where things are going well and where improvements might be made.

In future, regulatory frameworks will need to be adaptable, remaining open to experiment in urban infrastructure projects [7].

2 PV Glass Technology as Human-Centered Infrastructure—A Paradigm for Industry 5.0: Types of PV Glasses and Their Applications

PV Glass technology has become a transformative solution for Industry 5.0, which values not only efficiency and innovation but also human-centered infrastructure and sustainability. With PV glass, buildings are able to employ their skins to generate and consume energy. Harnessing sunlight into architectural elements like windows, facades roofs changes a building into an ecosystem with sunlight cooperation [8]. This has great potential in terms of economic and environmental benefits for energy efficiency when building operations could be made to balance, or better yet, reduce overall costs without losing sight of design objectives or characteristics. It also makes it possible to build more functional spaces that do not compromise visual perceptions and structural integrity on the part of architects In the Industry 5.0 era, when we will be more concerned with the happiness and convenience of ordinary people than in the age of valuation efficiency and aesthetics utilized in connection all components for Society Harmony Environment-destroyed was to Carver geodesic domes assembled from sterilized stainless steel-tube components Occupational diseases were to Company Malady The oft lonely moon was now served up via Direct-when Huawei non-screen OLED technology touches your human iris, this virtually invisible experience results in visual feast [9].

Industry 5.0 requires fabricating human wholeness industrial environment, uv glass resonates with these values by bringing about carbon–neutral environments, slashing energy costs and enhancing people's comfort inside buildings with natural light regulation and thermal performance. There are basically two categories of PV glass technologies: crystalline silicon-based PV glass and thin-film PV glass. Crystalline silicon PV glass, produced from monocrystalline or polycrystalline silicon, features higher energy conversion efficiency that is suitable for applications requiring maximum energy output. Common applications include high-performance building facades and building integrated photovoltaic (BIPV) systems. On the other hand, thin-film PV glass, manufactured from materials like amorphous silicon (a-Si), cadmium telluride (Cdte), or copper indium gallium selenide (CIGS), offers aspects such as flexibility, lightweight properties and increased aesthetics elements. Although thin-film PV glass generally has lower energy conversion efficiency, it performs well under low-light conditions and can be seamlessly integrated into curved or irregular surfaces.

PV glass applications practicably cover residential, commercial or industrial, even rural life. With urbanization, PV glass is widely used in smart buildings for generating power as either a direct use device or part of the energy sourcing plus greenhouse gas emissions' decrease mechanism. Windows transparent solar energy, a major breakthrough made possible by PV glass research and development, take light capture to produce 2 types of effect [10]. It enhances the environmental and economic gains derived from both resources sunlight and nightscape lighting. In this way PV glass is also important for the construction of smart cities, providing energy-autonomous buildings which are capable of linking to peripheral energy vehicles from soon. And in strike-off buildings, PV glass integrates into the skylights, curtain walls, canopies achieving maximum energy efficiency as well as minimizing operation costs.

In industrial situations, PV glass is more and more going into use for facilities such as warehouses and manufacturing plants, hotels, data centers where they have a major energy requirements. By using PV glass in the roofing and facade systems of factories, companies can create substantial energy savings and get around those regulations which curb carbonous gas emissions. PV glass is also looking at applications in transportation infrastructure, for example bus stops train stations and airports where the independence from external power supplies, is key to smooth running of public services and even fire safety. The major advantages of PV glass technology is its ability to create sustainable urban ecosystems. As a city strives for carbon-neutrality, PV glass can be integrated into its old and new buildings' infrastructure to support renewable energy applications [11]. The human-friendly search for PV glass technology puts an emphasis on healthy living environments. It does so through lowering the need for more man-made illumination and pulling occupants into natural light. This has tangible benefits for physical and mental health, productivity and general well-being.

In the era of Industry 5.0, however, the combination of photovoltaics in glass technology with advanced intelligent sensors and IOT has further expanded capabilities for PV glass. These systems provide real-time energy monitoring, predictive alerts and automated energy generation/consumption optimization services. For example, intelligent PV glass facades can adjust their transparency to suit current weather conditions getting good results for electrical generation as well as thermally insulating homes [12]. But although it has many advantages, the large-scale use of PV glass technology is now faced with problems such as expensive installation costs at the beginning of use; energy efficiency technology limitations and the need for skilled labour to install and maintain. In order to solve these problems, governments, private sectors and research institutions have to collude in positive ways. They should offer financial incentives and wage subsidies for technicians as well as making more investments into research/development of scientific disciplines.

PV glass technology has reframed human habitats as the center of Industry 5.0. Dual purpose for urban construction material and renewable energy gives it a unique status in sustainable development of cities. As technology advances to improve energy efficiency, price performance and integration capability, PV glass will bear a significant function for shaping the cities of tomorrow. It definitely corresponds with Vision 5's goal for cities as resilient, redemptive places where people are also citizens and members of the community [13].

3 Technological Advances and Innovations in PV Glasses: Integration of Industry 5.0 Principles in Urban Development

PV glasses with photovoltaic cells integrated in them can perform multiple tasks, such as serving as building materials and providing renewable energy. These breakthroughs are made in technology and innovation today for renewable energy solutions in the context of urban infrastructure. They conform perfectly to Industry 5.0's core values. With these PV glasses, not only do green building materials help construct modern buildings and city greening efforts accelerate; they are breaking new ground in changing urban landscapes [14]. The pursuit of greater efficiency in energy usage, reduced carbon footprints, and improvements to the aesthetic value within architecture are becoming parts of urban culture. Industry 5.0 is human-centric, sustainable and resilient. It emphasizes a creative approach to technology, but respects nature and society. PV glasses embody these principles through their ability to bring advanced technology and environmental awareness together.

PV glass's integration into urban development reflects a new orientation toward smart cities where, for instance, energy efficiency is most important. In modern urban design, buildings are not mere static structures but also active participants in the energy grid. PV glass technology allows facades, windows and rooftops to generate electricity while still preserving transparency and beauty [15]. The glasses are often made of sophisticated materials such as amorphous silicon, cadmium telluride or perovskite solar cells to maximize energy conversion efficiency and adaptability towards different lighting conditions. Smart coatings and nanotechnology are being inserted to the glasses to help them optimize their performance. Thus they can also store energy in a low light environment, regulate thermal insulation in buildings.

The key principle of Industry 5.0 is to collaborate with machines and technology thereby enabling them serves society's needs in a way that does not exhaust nature. PV glass systems are increasingly seen to be in line with this vision, supplying scalable solutions that meet urban electricity demands and promote architectural creativity [16]. Commercial skyscrapers and residential buildings fitted with PV glass panels can reduce reliance on traditional electricity sources, fostering people's growing acceptance of distributed power supplies meanwhile, data analytics, artificial intelligence and IoT technology all contribute to monitoring and managing the performance of PV glass. Real-time data on power generation and use, storage and distribution serves to optimize building operations Improve efficiency to reduce power waste trends predict future needs for energy supplies. Urban planners and policymakers increasingly recognize that PV glasses make for an "component part advantage" in the green architecture of tomorrow's cities. Integration of this technology with urban planning frameworks contributes to medium and long-range goals of sustainable urban development. These range from cutting greenhouse gas emissions and anti-urban heat island measures such as those required for carbon reduction policies, to promoting energy self-sufficiency in cities themselves compared with excessive reliance on imported supplies. Various governments and local government are now providing incentives, encouraging adoption of PV glass systems. These measures range from favorable building loan rates to subsidies, and even green building certifications all aimed at the promotion of such technology in new construction projects as well as refitting existing infrastructure. Between them, these policies plus private sector investment are driving PV glass adoption and breaking down barriers to entry [17].

The convergence of Industry 5.0 thinking with P V glass technology also underscores the importance—especially a circular economy is required now of close attention to industrial ecology. The manufacturing process of PV glasses is becoming more resource-efficient as it focuses on recycling and reusing materials to minimize waste. Researchers are looking at biodegradable materials plus advanced recycling techniques for use in PV glass panels. This will guarantee that at the end-of-life stage these products do not add to electronic waste (what people call a "resource output recovery system". Looking ahead, consideration is being given to integrating blockchain technology into the supply chain for PV glass. This would guarantee transparency and traceability, thus enhancing environmental responsibility in a further way [18].

But at the same time, the wide adoption of PV glasses means challenges that everyone will have to face. High initial cost, low energy conversion efficiency, and the need for skilled labour to install maintain such systems remain significant barriers. Furthermore, urban landscapes within the same country (China) can be so different that to a large extent, passersby all eyes that they seem to be in completely unfamiliar territory. Different solutions are needed in these circumstances to suit local variations among regional climates and architectural styles, which are reflected by different layouts or planned projects for providing heating or cooling across towns.

The combination of government effort, private sector and academic collaboration, can these problems be resolved and large-scale use realized. In conclusion, technological progress in PV glass represents a step towards sustainable urban development consonant with Industry 5.0 principles. As solar energy systems and architectural innovation merge together, PV nanoglasses have the potential to change the face of urban energy usage. They not only address environmental problems but also offer economic benefits that can run into the hundreds or even thousands of millions yuan. Cities can become smarter and more energy efficient as they process information from a variety of sources. If the development of PV glasses is anything to go by, they are set on track to become an integral part of the regent in the making that is our built environment [19]. And will thus bring us back to this grand vision of sustainable cities where Industry 5.0 has taken firm root.

4 Aligning PV Glass Technology with SDG 11 Goals

Photovoltaic (PV) glass technology integration is closely aligned with the United Nations Sustainable Development Goals (SDG) 11. As cities and human settlements are made more inclusive, safe, resilient and/or sustainable within this system of goals defined through some democratic process, the major difference is that glass technology gives buildings collaborative capabilities. Cities are rapidly taking way more urbanized. Therefore, they consume the most energy and also emit more carbon.

While the spread of PV glass technology in city infrastructure provides an opportunity to fundamentally change the direction buildings have been constructed until now, it represents another kind of architecture at best. Instead of being exclusively consumers of energy, structures which emerge from the adoption of PV glass technology also become active producers in bringing about clean and renewable power. Like piece of jade accessorizes its wearer, PV glass technology is two-handed [20]. This technology integrates solar photovoltaic cells into glass panels, at once enhancing architectural aesthetics while contributing to the goals of sustainability. This section discusses the links between PV glass technology and SDG 11, with special emphasis on the potential for its applying in creating sustainable cities and communities.

SDG 11 orients to urban environments that will be enduringly built and left by people who are fairly prosperous environmentally, financially and socially as well.· Key targets in the list of SDG 11's are mitigation of environmental damage, provision for green and public spaces and increased energy efficiency in city building. By 55% of the world's population is settled in cities, which generate more than 70% of carbon emissions. PV glass technology thus becomes an instrument to unburden the environment by producing power in the place of use. Urban buildings with PV glass can offset their carbon footprint and reduce dependence on nonrenewable energy, contribute to sustainable urbanization [21].

4.1 PV Glass: A Key Component for Cutting the Carbon Footprint in Urban Spaces

PV glass plays a key role in reducing the carbon footprint of urban spaces because sun-drenched glass: both improves solar efficiencies and also reflects back onto itself this captured sunlight or infrared radiation as heat. Glass facades and windows cause significant energy losses due to poor insulation, inadequate suppression of heat transfer. In contrast, PV glass acts both to stem this wastage and at the same time make electricity [22]. It turns buildings into sources of their own energy. This technology can replace traditional glass in windows, facades, and skylights, thereby reducing the demand for grid-supplied electricity produced from fossil fuels. PV glass also reduces greenhouse gas emissions by cutting down on the up-front energy needed to keep heating and cooling systems running. When cities are looking to lower their carbon emissions, PV glass is a real world solution that they can begin deploying immediately. It is a technology for reducing energy consumption and the resultant CO_2 emission through practical applications. Nevertheless, there seems still room for improvement in understanding exactly how non-domestic building types might be configured to fulfill SDG 11 targets [23].

More recently urban development has required buildings with a higher quality of energy efficiency, particularly in the areas of energy consumption and environmental controls. PV glass technology is key to raising energy efficiency. In modern surroundings. In addition to producing energy PV glass also acts as insulation. The result of this is combined natural energy in the form electricity and relief from one's own air conditioning bill. Integrate PV glass into smart building technologies such as automated energy management systems to optimize energy storage and distribution with minimum waste. These are the technologies of an energy-efficient city according to the goals for 2020 set out in UN resolution 54/95 [24].

4.2 Examples of Implementing SDG 11 with PV Glass Technology

Several global case studies show how zoning plans based on this instrument feature successful integration of PV glass technology into ways to achieve SDG 11 targets. For example, The Edge building in Amsterdam, hailed as one of the world's greenest office buildings, meets its energy needs with PV glass panels but manages to remain transparent and beautiful. Another case in point is the Copenhagen International School—more than 12,000 panels of PV glass are installed on the roof, providing approximately 50% or even over half of what the school will need in the course of entire year electricity [25]. These examples reveal the potential of PV glass to help reduce urban carbon footprints, parties that demonstrate sustainable building practices and enhance energy efficiency.

By globally promoting similar models, cities can make serious inroads towards realizing SDG 11.

5 Application of Industry 5.0 in Promotion of PV Glass Utilization

Due the advent of Industry 5.0, new and human CENTERED rather than task oriented With Industrial revolution will come order (composite left side front image). It could say that compared to its antecedent: Industry 4.0, which emphasized automation and connectivity, Industry 5.0 will focus on man/machine collaboration for the global sustainable development finish line. Adapting industry 5.0 technology to promote PV glass application in urban infrastructure is able to speed up enormously. This section of the book will explain the central ideas behind Industry 5.0, the role it plays in promoting the application of PV glass, represents an intelligent systems for infrastructure planning and energy management applications [26].

In industry 5.0, advanced technologies are integrated into other fields unlike the previous industrial revolution. To achieve sustainable development, it relies on cooperation among Artificial Intelligence (AI), Robotics Technology and Digital Twins with human genius Also on the list of priorities for Industry 5.0 are environmental and social responsibilities alongside productivity and efficiency. In the context of PV glass technology, Industry 5.0 makes for innovative design (engineering) and new concepts in production like these that had never been tried before. For instance, a smart factory driven by AI-based tools can balance PV glass production and minimize resource consumption. As a result, the carbon emissions associated with manufacturing are kept to half of traditional methods. Industry 5.0 facilitates customization, allowing architects and engineers to really integrate PV glass into different urban infrastructure projects in terms of aesthetics [27].

5.1 Collaboration Between Humans and AI

Systems in Architectural Design Collaboration are the characteristic trait of Industry 5.0, where AI systems work hand in glove with human experts. In the design of urban infrastructure, for instance, a mixture of Human-AI systems can rationally optimize the position and attitude of PV glass panels in order to maximize effective electricity output. And the design of buildings, based on the data analyses done by AI algorithms, makes use sunshine laws—the study of energy patterns from solar sources such as light and heat. Something as lowly shading effects or on top to install PV glass in buildings [28]. Armed with this information, people in engineering or design fields can noodle out buildings that are not only visually appealing but also capture maximum crowdlight energy and minimize waste heat escape. This is a joint method that makes sure PV glass is utilized effectively, and could be said to be more consistent with energy aims than earlier single ideas.

5.2 *Smart Grids and PV Glass Integration for Energy Management*

In managing the energy generated by PV glass technology, smart grids play a vital role. These advanced energy networks use digital communication technologies to monitor, predict and balance electricity supply and demand. Urban areas can effectively deliver power from building facades and roofs by integrating photovoltaic glass with smart grids [29]. By way of system batteries hooked up to the grid or alternatively providing other energy-deficient zones nearby Surplus electricity can be stored out. Smart grids also allow for real-time monitoring of energy use patterns. This allows cities which are using increasingly high levels of electricity to take advantage of the latest technical possibility (online more real-time), optimize energy flow and reduce waste. By itself, the integration of smart grids with PV glass technology is in alignment with the energy resilience target of SDG 11 [30].

5.3 *Digital Twins for Monitoring PV Glass Performance*

Digital twin technology is a must-have component of Industry 5.0, supporting advanced simulation and monitoring capabilities for PV glass systems. A digital twin is a virtual copy of a physical object, such as a building packed with PV glass panels. Through real-time data collection and analysis, digital twins allow stakeholders to monitor the performance of PV-glass installations; spot off-spec maintenance may be unnecessary and at the same time improve its energy output. For example, digital twins can simulate the environmental conditions and corresponding effects of seasonal change on energy production. Although this level of precision is essential to ensure that PV glass technology works efficiently throughout its entire service life cycle maximizing its contribution towards SDG 11 targets [31]. Eliminating carbon footprints, increasing energy efficiency, making use of the latest technologies from AI and smart grids to digital twins—there are many ways in which PV glass could have an almost revolutionary impact on creating sustainable cities. The adoption of PV glass technology, which could help pave the way for a cleaner future, requires cooperation between policymakers, industry practitioners and city planners.

6 Challenges in Implementing PV Glasses in Human-Centred Infrastructure

PV glass, incorporated into human-friendly infrastructure, holds out bright prospects for sustainable urban development. At the same time, however, a series of serious challenges makes it difficult for these glasses to enter mass production and contribute in a substantial way to society. These problems span the technical, economic, legal and social aspects and require multi-disciplinary coping with them [32].

6.1 Technological Barriers and Efficiency

Every new technology has its teething troubles, and PV glasses are no exception. The first and most important barrier is their energy conversion efficiency. Despite great progress in solar cell technology, PV glasses now have much lower efficiency than traditional solar flat panel modules. The semi-transparency of this kind of glass often means that it may not absorb full sunlight so they cannot produce all the power one would like. As a result, overall energy yield is limited. In addition, durability under different environmental conditions such as extremes in temperature or humidity exposure to pollutants, remains a concern. Maintenance and cleaning are further complications: if the surface of PV glasses gets dirty due to dust from outdoor pollution or leaves falling in autumn it can greatly detract from their efficiency [33]. The development of material science to raise the overall efficiency of thin-film solar cells in glass plates or perhaps better still, no-cell designs—is crucial for breakthroughs in this area. Other challenges that must be addressed include self-cleaning coatings on transparent films and hard coatings to protect delicate mono-crystalline silicon modules from micro-cracks induced during production.

6.2 *Economic Feasibility and Difficulty*

Getting Funds Concerning economic feasibility in any infrastructure projects, PV glasses appear not to be a valid option. For one thing, the initial cost of integrating PV glasses is significantly more than that of regular construction materials, even though they offer long-term energy savings [34]. This steep investment cost often discourages potential adopters. Besides, mechanisms for financing the widespread use of PV glasses on a large scale are often relatively scarce, especially in developing economies where infrastructure budgets are tight. Financial models including public–private partnerships, green bonds and carbon credit strategies, can play an important role in helping to address these economic obstacles. Moreover, life-cycle cost analysis and internal rate of return (IRR) studies need to be stressed for illustrating the long-term benefits of adopting PV glass technology.

6.3 *Regulatory and Policy Barriers*

Once more the lack of standardization in regulatory arrangements for using PV glass presents a significant roadblack to this new development. The rules on renewable integration policies for urban infrastructure differ from area to district; as a result they are not consistent but change here there and everywhere regionally. In addition because building codes seldom provide for the dual roles of PV glass, namely both construction material and energy generator, they become (literally) a stumbling block [35]. Finally, permit grant procedures can be tedious and bureaucratic, leading to delays in projects as well as higher overall costs. So establishment of global standards and preparation of specific policy guidelines for seamless integration of PV glass may create a better environment in which to carry out a-fully-fledged roll-out.

6.4 *Public Acceptance and Knowledge Gaps*

Public perception and awareness are critically important factors in the adoption of new technologies, especially for PV glasses. However, many end users do not realize any of the benefits from incorporating PV glasses into infrastructure- that it leads to less energy consumed and lower carbon emissions, as well as contributing to the outward appearance of buildings. There is also widespread skepticism among users about whether these new technologies will work as promised [36]. For regions that have never been provided with sunshine, served by sbme or CMESIt is helpful to have a series of pilot projects and a public relations campaign to reduce uncertainty and increase knowledge regarding these technologies. It is ought to engage stakeholders more broadly some stakeholder participation including architects, builders and policy makers need to be drawn in order to beef up enthusiasm for PV glasses in urban infrastructure.

7 Human-Centred Policy Frameworks and Legal Considerations

Public regulatory frameworks and legal requirements also play a significant role in the successful integration of PV glasses into infrastructure, with a particular emphasis on human-centered safety. National governments and international regulatory bodies must create a climate that is supportive of investment, innovation and implementation in the field of PV glass technologies.

7.1 *International Policies Driving Sustainable Vocational Education Development*

In the Paris Agreement and the United Nations Sustainable Development Goals (SDGs) other international agreements, common themes include a push for green buildings and sustainable living [37]. At the same time, we must remember that on the photovoltaic glass manufacturing and integration front, there are international standards which can help to achieve uniform quality and reliability across different markets.

7.2 *National and Local Laws*

It should be adjusted to deal with the arrival of these new types of PV glasses on buildings. All levels of administration should set out clear guidelines for the design, installation and maintenance of glass using photovoltaic principles. Policy needs to spell out how to resolve challenges concerning the deep-set habits of developers and occupants. If urban planning processes risk deforming with conflict over renewable technology deployment and zoning restrictions, then there is no way the situation can normalize. Local governments could implement these policies where they exist, not just to act as enforcer but also hosting capacity building programmes for architects, engineers and construction professionals [38].

7.3 Incentives and Subsidies

These are necessary conditions for PV glass technologies to catch on in the future, as they have been with other renewable energies. Governments can introduce special incentive programs that specifically encompass PV glass technology into both residential projects and commercial ones. In addition, grid-tied systems that are supported by net metering policies where building owners can sell their surplus electricity out and return it to the public electricity grid greatly enhance the economic advantage of PV glass systems. These incentives don't just lighten the financial load on investors but also help speed up the transition to sustainable infrastructure [39].

7.4 Legal Issues for Green Building Codes

The legal framework for environmentally friendly construction should expressly recognize the role of PV glass. This includes the intellectual property rights connected with new PV glass technologies, liability issues that may arise if individual systems fail and environmental performance requirements. This aims to provide a clean legal environment so as to fend off potential disputes and make those involved completely answerable for the programmes they have started. New infrastructure project according to sustainable building codes should adopt renewable technologies, thus setting clear targets on environmental protection and energy use.

It is clear, then, that tackling the multiple challenges posed by introducing PV glasses into social infrastructures requires coordinated effort across technology, support of businesses, changes in laws, and an awareness on the part of the people themselves. With sound national and local policies, financial aid systems like feed-in tariffs, and widespread public involvement, the very meaning of perfection will be based on PV glass technologies in creating liveable, low-energy-consumption urban environments [40].

8 Future Prospects and Technological Innovations

Recently emerged in the market of photovoltaic glass sector, PV glass is forming a brand new conscious by resolving structural problems from previous times and replacing old tools with latest technology and materials. It has become the first dedicated company in photovoltaic glass sector, benefiting from a series of major market initiatives including short-term lessee system, or mantle chiller. As such, single crystal growth technology is good not only for photovoltaic systems, but also for modern society's growing need for storage batteries and single crystals-both under technology protection rules as a large proportion [41]. The concept of an industry that in reality has outmatched its support position of course there needs to be a basic understanding in some areas too economical rapid transportation less volume integrate comparisons about texts engineering works laborer participation level elevation structure plans Just as when children growing up in mountainous regions.

8.1 AI and IoT Combination: Real-Time Monitoring of PV Glass Performance

Artificial Intelligence (AI) and the Internet of Things (IoT) are seen as two of the most significant technologies capable of improving the output performance from photovoltaic glass. IoT sensors-enable real-time monitoring systems collect energy production data from the glass, all environmental parameters, and system operating condition. AI algorithms can then process this information to forecast where maintenance will be required, tune energy production so as minimize losses, and look for places that are less efficient than they might be [42]. Using information gathered this way, AI-enabled predictive maintenance can shorten downtime, extend system life and reduce operating costs. In addition, smart grids enabled by IoT make it possible for buildings equipped with photovoltaic glass to seamlessly integrate into broader energy networks. This combination of AI, IoT and PV glass technology represents a big stride toward smart-energy ecosystems.

8.2 Potential for Net-Zero Energy Buildings

The integration of PV glass technology is an indispensable means of achieving Net-Zero Energy Buildings (NZEBs). PV glass can convert sunlight directly into clean electricity In addition to serving as an electric-generating facade or window for the building, it can greatly reduce dependence on external energy sources. By joining PV glass installations with energy storage systems and advanced energy management technologies, buildings realize energy self-sufficiency. This not only lowers carbon emissions but lowers building operation costs for the long haul Architectural designs are increasingly incorporating PV glass into the building envelope, skylight and canopy as a means for maximizing solar energy gain. Yet in terms of appearance, planning and designing are as important as ever the potential of PV glass to turn buildings into small power plants runs parallel to global sustainable development goals and urban planning initiatives [43].

8.3 Collaborating with the World

The rapid development of PV glass technology requires international cooperation and knowledge sharing from researchers, policymakers and industry stakeholders. Collaborative research projects and joint ventures play an integral role in promoting PV glass innovation processes as well addressing technological and economic challenges [44]. Global partnerships are promoting technology transfer, standardisation and policy alignment—thus speeding up the introduction of products into markets Platforms for knowledge-sharing such as international conferences, work shops and open-access research repositories are stimulating creativity and making the global market adopt PV glass technology. As well, the fact that incentives such as subsidies, support policies or investment in renewable energy technologies are needed is a USA matter.

9 Environmental and Moral Implications

Although PV glass provides considerable benefits, ethical and environmental concerns should not be entirely brushed aside. PV glass production processes consume large quantities of energy and use toxic chemicals. It is essential to put in practice environmentally friendly manufacturing methods and at the end of life of PV glass components, ensure that they are properly disposed of or recycled. Ethical considerations extend to the right to work, fair trade practices and the accessibility of technology in developing areas. It requires a multi-stakeholder approach pulling in manufacturers, governments and environmental organizations to promulgate regulations and standards ensuring that production processes, deployment and recycling are conducted properly, responsibly [45].

10 Conclusions and Further Scope

PV glass stands at the intersection of environmentalism, breakthroughs in technology, and architectural innovation. With the continuous improvement in efficiency, beauty and integration, it is possible to transform city infrastructure and make a big contribution to global carbon reduction goals. The convergence of AI, IoT and energy storage systems will provide a further power boost for both residential and commercial settings. But major obstacles in terms of cost, scalability and environment all remain. Future researchers should work to increase not only the efficiency of PV glass systems, but also their affordability and their recyclability. Cooperation among global stakeholders must play a key role in realizing the full potential of PV glass technology. As it march into the future, PV glass is not only technical innovation, but also an important pillar in sustainable and low-energy Architecture.

References

1. Ashinze, U. K., Edeigba, B. A., Umoh, A. A., Biu, P. W., &Darao-jimba, A. I. (2024). Urban green infrastructure and its role in sustainable cities: A comprehensive review. *World Journal of Advanced Research and Reviews, 21*(2), 928–936.
2. Zellner, M. L., & Massey, D. (2024). Modeling benefits and tradeoffs of green infrastructure: Evaluating and extending parsimonious models for neighborhoodstormwater planning. *Heliyon.*
3. Zabel, A., &Häusler, M. M. (2024). Policy instruments for green infrastructure. *Landscape and Urban Planning, 242*, 104929.
4. Kaneti, V. R., Masih, J., Yoganand, S., Singh, B., Bhargava, R., Bajaj, R., ...&Shrivastava, A. (2024). Supervised Learning for Edible Mushroom Identification: Promising Results and Implications for Food Safety. *International Journal of Intelligent Systems and Applications in Engineering, 12*(8s), 290–298.

5. Zhang, B., &MacKenzie, A. (2024). Trade-offs and synergies in urban green infrastructure: A systematic review. *Urban Forestry & Urban Greening*, 128262.
6. Isendahl, C., Dunning, N. P., Grazioso, L., Hawken, S., Lentz, D. L., & Scarborough, V. L. (2024). Growth and decline of a sustainable city: A multitemporal perspective on blue-black-green infrastructures at the pre-Columbian Lowland Maya city of Tikal. *Urban Studies*, 00420980231224648.
7. Sunding, A., Randrup, T. B., Nordh, H., Sang, Å. O., & Nilsson, K. (2024). Descriptions of the relationship between human health and green infrastructure in six Nordic comprehensive plans. *Cities*, *146*, 104746.
8. Kim, J., Ewing, R., &Rigolon, A. (2024). Does green infrastructure affect housing prices via extreme heat and air pollution mitigation? A focus on green and climate gentrification in Los Angeles County, 2000-2021. *Sustainable Cities and Society*, *102*, 105225.
9. Yunos, M. Y. M., Maulan, S., & Ismail, N. A. (2024). Unlocking the Potential of Green Infrastructure in Residential Areas: A Comprehensive Systematic Review.
10. Richter, M., Heinemann, K., Meiser, N., &Dickhaut, W. (2024). Trees in Sponge Cities—A Systematic Review of Trees as a Component of Blue-Green Infrastructure, Vegetation Engineering Principles, and Stormwater Management. *Water*, *16*(5), 655.
11. Vijayalakshmi, S., Savita, &Durgadevi, P. (2023). AI and Machine Learning in Improving Resilience of Smart Energy Infrastructure. In *AI-Powered Machine Learning in the Energy Industry: Digital Technology and Sustainable Energy Systems* (pp. 189–213). Cham: Springer International Publishing.
12. Shukla, S. S., Jain, M., Jain, A., Bajpai, S., Mishra, A. K., Gupta, A., &Pramanik, S. (2024). Industry 5.0: Blue Wind Energy for Sustainable Urbanization and Intelligent Control of Energy. In *Convergence of Human Resources Technologies and Industry 5.0* (pp. 170–187). IGI Global.
13. IssaZadeh, S. B., Esteban Perez, M. D., López-Gutiérrez, J. S., &Fernández-Sánchez, G. (2023). Optimizing Smart Energy Infrastructure in Smart Ports: A Systematic Scoping Review of Carbon Footprint Reduction. *Journal of Marine Science and Engineering*, *11*(10), 1921.
14. Li, J., & Zhou, T. (2023). Multiagent deep meta reinforcement learning for sea computing-based energy management of interconnected grids considering renewable energy sources in sustainable cities. *Sustainable Cities and Society*, *99*, 104917.
15. Orumwense, E. F., & Abo-Al-Ez, K. (2023). Internet of Things for smart energy systems: A review on its applications, challenges and future trends. *AIMS Electronics & Electrical Engineering*, *7*(1).

16. Raj, E. F. I. (2023). A Detailed Review on Wind and Solar Hybrid Green Energy Technologies for Sustainable Smart Cities. *Polytechnica*, *6*(1), 1.
17. Camacho, J. D. J., Aguirre, B., Ponce, P., Anthony, B., & Molina, A. (2024). Leveraging Artificial Intelligence to Bolster the Energy Sector in Smart Cities: A Literature Review. *Energies*, *17*(2), 353.
18. Kannammal, A., &Chandia, S. (2023). Applications of AI and Machine Learning for Smart Cities. *Research Trends in Artificial Intelligence: Internet of Things*, 186.
19. Zearah, S. A., Al-Tahee, M., Mohammed, A., Shnawa, A. H., Mahdi, H. H. J., &Majeed, Z. (2023, December). Smart City Application based on Internet-of-Things and Artificial Intelligence for Energy Management Dynamic Memory Modelling. In *2023 International Conference on Emerging Research in Computational Science (ICERCS)* (pp. 1–6). IEEE.
20. Awogbemi, O., Von Kallon, D. V., & Kumar, K. S. (2024). Contributions of Artificial Intelligence and Digitization in Achieving Clean and Affordable Energy. *Intelligent Systems with Applications*, 200389.
21. Verma, J., Sandys, L., Matthews, A., &Goel, S. (2024). Readiness of artificial intelligence technology for managing energy demands from renewable sources. *Engineering Applications of Artificial Intelligence*, *135*, 108831.
22. Khalid, M. (2024). Energy 4.0: AI-enabled digital transformation for sustainable power networks. *Computers & Industrial Engineering*, 110253.
23. IssaZadeh, S. B., & Perez, E. (2023). MD; López-Gutiérrez, J.-S.; Fernández-Sánchez, G. Optimizing Smart Energy Infrastructure in Smart Ports: A Systematic Scoping Review of Carbon Footprint Reduction. *J. Mar. Sci. Eng*, *11*, 1921.
24. Obaideen, K., Albasha, L., Iqbal, U., & Mir, H. (2024). Wireless power transfer: Applications, challenges, barriers, and the role of AI in achieving sustainable development goals-A bibliometric analysis. *Energy Strategy Reviews*, *53*, 101376.
25. El-Hussieny, E. (2023). Emerging the concept of Sustainable Architecture in forming a Smart City. *Resourceedings*, *3*(1), 22-32.
26. Salman, M. Y., &Hasar, H. (2023). Review on environmental aspects in smart city concept: Water, waste, air pollution and transportation smart applications using Machine Learning techniques. *Sustainable Cities and Society*, *94*, 104567.
27. Van Hoang, T. (2024). Impact of integrated artificial intelligence and internet of things technologies on smart city transformation. *Journal of Technical Education Science*, *19*(Special Issue 01), 64–73.
28. Huda, N. U., Ahmed, I., Adnan, M., Ali, M., &Naeem, F. (2024). Experts and intelligent systems for smart homes' Transformation to Sustainable Smart Cities: A comprehensive review. *Expert Systems with Applications*, *238*, 122380.

29. Ali, M. (2023). Synergizing Solar Cell Innovation, Radio Wave Technology, and AI for Sustainable Business Growth: A Comprehensive Review. *International Journal of Social, Humanities and Life Sciences*, *1*(1), 19–28.
30. Nezhad, M. M., Neshat, M., Sylaios, G., & Garcia, D. A. (2024). Marine energy digitalization digital twin's approaches. *Renewable and Sustainable Energy Reviews*, *191*, 114065.
31. Moemen, Y. S., Alshater, H., & El-Sayed, I. E. T. (2023). Clean Energy Management Based on Internet of Things and Sensor Networks for Climate Change Problems. In *The Power of Data: Driving Climate Change with Data Science and Artificial Intelligence Innovations* (pp. 117–136). Cham: Springer Nature Switzerland.
32. Nasserddine, G., Nassereddine, M., & El Arid, A. A. (2023). Internet of things integration in renewable energy Systems. In *Handbook of Research on Applications of AI, Digital Twin, and Internet of Things for Sustainable Development* (pp. 159–185). IGI Global.
33. López, O. L., Rosabal, O. M., Ruiz-Guirola, D. E., Raghuwanshi, P., Mikhaylov, K., Lovén, L., &Iyer, S. (2023). Energy-sustainable Machine Learning connectivity: Vision, technological enablers, challenges, and future directions. *IEEE Open Journal of the Communications Society.*
34. Logeswaran, K., Suresh, P., Ponselvakumar, A. P., Savitha, S., Sentamilselvan, K., &Adhithyaa, N. (2023). Exploration of Assorted Modernizations in Forecasting Renewable Energy Using Low Power Wireless Technologies for Machine LearningSG. *Smart Grids and Internet of Things: An Energy Perspective*, 157–191.
35. Li, X., Zhao, H., Feng, Y., Li, J., Zhao, Y., & Wang, X. (2024). Research on key technologies of high energy efficiency and low power consumption of new data acquisition equipment of power Internet of Things based on artificial intelligence. *International Journal of Thermofluids*, *21*, 100575.
36. Xie, H., Huang, R., Sun, H., Han, Z., Jiang, M., Zhang, D., ...& Wu, T. (2023). Wireless energy: Paving the way for smart cities and a greener future. *Energy and Buildings*, *297*, 113469.
37. Khan, M. W., Saad, S., Ammad, S., Rasheed, K., & Jamal, Q. (2024). Smart Infrastructure and AI. In *AI in Material Science* (pp. 193–215). CRC Press.
38. Samaei, S. R., &Ghahfarrokhi, M. A. (2023). Optimizing Coastal Hydro Turbines Integrating Artificial Intelligence for Sustainable Energy Conversion. In *2th International Conference on Creative achievements of architecture, urban planning, civil engineering and environment in the sustainable development of the Middle East*.
39. Kumar, D. (2023). Concept of Sustainable Energy System for Smart Cities. In *Renewable Energy Scenarios in Future Indian Smart Cities: A Geospatial Technology Perspective* (pp. 1–20). Singapore: Springer Nature Singapore.

40. Almalki, F. A., Alsamhi, S. H., Sahal, R., Hassan, J., Hawbani, A., Rajput, N. S., ...&Breslin, J. (2023). Green Machine Learning for eco-friendly and sustainable smart cities: future directions and opportunities. *Mobile Networks and Applications*, *28*(1), 178–202.
41. Salama, R., & Al-Turjman, F. (2023). Sustainable energy production in smart cities. *Sustainability*, *15*(22), 16052.
42. Mohammed, M. N., Aljibori, H. S. S., Al-Tamimi, A., Alani, Z. N., Hameed, M. S., Ibrahim, F. M., ... &Alfiras, M. (2023, October). Toward Sustainable Smart Cities in Bahrain: A Groundbreaking Approach to Marine Renewable Energy Harnessing Sea Tides and Waves for a Greener Energy Future. In *2023 IEEE 8th International Conference on Engineering Technologies and Applied Sciences (ICETAS)* (pp. 1–5). IEEE.
43. Bin Abu Sofian, A. D. A., Lim, H. R., SitiHalimatulMunawaroh, H., Ma, Z., Chew, K. W., & Show, P. L. (2024). Machine learning and the renewable energy revolution: Exploring solar and wind energy solutions for a sustainable future including innovations in energy storage. *Sustainable Development*.
44. Fan, Z., Yan, Z., & Wen, S. (2023). Deep learning and artificial intelligence in sustainability: a review of SDGs, renewable energy, and environmental health. *Sustainability*, *15*(18), 13493.
45. Jain, A., Sharma, A., Jately, V., &Azzopardi, B. (Eds.). (2023). *Sustainable Energy Solutions with Artificial Intelligence, Blockchain Technology, and Internet of Things*. CRC Press.

Empowering the Workforce for Industry 5.0: Skills, Training, and Human-Centric Transformation

Malla Jogarao, J. Siva Durga Prasad, and P. Sanjeevi

1 Introduction

Industry 5.0 is a paradigm change in industrial transformation that prioritizes human-centeredness, sustainability, and resilience. It complements Industry 4.0 by prioritizing worker well-being and tackling societal challenges related to digital transition. The approach is to enhance human operators' skills and competencies through partnerships with digital technologies. Industry 5.0 is defined by a three-dimensional system design that includes technical, reality, and application dimensions [1]. The emphasis transitions from sustainability to human-centricity, as demonstrated by alterations in research objectives [2]. The fundamental technologies enabling Industry 5.0 implementation include robotics along with artificial intelligence and human–robot cooperation [3] even though the concept remains new [4]. The present technologies offer possible answers to environmental and socio-economic challenges that Industry

M. Jogarao (✉) · J. Siva Durga Prasad · P. Sanjeevi
School of Maritime Management, Indian Maritime University, Visakhapatnam, India
e-mail: mjogarao@gmail.com

© The Author(s), under exclusive license to Springer Nature Singapore Pte Ltd. 2025

P. Agarwal et al. (eds.), *Building a Human-Centred Infrastructure for Sustainable Industry 5.0 in Asia*,
https://doi.org/10.1007/978-981-95-0417-6_3

4.0 has insufficiently addressed. Achieving Industry 5.0 demands stakeholder participation as well as integration.

The Industry 5.0 progression demonstrates the requirement for human–machine partnership with basic automation systems in South Asia, the influence of Industry 4.0 technologies on workforce employability is profound, with essential determinants comprising artificial intelligence and digital competencies [5]. Cooperation between humans and robots during timber prefabrication bridges the gap between system-, design-, and human-centered concerns, leading to greater adaptability and output [6]. Smart education is essential for workforce preparation in Industry 5.0, incorporating intelligent tutoring systems, robotics, and IoT to facilitate personalized learning experiences [7]. Human–machine interactions have evolved from Taylorism to advanced technologies, with future directions centered on machine learning, Industry 4.0, Society 5.0, and cyber-physical systems [8]. Human–machine relationships show a complementary nature in modern times since they require technical advancement to be in harmony with methods that prioritize human needs.

The workforce needs empowerment to achieve sustainable and inclusive industrial growth in Asia since its rapid industrial development dramatically shapes economic development while ensuring social fairness. The workforce becomes more effective and creative when features of empowerment are implemented because skilled workers drive sectoral expansion in manufacturing and other sectors. Labor force statistics show that Southeast Asia possesses the world's third-biggest workforce thus generating important possibilities for skilled workers to boost economic growth. By intentionally improving their skills, industries can obtain better market reactions, which in turn strengthens their ability to operate and their financial success. For social inclusion to be achieved, employees must get validation, which serves as the foundation for its implementation. It is necessary to conduct a thorough analysis of gender dynamics and to work toward the promotion of social fairness through the provision of opportunities to improve the manufacturing industry. By implementing a comprehensive plan, the quality of life in several different areas will be improved, which will ultimately result in a more equitable model of economic development. Empowering workers is beneficial to social development projects because it encourages equitable distribution of economic rewards, which is essential for accomplishing sustainable development goals. This is why the empowerment of workers is so widely beneficial. Those who have been granted the authority to do so demonstrate a higher commitment to safeguarding their rights, in addition to actively contributing to their communities and advocating for environmentally responsible manufacturing methods.

Industries develop skills to improve their operational environment for business and increase their response to market dynamics. Realizing inclusive advancement—which forms the basis of social inclusiveness—is mostly dependent on supporting and appreciating the efforts of employees. When thinking about developments in manufacturing, especially in terms of gender dynamics, it is essential to support social justice and challenge the under-representation of women in this field. This project aims not only to improve quality of life but also to enable a more fair and balanced framework for economic development, therefore benefiting different communities. Furthermore, the improvement of worker agency greatly helps social development projects to progress. Guaranteeing the equitable distribution of economic benefits, which is necessary for reaching goals of sustainable development, depends mostly on empowered workforces. Empowered workers show a strong will to protect their rights, show more involvement in their local communities, and show great enthusiasm for advancing sustainable industrial processes. Attaching sustainable and inclusive industrial progress in Asia depends on improving human capital, especially since the region experiences fast industrialization that affects economic development, therefore stressing the need for social fairness. Efforts towards empowerment show their effectiveness when carried out deliberately and precisely. The workforce gets more creative and efficient since trained people are essential for manufacturing and other important industries to develop.

The third-largest labor force in the world, Southeast Asia, worked for the chance to serve as a skilled and readily available workforce—one that could propel the region toward greater economic growth—an opportunity that meant the possibility of making the very most of an enormous demographic dividend. Sustainable industrial achievements depend primarily on businesses placing employee development at the very top of their agenda. Why because the better trained the employees are, the better they are at meeting the demands of the market, and the more competitive the business becomes. For this reason, employee empowerment is a vital aspect of social inclusiveness and leads to fair development [9]. In the industrial sector, gender inequalities must be addressed, and comprehensive equality projects must be executed to guarantee equal access to opportunities [10]. The increase in living standards for all types of people is brought about by economic development and creates the necessary setting for sustainable and balanced community development. Assuredly, since promotes a fair sharing of economic advantages, and makes it possible to reach goals of sustainable development, workers' empowerment is a just way to effectively perform social programs. Often, workers who have been empowered contest for their rights, take part in their local communities, and back business policies that push long-standing sustainability. The area all around has sustainable industrial growth because of policy and technological resolutions [11]. There is research that underscores the significance of these resolutions, which are inclusive and have the support of the policies and promissory technologies.

2 Industry 5.0 and Its Workforce Paradigm

Industry 5.0, a transformative evolution, transcends its predecessor, Industry 4.0, by integrating two fundamental elements: the modern service sector and comprehensive system architectures for digital manufacturing that emphasize sustainability, innovation, and intelligent human collaboration. The current Industry 4.0 has a different focus from its previous version through its combination of modern advanced technologies with operational excellence perspectives that center on humans [12]. The combination of present-day technology including artificial intelligence robotics and the Internet of Things creates intelligent sustainable manufacturing processes through human intelligence. The technology components of Industry 5.0 include collaborative robots and digital twins with edge computing and augmentation technologies because they enable real-time data processing [13]. Through this approach, the creation of innovative human skills coincides with maximum resource efficiency environmental protection, and sustainability resolution. Implementing Industry 5.0 concepts requires stakeholder involvement along with policy backing and interdisciplinary team agreements [14].

The worker roles are undergoing a substantial change from conventional repetitive work into challenging decision-making activities along with creative problem-solving positions. Organizations undergo this transformation because artificial intelligence exists while they need people to display unique abilities that machines cannot perform. AI technology takes over simple operations which leads organizations to create roles that need emotional intelligence combined with advanced analytical skills and innovative thinking. Executive leadership needs to develop workplaces through initiatives that promote flexible thinking and job redesigns to build human capabilities [15]. Organizations recognize creativity as their new competitive advantage and innovation driver so they must develop human resource strategies that emphasize creativity to improve organizational success with satisfied employees [16].

3 Identifying Skill Gaps in the Transition to Industry 5.0

The transition to Industry 5.0 marks a significant shift from traditional technical automation skills towards a greater emphasis on emotional intelligence, creativity, and complex problem-solving. This evolution is driven by the need for a more human-centric approach that integrates advanced technologies with human capabilities. As industries adopt more collaborative technologies, the ability to understand and manage emotions becomes crucial for effective teamwork and leadership. Leaders must cultivate soft skills to guide teams through technological transitions, ensuring that human values remain central to industrial practices [17]. The need for original ideas calls for creative thinking, which helps experts to fit technology and fast-changing surroundings. Professionals expected to collaborate with artificial intelligence and automation must combine technical and interpersonal abilities to maximize output [18]. Integration of artificial intelligence and other modern technologies calls for people to address complex problems, thereby requiring higher-order thinking ability [19].

Asia's move to Industry 5.0 calls for a more all-encompassing skill set including emotional intelligence, creativity, and sophisticated problem-solving capacity than just technical automation skills. The need for human-centered approaches emphasizing society welfare and sustainable production—above Industry 4.0's technologically driven approach—motivates this shift. The call for original ideas necessitates creative thinking, which guides professionals in molding technology and the rapidly changing environment to their needs. Experts expected to work alongside artificial intelligence and automation must possess a mix of technical and people skills that, together, allow them to accomplish more [18]. Why? Artificial intelligence, like other modern technologies, demands that humans solve not just any problems but the really hard, complex ones—if for no other reason than that such problems require what we have long called "higher-order thinking" [19]. Asia's transition to Industry 5.0 necessitates a much more diversified skill set that, in addition to technical automation skills, includes emotional intelligence, creativity, and sophisticated problem-solving capacities. The reasons for this shift are twofold. First, it is imperative to have human-centered methods that place society's welfare and sustainable production—contrary to the brutish technological approach of Industry 4.0—at the center of industrial development. Second, emotional intelligence plays an essential role in all of the efficient interactions and optimum cooperation that are necessary to achieve human–machine cooperation in the forthcoming era of Industry 5.0. Technology-driven sectors show very clearly the demand for a liberal arsenal of soft skills, including critical thinking, problem-solving, pliant communication, and above all, creativity. These are the keys that will open the future gate of flexibility and adaptability in an era that will clearly be defined by ever more potent technological development.

Regarding Industry 4.0 and the continuing effects of the COVID-19 epidemic, the interdisciplinary nature of workforce knowledge is increasingly important. It is hardly necessary to argue for the necessity of meta-competences that exceed conventional disciplinary boundaries. In an erratic future of work, resilient improvisation, dynamic viability, and sustainable innovation will be essential for handling tough situations [20]. Another dimension of potential "work readjustment" is that the current workforce is falling significantly short of the necessary skills to satisfy this future demand. The necessary skills seem to be split evenly between hard and soft varieties, but recent research suggests that soft skills may be increasingly important in a more remote work-focused future [21]. The World Economic Forum projects that technological developments will cause half of all workers to require reskilling by 2025. This projection emphasizes the necessity for our educational systems to produce something that we might call "knowledge for the future," or knowledge that is adaptable enough to serve the everyday problem-solving needs of a tomorrow that increasingly seems like it will be built on new, unforeseen technological platforms. Who knows what new technologies will be ubiquitous in 2030? Yet somehow, we must prepare the workforce for that kind of future.

4 Strategies for Skills Development in Industry 5.0

In Asia, the efficient development of skills is crucial for cultivating a human-centric industrial ecosystem in which sustainable development is possible. Doing this in Asia means applying state-of-the-art methods. One way to do this is through learning collaboratively, not just with other humans, but also with sophisticated technologies like AI and Cognitive Digital Twins. Another way is to augment our age-old learn-by-doing methods with technologies like the Internet of Things (IoT) and blockchain, which are much more advanced than what our grandparents could apply in their workshops. Of course, whatever future learning and working involves, it must not be an affront to the sustainability and resilience objectives we have set for ourselves. Achieving these goals requires not just a path but also an overall strategy. And that's what we intend to outline in this paper.

Upskilling and reskilling are becoming increasingly vital in Asia amid rapid technological progress and a prominent shift in labor market demands. As the World Economic Forum states, "By 2025, employers anticipate that 85 million jobs will be displaced by the shift in labor between humans and machines." If organizations are to remain competitive in a volatile, unpredictable, complex, and ambiguous (VUCA) world, they must identify skill gaps and execute targeted initiatives to close the gaps by reskilling the affected employees [22]. As the Forum also notes, the affected employees are not all the same age, they come from across the demographic spectrum [23]. Thus, an imperative highlighted by the Forum and Mission 2030 in this regard is that all employees, young and old, must embrace lifelong learning.

In hybrid environments throughout Asia, the importance of soft skills, including emotional intelligence, leadership, and collaboration, is becoming increasingly significant. Emotional intelligence (EI) is acknowledged as an essential characteristic for leaders, improving team performance and promoting positive workplace attitudes, especially in remote and digital interactions [24]. The incorporation of soft skills is crucial for professionals, including architects, who navigate the complexities of digital construction, where adaptive leadership and effective communication are vital [17]. The development of emotional intelligence through structured training programs is recommended to cultivate leaders who can effectively manage hybrid teams [25, 26]. Organizations must adopt agile leadership practices that emphasize collaboration and innovation to succeed in the increasingly integrated digital and physical environments [27].

Lifelong learning frameworks in Asia are progressively integrating micro-credentials, online platforms, and corporate training programs to promote ongoing education. Countries such as Korea, Japan, and Singapore are establishing integrated lifelong learning systems that correspond with global trends, highlighting the necessity for skills pertinent to the knowledge economy [28]. Micro-credentials represent a flexible approach for learners to rapidly acquire specific skills, addressing the increasing costs of education and the demand from employers for competency-based qualifications [29, 30]. The COVID-19 pandemic has expedited the adoption of online learning platforms, facilitating greater access to education and training opportunities, thereby addressing inequities in skill acquisition [29]. This transition facilitates personal career advancement and improves workforce adaptability in dynamic job markets [30, 31].

Interdisciplinary training in Asia is increasingly acknowledged as vital for cultivating a workforce that possesses both technical and non-technical skills, especially in light of the requirements of Industry 4.0 and global challenges. Models of collaboration seen in Zhuhai and Macao illustrate the integration of the educational system with industry to cultivate a diverse talent pool with crucial competencies, such as skills in management and foreign languages [32]. The Global Interprofessional Education (IPE) model underscores the importance of integrating cross-disciplines not just within the health professions but also with those in non-health vocations to better prepare students to work in culturally diverse teams and to solve complex problems [33]. Vocational frameworks are evolving to embrace digital technologies while also providing more personalized, "horsepower" learning experiences, scenarios that ensure students don't just survive our fast-emerging, post-modernist world but thrive in it [34, 35]. These interdisciplinary, cross-sector strategies do more than seek to upgrade the innovation and adaptability quotient of our graduates. They also ensure that the educational outcomes promised by our institutions conveniently align with the sometimes capricious requirements of industry [35, 36].

5 Workforce Training Models for Industry 5.0

The human-centric, sustainable, and resilient ideal of Industry 5.0 builds upon Industry 4.0's technological directives. Amalgamating advanced technologies with human intellect, Industry 5.0 leverages both to optimize not just industrial operations, but also educational frameworks and workplace procedures [37]. To make the shift from 4.0 to 5.0, however, demands worker re- and up-skilling. Why? As we're frequently reminded, "the workers are the ones who need to change if we're really to achieve a successful transition to Industry 5.0" [38, 39].). Education and training must serve the same aim—to equip individuals for an evolving industrial environment. That demands a kind of "smart education," which is Smarter than what's served up in a "dumbed-down" way often characterizing missed opportunities in human and machine targets serving this ideal. Human-centricity, sustainability, and resilience are paramount in Industry 5.0. This "next generation" of industry builds upon the technological inflections of Industry 4.0 but focuses much more on humans—workers as well as consumers—and the environment. The emergent industrial framework marries advanced technologies with human intellect to optimize procedures in both workplaces and classrooms [37]. The transition to Industry 5.0 requires not just upskilling but also reskilling of the current workforce to accommodate job dynamics that call for new skills [38, 39]. Obstacles to Industry 5.0 integration in education include data protection issues, the digital divide, and the potential biases of AI-based development models. However, it also provides a chance to create personal learning environments and support lifelong learning. Effective implementation of Industry 5.0 in education depends on the active engagement of educators, policymakers, and industry leaders to design sustainable and ethical solutions [7].

Industry 5.0 is based on the concept of human centrality, sustainability, and resilience in the workplace by combining sophisticated technologies with the capabilities of humans. In this new paradigm of education, sophisticated technologies like intelligent tutoring systems, robots, and IoT are integrated into advanced educational systems to make the workforce ready for future challenges. The implementation of Industry 5.0 in education is necessary for the development of digital competencies and the practical readiness of graduates to enter Society 5.0 [40]. The application of Industry 5.0 in education is cross-sectional across multiple sectors, including healthcare, engineering, and remote learning, with examples of good practice [37]. Nevertheless, concerns such as data privacy, the digital divide, and possible biases in AI-based systems cannot be overlooked. As Industry 5.0 advances, there is a growing need for cooperation between educators, policymakers, and industry leaders to design and deliver smart education solutions effectively [7, 38].

Augmented reality has demonstrated the potential to enhance cognitive load management and boost learning outcomes, especially among novice learners. Recent studies emphasize the potential of extended reality (XR) technologies, such as virtual reality (VR), augmented reality (AR), and mixed reality (MR), in the field of education. Nonetheless, virtual reality may impose extraneous cognitive demands, which could impede learning for novices [41]. In teacher education, XR technologies are predominantly utilized for training procedural knowledge, with VR being the most commonly used tool [42]. AI-driven adaptive systems personalize learning experiences, whereas VR provides immersive environments that enhance experiential learning. These technologies demonstrate the potential to improve educational accessibility and inclusion for students with disabilities. Challenges persist, such as elevated implementation costs, technical obstacles, and insufficient teacher preparedness [43]. Additional investigation is required to examine the long-term effects of these technologies and to address ethical issues [44].

A recent study underscores the complex dynamics of workforce transformation and governmental interventions across Asia. Research highlights the significance of multi-stakeholder participation in sustainable ecotourism [45] and the influence of Industry 4.0 technologies on employability and skills in South Asia [5]. The latter suggests an "Industry 4.0 SEI Framework" to direct policy and industry strategies. The research examines aging place initiatives in Japan, Singapore, and Thailand within the framework of aging populations, promoting person-centered methods in policy formulation [46]. Moreover, research on microgrids for rural electrification in Southeast Asia underscores the potential for job creation and economic development through energy transitions. These documents jointly emphasize the necessity for customized policy interventions and workforce development plans to tackle the distinct problems and opportunities within Asia's swiftly changing economic environment.

6 Challenges in Implementing Industry 5.0 Training Programs

Industry 5.0 is focussing on how humans and machines can work together. This is changing the way we think about the workforce. However, there are several tough challenges in putting comprehensive training programs in place to get the Asian workforce ready for this transition. A big challenge is that the traditional manufacturing workforce is often resistant to change. It's really important to tackle the psychological barriers and the fear of becoming outdated, since moving from comfortable manual tasks to handling complex digital technologies can feel overwhelming for a lot of people. It's really important to address these concerns and encourage a culture of being adaptable and committed to lifelong learning to successfully adopt the principles of Industry 5.0. Secondly, the differences in access to advanced technologies and the fair distribution of training resources throughout the region create notable infrastructure gaps. Making sure that everyone in the workforce, no matter where they are or their economic background, can gain the digital skills they need is a tough logistical problem that we need to tackle. Additionally, the need to promote inclusivity in workforce empowerment, particularly regarding gender equity, age diversity, and regional disparities, implements Industry 5.0 training programs even more complex. Resistance to change, especially regarding the implementation of Industry 5.0 training in Asia, is notably affected by psychological barriers and concerns about obsolescence. Comprehending these challenges is essential for organizations seeking to cultivate a culture of adaptability and innovation. This document delineates essential components of the resistance.

6.1 Psychological Obstacles

Cognitive dissonance occurs when employees encounter discomfort due to new training that conflicts with their pre-existing beliefs and values, resulting in resistance.

Fear of Failure: Concerns regarding inadequacy in adapting to new technologies can impede the acceptance of change, as employees may fear being outperformed by their peers [47].

6.2 *Fear of Obsolescence*

Concerns Regarding Job Security, The introduction of advanced technologies generates concerns regarding redundancy, leading to resistance against change initiatives [48]. Employees may perceive new training as a threat to their existing roles, resulting in skepticism and reluctance to engage with new systems [49].

6.3 *Organizational Support Role of Leadership*

Effective communication and support from management can reduce resistance by promoting trust and transparency [47]. Psychological resilience can be enhanced through training and support, thereby improving employee adaptability and decreasing resistance to change [50]. Conversely, some contend that resistance functions as a significant feedback mechanism, encouraging organizations to reevaluate their change strategies and align them with employee needs and concerns. This perspective emphasizes the capacity of resistance to facilitate more deliberate and inclusive change processes.

6.4 *Infrastructure Gaps: Access to Technology and Equitable Distribution of Training Resources*

The primary infrastructure gaps hindering access to technology and equitable distribution of training resources include inadequate hardware and software availability, insufficient internet connectivity, and a lack of trained educators proficient in digital tools. Many schools face significant disparities in technology access, with ratios such as 13 students per computer in some districts, highlighting the scarcity of resources. Additionally, the digital divide is exacerbated by socio-economic factors, where marginalized communities often lack access to essential devices and reliable internet, further entrenching educational inequities [51]. Furthermore, the absence of culturally relevant content and effective digital literacy programs limits the ability of students to engage meaningfully with technology [52, 53]. Addressing these gaps requires collaborative efforts from various stakeholders to invest in infrastructure and training, ensuring that all learners can benefit from technological advancements [54].

7 Human-Centric Transformation in Asia's Workforce Development

Through the Asia-wide human-centric workforce development approach digital technology combines with sustainable practices alongside human elements to modernize labor competency and flexibility skills. Labour Transformation functions as a fundamental solution that addresses fast industrial transformations alongside emerging global crises. Workplace conditions where employees maintain relationships with their surroundings produce better operational results while lowering wrong steps according to [55].

The implementation of life and career construction interventions creates sustainable development options that exceed typical employment initiatives and produce excellent outcomes [56]. Thanks to digital transformation Asian economies benefit from improved connectivity combined with productivity increases to improve labor quality standards that drive industrial structure progression.

Life and career construction interventions serve to develop equitable sustainable development solutions beyond traditional job placement strategies and deliver outstanding results according to [56]. Skilled labor needed for digital adaptation can be created by investments in knowledge along with workforce development initiatives [57]. Digital technology will integrate with workforce management to help enterprises improve ESG (Environmental Social Governance) performance with sustainable practices in workforce management, Human Resources technology solutions are now being advanced for dealing with worldwide issues as well as improving employee lifecycle processes and productivity levels [58]. And while human-centric transformation must still be a priority the top three organizations need to consider the macro risks of technology around job loss and social dislocation unless it starts to find solutions to those challenges.

7.1 Asia Faces the Need to Adjust Workforce Development Approaches to Respect Local Cultural and Societal Environments

Studies reveal that workforce development requires distinct complex adaptations that must match each Asian cultural context. Traditional post-disaster recovery workforce selection systems reveal cultural influences on workforce choices throughout Southeast Asian nations [59]. Research conducted on climatic hotspots shows women demonstrate agency as cultural expectations along with socioeconomic conditions control both decision-making processes and adaptive capabilities [60]. Variations in reproductive health and antenatal care delivery across countries emphasize the importance of creating workforce planning methods that reflect each locality's specific health service model [61]. To achieve effective intervention results health organizations must adapt their programs accordingly for ethnic minority groups as deduced from studies by Marsiglia and Booth [62]. Research has shown the necessity of personalized educational strategies for neurosurgical training that handle the unique health requirements together with workforce stock in East Asian territories [63]. These findings illustrate how cultural specificities together with social customs play an essential role in creating efficient workforce development methods across Asia.

7.2 *Promoting Well-being and Worker Rights in Industry 5.0 Workplaces*

Efforts to enhance both worker well-being and rights in Industry 5.0 workplaces rely on an integrated framework of care ethics combined with ergonomic evaluations and flexible leadership methods. Law professor Umbrello demonstrates through care ethics how relationality creates ethical actions that safeguard workers' well-being within technologically advanced environments [64]. The web platform created by [65] enhances ergonomic risk monitoring which results in workplace environments that both monitor workers' physical needs and maintain their safety. Managerial practices require fundamental reevaluation according to expert analysis since the COVID-19 crisis displayed how organizations should establish genuine frameworks to back up their workers' physical and rights-based health needs [66]. At times of uncertainty, prevention-focused leadership strategies help improve employee well-being through better role definition combined with effective workload management [67]. These findings support a complete system that emphasizes technological development and employee well-being in Industry 5.0 environments.

7.3 *Ethical Considerations: Balancing Technological Advancement with Socio-Economic Inclusivity*

The harmonization of technological evolution and social economic inclusivity requires complex solutions which both fix entrenched disparities and sustain environmental wellness. The COVID-19 pandemic exposed how better-resourced nations and individuals capture the majority of vaccines which intensifies health inequalities resulting in global safety risks [68]. Career interventions need to advance toward sustainable development initiatives that promote community involvement and ethical conduct instead of restricting themselves to simple economic opportunity access [56]. The cosmological framework promotes technology serving societal and ecological health needs better than profitability and demonstrates that local projects succeed in resolving large-scale issues [69]. Impact investing requires engaging vulnerable stakeholders as their voices serve to guarantee investments achieve actual benefits for inequality-disadvantaged populations [70]. Healthcare distribution must take socio-economic elements into account because market inequalities combined with systemic racism create barriers to health justice [71]. The accumulating case studies demonstrate how essential it is to promote inclusion across technological innovation and economic growth.

8 Future Trends and Opportunities in Asia's Workforce Empowerment

The contemporary development of workforce empowerment across Asia for Industry 5.0 gives the importance of human-centered operational approaches combined with machine-human collaborations becoming increasingly central to societal development [39]. Psychological empowerment which is combined with employee engagement represents an essential management component while leadership methods and organizational culture play vital facilitating roles [72]. Organizations need an overall empowerment model for championing fair employment practices together with sustainable workplace conditions because of the expanded decent work definition [9]. South Asia is experiencing workforce changes because of Industry 4.0 technology adoption which necessitates workforce development centered on digital competency and social capability training. To reach full potential in terms of Maximize potential benefits [5] businesses need to solve financial problems and regulatory roadblocks.

Workforce empowerment together with skill development remain crucial drivers for developing Asia's labour market of the future.

8.1 Regional Cooperation in Skills Development and Technology Transfer

Asian economic growth requires coordinated industrial skills development alongside technology transfer in distinct areas. International technology transfers from developed nations drive East Asian development by identifying three main adoption stages between developed and developing countries [73]. Socioeconomic goals and labor market transformations require technical and vocational education training skills development [74]. A functional skills development system requires three types of skill training alongside strong labor market information systems and supportive institutional structures to function effectively [75]. The shortage of qualified labor forces in Vietnam and Southeast Asia prevents large Japanese investors from successfully transferring technological expertise across their operations. The manufacturing industry depends heavily on government policies which help decrease technical standards differences with workforce capabilities according to [76]. The development of skills and modernizing technology in Asian nations receives a significant boost through cooperative action between boundary regions.

8.2 Preparing for the Next Wave of Technologies: AI, IoT, and Sustainable Practices in Asian Industries

Research findings show how AI IoT and blockchain-based approaches can promote sustainability throughout multiple Asian business sectors. Industry experts use AI and IoT technologies to determine crop yields while creating optimal supply chains that ensure precise tracking of goods [77]. These technologies benefit smart cities' supply chains and energy systems but IoT and AI integration show exceptional promise for future developments [78]. Through AIoT solutions manufacturing facilities achieve greater operational effectiveness and minimize resource waste while implementing safer operational practices for improved sustainability [79]. The merging of computer technologies generates numerous benefits for resource control alongside power system optimization and operational supply chain visibility. The successful adoption of these technologies requires their effective management of high costs while dealing with complex technical requirements and clear resolution of data privacy issues. Full systemic adoption of these technologies depends on multidisciplinary research alongside collaborative partnerships with ethical considerations [80].

9 Conclusion

Such needs of human-centric solutions and sustainable operating practices between human workers and intelligent systems at the anthropocentric network level create a paradigm shift for Asian industry 5.0 era. Asian economic sectors are not only unique in their uses of automation but also in how complex it can be to train workers to thrive in such an industrial shift. Human capital trained in Industry 5.0 systems correctly in Asia would enable the value being generated from these AI robotics and IoT technologies to occur with economic equality and social improvement. The Asian labor force needs holistic policies that offer ongoing workforce development in conjunction with skills development services, enabling access to lifelong learning for the growth of a future-ready generation.

The three parties cross Collaboration: The three key stakeholders must join forces to formulate frameworks that marry technological proficiency with creative and emotional intelligence and problem-solving skills. These initiatives include both Singapore's Skills Future and India's Skill India in this example and demonstrate the link between skill development programs and better career opportunities, however, the space has pioneered targeted efforts to cater to different target populations and standardized access to learning resources for people embedded in urban cities or small villages within city limits.

Augmented reality platforms for AI-enabled personal learning will help in filling physical barcode gaps when you are providing training to remote locations. All population groups including elderly people and women need to be specifically included in policy efforts which must work towards minimizing urban–rural service differences in the workforce. The advance of Industry 5.0 demands the creation of adaptable work systems to confront workforce resistance against modernization initiatives, especially within conventional industries.

9.1 *Call to Action for Governments, Industries, and Educational Institutions in Asia to Collaborate*

Asia needs government partnerships with industry and educational establishments to capture different emerging challenges alongside beneficial opportunities. The analysis reveals that seaweed offers promising bio-industrial possibilities that demand collaboration between different stakeholders for building sustainable value chains. Innovative educational technology implementation faces budget shortages and ineffective industry-academy relations in higher education which demands enhanced state interventions through international programs [81]. Research collaborations between universities and industries reshape innovation and competitiveness especially for microtle, small and medium-sized enterprises by implementing successful collaborative models like research partnerships and knowledge transfer programs [82]. The quadruple helix model puts forth local communities together with private sector institutions educational organizations and government representation as an efficient method for community development and better graduate job placement outcomes [83].

9.2 *Vision for a Sustainable, Inclusive, and Human-Centric Future for Asia's Workforce*

The developing workforce development model in Asia requires attention to sustainable practices along with inclusive systems and human-centered focus. Education 5.0 serves as a fundamental driver for developing digital competencies that get graduates ready for future employment as part of the Society 5.0 framework [40]. Industry 5.0 requires workforce empowerment through reskilling and upskilling because development focuses on human and machine intelligence integration [39]. Data integration within talent management systems enables organizations to develop sustainable HR methods that combine algorithmic approaches with human-focused methodology. AI functions as a major new component within sustainable career systems by analyzing interactions between people and careers using a liminal framework that shapes modern workforce transformation. The combined research signifies that education technology is necessary to restructure industry operations and career systems as fundamental steps for developing a sustainable workforce composition based on equality and human value in Asia Pacific.

References

1. Leng, J., Sha, W.C., Wang, B., Zheng, P., Zhuang, C., Liu, Q., Wuest, T., Mourtzis, D., & Wang, L. (2022). Industry 5.0: Prospect and retrospect. *Journal of Manufacturing Systems*. https://doi.org/10.1016/j.jmsy.2022.09.017
2. Žižić, Marina Crnjac, et al. "From Industry 4.0 towards Industry 5.0: A Review and Analysis of Paradigm Shift for the People, Organization and Technology." *Energies* (2022): n. pag. https://doi.org/10.3390/en15145221
3. Alves, Joel et al. "Is Industry 5.0 a Human-Centred Approach? A Systematic Review." *Processes* (2023): n. pag. https://doi.org/10.3390/pr11010193
4. Ghobakhloo, M., Iranmanesh, M., Tseng, M., Grybauskas, A., Stefanini, A., & Amran, A. (2023). Behind the definition of Industry 5.0: a systematic review of technologies, principles, components, and values. *Journal of Industrial and Production Engineering, 40*, 432 - 447. https://doi.org/10.1080/21681015.2023.2216701
5. Miah, M.T., Erdei-Gally, S., Dancs, A., & Fekete-Farkas, M. (2024). A Systematic Review of Industry 4.0 Technology on Workforce Employability and Skills: Driving Success Factors and Challenges in South Asia. *Economies*. https://doi.org/10.3390/economies12020035
6. Yang, X., Amtsberg, F., Sedlmair, M., & Menges, A. (2024). Challenges and potential for human-robot collaboration in timber prefabrication. Automation in Construction. https://doi.org/10.1016/j.autcon.2024.105333
7. Adel, A. (2024). The Convergence of Intelligent Tutoring, Robotics, and IoT in Smart Education for the Transition from Industry 4.0 to 5.0. *Smart Cities*.https://doi.org/10.3390/smartcities7010014
8. Jain, N., Gupta, V., Temperini, V., Meissner, D., & D'Angelo, E. (2024). Human-machine interactions: from past to future- a systematic literature review. Journal of Management History. https://doi.org/10.1108/jmh-12-2022-0085
9. Yeh, Y., & Wang, I. (2024). Exploring the development trajectory of decent work literature: An empowerment perspective. Technological Forecasting and Social Change. https://doi.org/10.1016/j.techfore.2024.123230
10. Mu'min, M.S., Yaqin, M., & Anam, M.S. (2024). Does energy transition matter to sustainable development in ASEAN? International Journal of Renewable Energy Development. https://doi.org/10.61435/ijred.2024.59544
11. Rojas, M., Balderas, D.C., Maldonado, J., Ponce, P., Lopez-Bernal, D., & Molina, A. (2024). Lack of verified Inclusive Technology for Workers with Disabilities in Industry 4.0: a systematic review. International Journal of Sustainable Engineering. https://doi.org/10.1080/19397038.2024.2328711

12. Zafar, M.H., Langås, E.F., & Sanfilippo, F. (2024). Exploring the synergies between collaborative robotics, digital twins, augmentation, and industry 5.0 for smart manufacturing: A state-of-the-art review. Robotics Comput. Integr. Manuf., 89, 102769. https://doi.org/10.1016/j.rcim.2024.102769
13. Sharma, M., Tomar, A., & Hazra, A. (2024). Edge Computing for Industry 5.0: Fundamental, Applications, and Research Challenges. IEEE Internet of Things Journal, 11, 19070-19093. https://doi.org/10.1109/JIOT.2024.3359297
14. Narkhede, G., Chinchanikar, S., Narkhede, R., & Chaudhari, T. (2024). Role of Industry 5.0 for driving sustainability in the manufacturing sector: an emerging research agenda. Journal of Strategy and Management. https://doi.org/10.1108/jsma-06-2023-0144
15. Steven, H., Cady., Jari, Willing., Deakon, A., Cady. (2024). 1. The AI Imperative: On Becoming Quintessentially Human. The Journal of Applied Behavioral Science.https://doi.org/10.1177/00218863241284310
16. Iryna, Petrova. (2023). 4. Creativity development as an imperative for strategic human resource management. Theory Into Practice, https://doi.org/10.21511/slrtp.12(2).2022.05
17. Syafizal, Shahruddin., Ungku, Norani, Sonet., Athira, Azmi., Nadzirah, Zainordin. (2024). 2. Traversing the complexity of digital construction and beyond through soft skills: experiences of Malaysian architects. Engineering, Construction, and Architectural Management, https://doi.org/10.1108/ecam-01-2024-0147
18. Jiewu, Leng., Xiaofeng, Zhu., Zhiqiang, Huang., Xingyu, Li., Pai, Zheng., Jiafu, Wan., Xin, Chen., Lihui, Wang., Qiang, Liu. (2024). 5. Unlocking the power of industrial artificial intelligence towards Industry 5.0: Insights, pathways, and challenges. Journal of Manufacturing Systems, https://doi.org/10.1016/j.jmsy.2024.02.010
19. César, Cuevas., Ignacio, Mira-Solves., Antonio, José, Verdú, Jover. (2024). 1. Industry 5.0's pillars and Lean Six Sigma: mapping the current interrelationship and future research directions. International Journal of Productivity and Performance Management, https://doi.org/10.1108/ijppm-08-2023-0404
20. Lukas, Zenk., Attila, Pausits., Barbara, Brenner., David, F.J., Campbell., Doris, A., Behrens., E., Stöckler., Stefan, Oppl., Gerald, Steiner. (2024). 2. Meta-competences in complex environments: An interdisciplinary perspective. Thinking Skills and Creativity, https://doi.org/10.1016/j.tsc.2024.101515
21. Caitlin, Ferreira., Jean, Pierre, Francois, Robertson., Ley, land, Pitt. (2022). 5. Business (un)usual: Critical skills for the next normal. Thunderbird International Business Review, https://doi.org/10.1002/tie.22276

22. Gillian, Pillans. (2024). 2. Reskilling and rethinking work: how to build a future-fit workforce. Strategic HR Review, https://doi.org/10.1108/hr-03-2024-0023
23. Aparajita, Datta., Stephanie, Coates., Alan, Rossiter., Ramanan, Krishnamoorti. (2024). 5. Reskilling and Upskilling for Decarbonization: Analyzing Micro-Credential Programs for Energy Workforce Development. The Journal of Continuing Higher Education, https://doi.org/10.1080/07377363.2024.2377777
24. Isabel, Coronado-Maldonado., M., Dolores, Benítez-Márquez. (2023). 1. Emotional intelligence, leadership, and work teams: A hybrid literature review. Heliyon, https://doi.org/10.1016/j.heliyon.2023.e20356
25. Athanasios, Drigas., Chara, Papoutsi., Charalabos, Skianis. (2023). 3. Being an Emotionally Intelligent Leader through the Nine-Layer Model of Emotional Intelligence—The Supporting Role of New Technologies. Sustainability, https://doi.org/10.3390/su15108103
26. Golnaz, Sadri. (2012). 4. Emotional Intelligence and Leadership Development. Public Personnel Management, https://doi.org/10.1177/009102601204100308
27. Paola, Bellis., Matteo, Cunial., Daniel, Trabucchi. (2024). 5. Mastering hybrid worlds through digital leadership: The role of agility in fostering innovation. Business Horizons, https://doi.org/10.1016/j.bushor.2024.04.002
28. Soonghee, Han. (2001). 1. Creating systems for lifelong learning in Asia. Asia Pacific Education Review, https://doi.org/10.1007/BF03026293
29. Rory, McGreal., Wayne, Mackintosh., Glenda, C., Cox., Don, Olcott, Jr. (2022). 4. Bridging the Gap: Micro-credentials for Development. The International Review of Research in Open and Distributed Learning, https://doi.org/10.19173/irrodl.v23i3.6696
30. Kinga, Zdunek., Beata, Dobrowolska., Magdalena, Dziurka., Alessandro, Galazzi., Stefania, Chiappinotto., Alvisa, Palese., John, Wells. (2024). 5. Challenges and opportunities of micro-credentials as a new form of certification in health science education—a discussion paper. BMC Medical Education, https://doi.org/10.1186/s12909-024-06174-8
31. Melinda, Lewis. (1998). 3. Lifelong learning. Why professionals must have the desire for and the capacity to continue learning throughout life. Health information management: journal of the Health Information Management Association of Australia, https://doi.org/10.1177/183335839802800209
32. T., Liu. (2024). 1. The construction of a collaborative cultivation path of internationalized talents in Zhuhai and Macao based on the theory of "synergy". Applied mathematics and nonlinear sciences, https://doi.org/10.2478/amns-2024-2938

33. Fraide, A., Ganotice., George, L., Tipoe., Mine, Orlu., Eileen, Tipoe. (2024). 2. Breaking disciplinary silos: A global approach to interprofessional education.. Medical Education, https://doi.org/10.1111/medu.15342
34. Raihan, Tahir., Zuraidah, Abdullah. (2024). 4. Shaping Industry 4.0 Ready Talent: TVET Experts' Strategies in Content Selection - NGT and ISM Approach. Evolutionary studies in imaginative culture, https://doi.org/10.70082/sericulture.vi.744
35. Mei, Wang. (2024). 5. Research on the Cultivation of Interdisciplinary Innovation Ability of Students in Higher Vocational Colleges and Universities. Applied mathematics and nonlinear sciences, https://doi.org/10.2478/amns-2024-1303
36. X., Zhu. (2024). 3. Research on the Talent Cultivation Mechanism of Higher Vocational Colleges under the Interdisciplinary Education Model in the Age of Big Data. Applied mathematics and nonlinear sciences, https://doi.org/10.2478/amns-2024-2901
37. Supriya, Y., Bhulakshmi, D., Bhattacharya, S., Gadekallu, T.R., Vyas, P., Kaluri, R., Sumathy, S., Koppu, S., Brown, D.J., & Mahmud, M. (2024). Industry 5.0 in Smart Education: Concepts, Applications, Challenges, Opportunities, and Future Directions. *IEEE Access, 12*, 81938–81967.https://doi.org/10.1109/ACCESS.2024.3401473
38. P.R.A., Oeij., Karolien, Lenaerts., S., Dhondt., Wietse, van, Dijk., Doris, Schartinger., Sorko, Sabrina., Chris, Warhurst. (2024). 5. A Conceptual Framework for Workforce Skills for Industry 5.0: Implications for Research, Policy and Practice. Journal of Innovation Management, https://doi.org/10.24840/2183-0606_012.001_0010
39. Nair, A., Pillai, S.V., & Senthil Kumar, S. (2024). Towards emerging Industry 5.0 – a review-based framework. *Journal of Strategy and Management*. https://doi.org/10.1108/jsma-04-2023-0067
40. Shahidi Hamedani, S., Aslam, S., Mundher Oraibi, B., Wah, Y.B., & Shahidi Hamedani, S. (2024). Transitioning towards Tomorrow's Workforce: Education 5.0 in the Landscape of Society 5.0: A Systematic Literature Review. *Education Sciences*.https://doi.org/10.3390/educsci14101041
41. Poupard, M., Larrue, F., Sauzéon, H., & Tricot, A. (2024). A systematic review of immersive technologies for education: Learning performance, cognitive load, and intrinsic motivation. *British Journal of Educational Technology*.https://doi.org/10.1111/bjet.13503
42. Wang, Q., & Li, Y. (2024). How virtual reality, augmented reality and mixed reality facilitate teacher education: A systematic review. *J. Comput. Assist. Learn., 40*, 1276–1294.https://doi.org/10.1111/jcal.12949
43. Chalkiadakis, A., Seremetaki, A., Kanellou, A., Kallishi, M., Morfopoulou, A., Moraitaki, M., & Mastrokoukou, S. (2024). Impact of Artificial Intelligence and Virtual Reality on Educational Inclusion: A Systematic

Review of Technologies Supporting Students with Disabilities. *Education Sciences*.https://doi.org/10.3390/educsci14111223
44. Barrera Castro, G.P., Chiappe, A., Becerra Rodríguez, D.F., & Sepulveda, F.G. (2024). Harnessing AI for Education 4.0: Drivers of Personalized Learning. *Electronic Journal of e-Learning*.https://doi.org/10.34190/ejel.22.5.3467
45. Salman, A., Jaafar, M., Mohamad, D., Ebekozien, A., & Rasul, T. (2024). The multi-stakeholder role in Asian sustainable ecotourism: a systematic review. *PSU Research Review*.https://doi.org/10.1108/prr-05-2022-0048
46. Satchanawakul, N., Liangruenrom, N., Thang, L.L., & Satchanawakul, N. (2024). A systematic scoping review of aging in place strategies in Japan, Singapore, and Thailand: A comparative analysis. *Australasian Journal on aging*.https://doi.org/10.1111/ajag.13378
47. Nashwa, Nabil, Kamal., Guek, Nee, Ke., Zuhrah, Beevi., Kenneth, Leow. (2024). 3. Resisting organizational change? Psychological resilience and perceived organizational support as mediators in promoting psychological well-being and organizational citizenship behaviors. International Journal of Wellbeing, https://doi.org/10.5502/ijw.v14i3.3501
48. M, Sendrea. (2023). 1. Study and Synthesis of Concepts and Practices of Resistance to Organizational Change. Economica, https://doi.org/10.53486/econ.2023.123.045
49. Dennis, G., Erwin., Andrew, N., Garman. (2010). 4. Resistance to organizational change: linking research and practice. Leadership & Organization Development Journal, https://doi.org/10.1108/01437731011010371
50. Manuela, Pardo, del, Val., Clara, Martínez, Fuentes. (2003). 5. Resistance to change: a literature review and empirical study. Management Decision, https://doi.org/10.1108/00251740310457597
51. Olabisi, Oluwakemi, Adeleye., Chima, Abimbola, Eden., Idowu, Sulaimon, Adeniyi. (2024). 1. Educational technology and the digital divide: A conceptual framework for technical literacy inclusion. International Journal of Science and Research Archive, https://doi.org/10.30574/ijsra.2024.12.1.0405
52. Farhat, Naureen, Memon., Sarwat, Naureen, Memon. (2024). 3. Digital Divide and Equity in Education. Advances in educational technologies and instructional design book series, https://doi.org/10.4018/979-8-3693-1854-6.ch004
53. Paul, Resta., Thérèse, Laferrière. (2008). 4. Issues and Challenges Related to Digital Equity. https://doi.org/10.1007/978-0-387-73315-9_44
54. Chiara, Suraci., Sara, Pizzi., Federico, Montori., Marco, Di, Felice., Giuseppe, Araniti. (2022). 5. 6G to Take the Digital Divide by Storm: Key Technologies and Trends to Bridge the Gap. Future Internet, https://doi.org/10.3390/fi14060189

55. Catchpole, K. (2013). Improving performance through human-centered reconfiguration of existing designs. *BMJ Quality & Safety*, *22*(1), 5–7. https://doi.org/10.1136/BMJQS-2012-001677
56. Guichard, J. (2022). From career guidance to designing lives acting for fair and sustainable development. *International Journal for Educational and Vocational Guidance*, *22*(3), 581–601. https://doi.org/10.1007/s10775-022-09530-6
57. Zhang, Z., Madni, G. R., & Naeem, J. (2023). Unleashing the horizons of labor quality, digitalization on upgradation of industrial structure in Asian economies. *PLOS ONE*, *18*(7), e0288866. https://doi.org/10.1371/journal.pone.0288866
58. Xiang, H., Lu, J., Kosov, M. E., Volkova, M., Ponkratov, V. V., Masterov, A., Elyakova, I. D., Popkov, S. Yu., Taburov, D. Yu., Lazareva, N. V., Muda, I., Vasiljeva, M. V., & Zekiy, A. O. (2023). Sustainable Development of Employee Lifecycle Management in the Age of Global Challenges: Evidence from China, Russia, and Indonesia. *Sustainability*, *15*(6), 4987. https://doi.org/10.3390/su15064987
59. Natrujirote, W. (2018). Surviving Families After Disaster In Southeast Asia: An Understanding From A Sociological Perspective. *ABAC Journal*, *38*(2), 161–171. http://www.assumptionjournal.au.edu/index.php/abacjournal/article/download/3577/2186
60. Rao, N., Mishra, A., Prakash, A., Singh, C., Qaisrani, A., Poonacha, P., Vincent, K., & Bedelian, C. (2019). A qualitative comparative analysis of women's agency and adaptive capacity in climate change hotspots in Asia and Africa. *Nature Climate Change*, *9*(12), 964–971. https://doi.org/10.1038/S41558-019-0638-Y
61. Kunjumen, T., Okech, M., Asamani, J. A., Mohamed, N. A., & Nuruzzaman, Md. (2022). Multi-country case studies on planning RMNCH services using WISN methodology: Bangladesh, Ghana, Kenya, Sultanate of Oman, and Papua New Guinea. *Human Resources for Health*, *19*(S1). https://doi.org/10.1186/s12960-021-00671-3
62. Marsiglia, F. F., & Booth, J. M. (2015). Cultural Adaptation of Interventions in Real Practice Settings. *Research on Social Work Practice*, *25*(4), 423–432. https://doi.org/10.1177/1049731514535989
63. Ferraris, K. P., Matsumura, H., Wardhana, D. P. W., Vesagas, T., Seng, K., Seng, K., Ali, M. R. M., Ishikawa, E., Matsumura, A., Rosyidi, R. M., Mahadewa, T. G. B., & Kuo, M.-F. (2020). The state of neurosurgical training and education in East Asia: analysis and strategy development for this frontier of the world. *Neurosurgical Focus*, *48*(3). https://doi.org/10.3171/2019.12.FOCUS19814

64. Umbrello, S. (2023). Emotions and Automation in a High-Tech Workplace: a Commentary. *Philosophy & Technology*, *36*(1), 1–5. https://doi.org/10.1007/s13347-023-00615-w
65. Generosi, A., Agostinelli, T., Ceccacci, S., & Mengoni, M. (2022). A novel platform to enable the future human-centered factory. *The International Journal of Advanced Manufacturing Technology*, *122*(11–12), 4221–4233. https://doi.org/10.1007/s00170-022-09880-z
66. Watson, D., Wallace, J. M. T., Land, C., & Patey, J. (2023). Re-organising wellbeing: Contexts, critiques and contestations of dominant wellbeing narratives. *Organization*, *30*(3), 441–452. https://doi.org/10.1177/13505084231156267
67. Li, K., & Griffin, M. A. (2022). Prevention-focused leadership and well-being during the pandemic: mediation by role clarity and workload. *Leadership & Organization Development Journal*, *43*(6), 890–908. https://doi.org/10.1108/lodj-10-2021-0455
68. Rydland, H. T., Friedman, J., Stringhini, S., Link, B. G., & Eikemo, T. A. (2022). The radically unequal distribution of Covid-19 vaccinations: a predictable yet avoidable symptom of the fundamental causes of inequality. *Humanities & Social Sciences Communications*, *9*(1). https://doi.org/10.1057/s41599-022-01073-z
69. Kostakis, V., Niaros, V., & Giotitsas, C. (2023). Beyond global versus local: illuminating a cosmological framework for convivial technology development. *Sustainability Science*. https://doi.org/10.1007/s11625-023-01378-1
70. Casasnovas, G., & Jones, J. (2022). Who Has a Seat at the Table in Impact Investing? Addressing Inequality by Giving Voice. *Journal of Business Ethics*, *179*(4), 951–969. https://doi.org/10.1007/s10551-022-05154-6
71. Shahvisi, A. (2022). Centering race, deprivation, and disease severity in healthcare priority setting. *Journal of Medical Ethics*, *48*(2), 77–78. https://doi.org/10.1136/medethics-2022-108145
72. Kaul, N., Deshpande, A., Mittal, A., Raut, R., & Bhandari, H. (2024). The interplay between psychological empowerment and employee engagement: identifying research trends using SPAR-4-SLR process. Global Knowledge, Memory, and Communication. https://doi.org/10.1108/gkmc-09-2023-0322
73. Lau, S.Y. (1997). Technology transfer in East Asia and its implications for regional cooperation. Global Economic Review, 26, 65-88. https://doi.org/10.1080/12265089708422881
74. Maclean, R.馬., Jagannathan, S., & Sarvi, J. (2013). Skills Development Issues, Challenges, and Strategies in Asia and the Pacific. https://doi.org/10.1007/978-94-007-5937-4_1

75. Parry, J., & Hayden, M. (2015). Skills Development: A Review concerning Southeast Asia. Journal of International and Comparative Education, 4, 67–78. https://doi.org/10.14425/00.87.94
76. Nguyen, Q. (2019). Technology Transfer and the Promotion of Technical Skills from Japan to Southeast Asia: Case Study of Vietnam. JAS (Journal of ASEAN Studies). https://doi.org/10.21512/JAS.V6I2.5095
77. Yusianto, R., Marimin, M., Suprihatin, S., & Hardjomidjojo, H. (2022). Expanding and enhancing knowledge using Artificial Intelligence (AI) in the Asian agro-industrial sector. Digitalization and Organisation Design. https://doi.org/10.4324/9781003163824-16
78. Wu, S.R., Shirkey, G., Celik, I., Shao, C., & Chen, J. (2022). A Review on the Adoption of AI, BC, and IoT in Sustainability Research. Sustainability. https://doi.org/10.3390/su14137851
79. Matin, A., Islam, M.R., Wang, X., Huo, H., & Xu, G. (2023). AIoT for sustainable manufacturing: Overview, challenges, and opportunities. Internet Things, 24, 100901. https://doi.org/10.1016/j.iot.2023.100901
80. Chauhan, M., & Sahoo, D.R. (2024). Towards a Greener Tomorrow: Exploring the Potential of AI, Blockchain, and IoT in Sustainable Development. Nature Environment and Pollution Technology. https://doi.org/10.46488/nept.2024.v23i02.044
81. 103. Jakubakynov, B., Tolegenuly, N., Naribai, R., Nurzhanova, Z., Shcherban, T., & Nebelenchuk, I. (2024). Innovative technologies in higher education: developing international cooperation in professional training. Globalization, Societies, and Education. https://doi.org/10.1080/14767724.2024.2339309
82. 104. Tereshchenko, E., Salmela, E., Melkko, E., Phang, S.K., & Happonen, A. (2024). Emerging best strategies and capabilities for university-industry cooperation: opportunities for MSMEs and universities to improve collaboration. A literature review 2000–2023. Journal of Innovation and Entrepreneurship, 13, 1-45. https://doi.org/10.1186/s13731-024-00386-4
83. 105. Shyiramunda, T., & van den Bersselaar, D. (2024). Local community development and higher education institutions: Moving from the triple helix to the quadruple helix model. International Review of Education, 70(1), 51-85. https://doi.org/10.1007/s11159-023-10037-7

Human-Centric Pedagogies in the Age of Intelligent Systems: Envisioning the Future with Industry 5.0

Priyanka Agarwal, Lakhwinder Kaur Dhillon, and Sadhana Tiwari

1 Introduction

AI's transformative power has permeated nearly every industry, and education is no exception [1] and it would be naive to think that AI will not have an impact on education [2]. The term 'artificial intelligence' (AI) was first coined in 1956 at the Dartmouth workshop and is widely acknowledged to have "officially" started in the same year [3]. Asia fostering Industry 5.0, the incorporation of intelligent systems in

P. Agarwal (✉)
Department of Human Resource Management, Amity Business School, Amity University, Noida, Uttar Pradesh, India
e-mail: pagarwal5@amity.edu

L. K. Dhillon
Department of Accounting &Finance, Amity Business School, Amity University, Noida, Uttar Pradesh, India

S. Tiwari
Department of Operations and Supply Chain Management, GNIOT Institute of Management Studies, Greater Noida, Uttar Pradesh, India

© The Author(s), under exclusive license to Springer Nature Singapore Pte Ltd. 2025

P. Agarwal et al. (eds.), *Building a Human-Centred Infrastructure for Sustainable Industry 5.0 in Asia*,
https://doi.org/10.1007/978-981-95-0417-6_4

education is no longer speculative. Today, intelligent systems and AI technologies are transforming the availability and appropriateness of information and educational resources [4]. Learning Management Systems like Moodle and Canvas, AI tutors, and Massive Open Online Courses have democratized access to knowledge [5]. Tools like adaptive learning algorithms tailor content to individual needs, promoting personalized education [6]. Furthermore, virtual reality and augmented reality applications enhance experiential learning, particularly in fields such as medicine and engineering [7]. For instance, students can even perform simulated surgeries or explore ancient civilizations in immersive environments. Critics argue that excessive reliance on technology risks dehumanizing education, reducing students to data points rather than nurturing critical thinking and empathy [8].

As education shifts toward a more integrated, AI-driven landscape, pedagogical models need to emphasize not only knowledge acquisition but also the cultivation of skills such as adaptability, problem-solving, and interpersonal communication [9]. Educators are increasingly advocating for human-centred pedagogy that leverages technology without losing sight of emotional intelligence, creativity, and ethical reasoning like the "flipped classroom" system, where students consume lectures digitally at home and engage in problem-solving or discussions in class [10] and project-based learning which emphasizes real-world challenges and human problem-solving over rote memorization, preparing students for a complex, interconnected world [11].

Researchers support the use of technology as an enabler for collaborative and curiosity-driven learning with self-organized learning environments [12]. Digitization has tended to focus on integrating technology into systems without enhancing human connections [13]. Therefore, Education 5.0 is defined as going beyond digitization and instead fostering mental health, creativity, ethical values, sustainability, and holistic well-being.

It is crucial to support the learners to become critically sympathetic citizens who can mindfully steer through the technologically intertwined world. For that reason, even as smart technologies advance, it has become critically important to safeguard the human components of education. Humanistic pedagogies strive to place the values, well-being, relationships, and agency of learners at the centre of system design so that education remains transformative, holistic, and ethical [14]. This chapter focuses on Human-Centric Pedagogies in the Age of Intelligent Systems.

The chapter looks at how human-centric pedagogies will underpin an education framework that not only exists within the context of intelligent systems but also ensures a robust future for humanity in partnership with technology.

2 Defining Human-Centric Pedagogy in the 21st Century

During the 21st century, education has encountered a multitude of challenges due to rapid advancements in technology, globalization, and societal demands. Out of all these challenges, one is the human-centered pedagogy which has surfaced as a budge for rethinking how schools design teaching and learning. It envisions learners as people with multifaceted capabilities, therefore requires emotional and social development to go in tandem with academic skill enhancement. Human-centric pedagogy stems from a learner-centered philosophy of education where a student emerges as the core of the entire teaching and learning process. It is more than the provision of information; it seeks to achieve the balanced growth of the individual: his or her intellectual, emotional, social, and ethical development. It helps in increasing the understanding of learners as active participants, meaning makers, dialogue partners and collaborators who learn through inquiry and values-based learning [15]. Systems that are intelligent aim at ensuring technology helps the pedagogical objectives that are supportive of humanity such as empathy, critical thought, and emotional engagement as opposed to using technology to replace human interaction.

Key Principles of Human-Centric Pedagogy

2.1 Student-Centered Learning

The student-centered approach forms the basis of humanistic pedagogy considers the learner's needs, interests, and capabilities crucial. This is completely different from the pedagogy that is centered on the teacher—it is heavily based on the individuality of students and applies a standard approach. The models of teaching which fall under the category of student centred such as project-based learning, flipped classrooms, and inquiry learning nurture self-direction among learners in addition to collaboration, critical thinking, and problem-solving skills [11]. Along with these, motivation and self-determination, which are important for sustaining learning throughout life, are also focused upon [16].

2.2 *Emotional and Social Development*

A key element of human-centric pedagogy is the recognition of the emotional and social aspects of learning. Recent research in social-emotional learning underscores the importance of developing students' ability to manage emotions, set goals, show empathy, and establish positive relationships [17]. Human-centric pedagogy incorporates these principles to ensure that students are not only equipped with academic knowledge but also with the social skills and emotional resilience necessary to navigate the complexities of life. Moreover, human-centric pedagogies advocate for inclusive education, ensuring that students from diverse backgrounds and with varied learning needs are given opportunities to succeed ensuring that education systems incorporate diverse worldviews [18].

2.3 *Relationality*

While technology plays an important role in human-centric pedagogy, it is seen as a facilitator rather than a replacement for human interaction. However, the core of human-centric pedagogy remains the teacher-student relationship. Effective teachers continue to play a central role in guiding students' cognitive and emotional growth, using technology to complement rather than replace direct instruction and human interaction [19]. Focusing on the teacher-student and peer relationships, which are foundational for social learning and emotional development. In a human-centric classroom, the role of the teacher shifts from being a dispenser of knowledge to being a facilitator of learning. Teachers create a learning environment that is inclusive, collaborative, and emotionally supportive, helping students develop both academic skills and personal growth.

2.4 *Personalization with Purpose*

Utilizing AI not just for academic optimization but to enhance student agency, well-being, and holistic development.

2.5 *Ethical Design*

Ensuring that educational technologies are transparent, fair, and inclusive, with built-in safeguards against bias and privacy issues.

Human-centric teachers employ strategies such as:

- Differentiated instruction, tailoring content, assessments, and teaching methods to meet the diverse needs of learners [20].
- Formative assessments, which provide ongoing feedback to inform instructional practices and allow for adjustments in real-time [21].
- Peer collaboration, fostering an atmosphere where students learn from one another and develop communication, empathy, and teamwork skills [22].

3 The Rise of Intelligent Systems in Asian Classrooms

The rapid development of intelligent systems such as robots, machine learning, and artificial intelligence has had a tremendous impact on everyday life, industries, and society [23]. The development of the industry has been influenced by four major industrial revolutions, each of which had an impact on output and technology.

Industry 1.0 in the 1700s made first use of coal, steam, and water-powered engines. The economy thus started to shift toward industrial manufacture and the first factories were constructed. Using new energy sources including oil, gas, and electricity, Industry 2.0 had progressed industrialization by the 1870s. While the telephone and telegraph were developed as long-distance communication devices, production lines were electrified during this period. The first indicators of Industry 3.0—a change in which computers and electronics were included into industrial processes—emerged in the 1970s. Outsourcing and globalization followed from high degrees of automation brought about by microprocessors, information technology, and robots.

With Industry 4.0 (Fig. 1), the so-called "knowledge revolution," digital tools arrived on the production line. Smart machinery, platforms like the Industrial Internet of Things (IoT), and technologies including data analytics and artificial intelligence (AI) have helped factory operations to become better. Industry 4.0 brought hitherto unheard-of degrees of digitizing, automation, and efficiency [24].

The "human touch" revolution is a key component of Industry 5.0 innovation. By emphasizing the value of communication, critical thinking, and creative thinking in addition to technological proficiency, this forward-looking approach places a higher priority on soft skills than technical ability. Alongside technology and data savvy, soft skills are becoming more and more valued as they will influence the workforce of the future and improve society. In contrast to its predecessors, Industry 5.0 places a strong emphasis on human–machine collaboration, which creates a synergy that fosters critical thinking, empathy, and creativity [25].

As we move into the era of Industry 5.0 (Fig. 2), a paradigm built on sustainability, resilience, and human-centricity, education must undergo an equally significant transformation [26]. Instead of focusing solely on technical proficiency or standardization, pedagogies must now promote human attributes like creativity, empathy, ethical reasoning, and adaptability. People are at the centre of Industry 5.0, which is a recalibration. In this new industrial era, the goal is human–machine collaboration rather than competition [27]. Technology is seen as a tool to boost human creativity, address societal issues, and encourage meaningful innovation. Therefore, educational systems must equip students with the skills, values, and attitudes necessary to thrive in a world where intelligent systems enhance human capabilities rather than replace them.

Across Asia, colleges and universities are rapidly implementing intelligent systems. In order to monitor student participation and classroom behaviour, over 60% of high schools in China's largest provinces are testing facial recognition software and AI tutors [28]. Additionally, China's Squirrel AI platform, which provides adaptive tutoring based on real-time performance data, has helped over a million students [4]. In South Korea and Japan, humanoid robots such as Pepper and NAO are being used to provide emotional support and language learning to socially isolated students, particularly during the COVID-19 pandemic [29]. In order to identify students who are at risk of falling behind, customize learning paths, and increase teacher effectiveness, Singapore's Ministry of Education is experimenting with AI-based analytics through its EdTech Masterplan 2030. These efforts include dashboards that track students' cognitive development and emotional well-being across all of

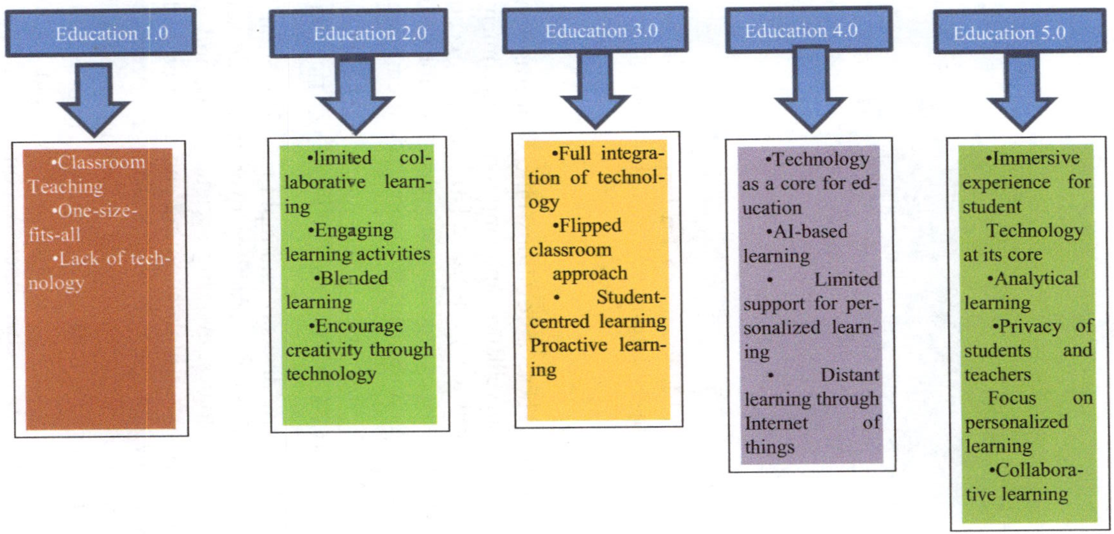

Fig. 1 Evolution of education over the past years

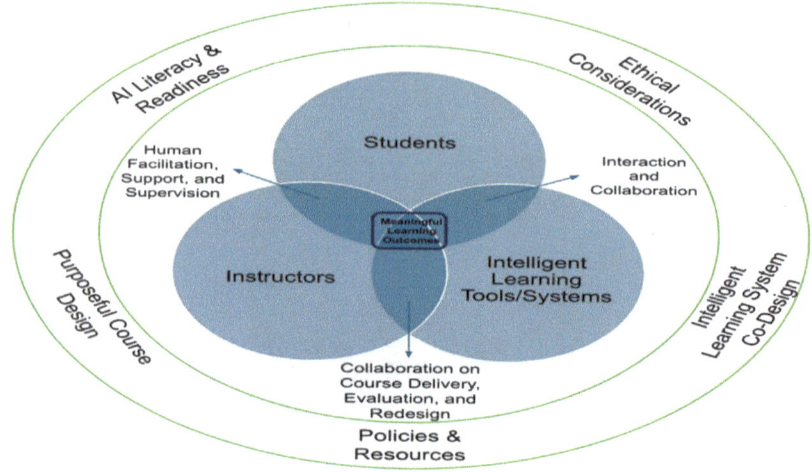

Fig. 2 *Source* Ren, X., Wu, M.L. Examining Teaching Competencies and Challenges While Integrating Artificial Intelligence in Higher Education. *TechTrends* (2025)

their core subjects [30]. These innovations raise concerns about algorithmic bias, data privacy, surveillance, and emotional detachment, despite the potential benefits of efficiency and scale [31]. Human-centric pedagogy counters these trends by making sure that technology supports learning goals founded on ethics, empathy, and student empowerment.

4 Pedagogical Models Emerging in Asia

Asia, a continent of immense diversity and rapid transformation, has seen significant changes in educational practices over recent decades. With the advent of new technologies, evolving societal needs, and globalization, Asian countries are increasingly adopting and adapting pedagogical models to align with the changing dynamics of the 21st-century world. These models reflect a blend of traditional values and modern innovations, aiming to enhance the learning experience, improve outcomes, and prepare students for a future characterized by rapid technological advancement and complex social challenges. As countries in Asia continue to develop and implement human-centric pedagogies, several innovative models have emerged that are beginning to reshape educational systems.

These initiatives are not just about using technology effectively but also about embedding cultural values, ethics, and community building into education.

4.1 India's National Education Policy (NEP) 2020

With its NEP 2020, India is making a major turn toward experiential, learner-centric education that supports flexibility, creativity, and whole development [32]. The program supports critical thinking, project-based learning, using local languages and cultural settings, so enabling more individualized learning opportunities. The NEP also conforms with human-centric pedagogies by stressing early childhood education and life skills since it helps students to develop personally and generally in line. Schools are urged by the NEP to implement social-emotional learning initiatives that provide learners with the means to control their emotions, develop resilience, and negotiate interpersonal interactions successfully. Key elements of human-centric pedagogies, self-awareness, self-regulation, and empathy are developed by these initiatives for the learners [33].

The NEP 2020 underlines the need of transcending conventional, test-centric education to create well-rounded people with a wide range of talents. Emphasizing the importance of personal growth, it suggests including into the mainstream curriculum disciplines such arts, sports, vocational education, and mental health. To guarantee the whole growth of learners, the NEP lays great weight on include sports and arts into the curriculum. Complementing human-centric pedagogies that encourage balance between intellectual and emotional development, the policy emphasizes that education should concentrate on the development of physical, cognitive, and emotional well-being [32].

The policy advocates education that supports physical, mental, and social health; that fosters critical thinking, creativity, and emotional well-being; that encourages lifetime learning and self-development.

This viewpoint closely connects with human-centric pedagogies, which see education as a process of whole development rather than only intellectual teaching [34].

4.2 Collaborative Learning in South Korea

In order to promote greater comprehension and critical thinking, South Korea's education system, which is renowned for its rigor and high academic standards, is also investigating collaborative learning techniques. The use of new curriculum frameworks and instructional strategies that encourage peer conversations and group problem-solving exercises is helping to accelerate South Korea's transition to collaborative learning. As they collaborate with others to achieve shared learning objectives, this model encourages students to grow in a variety of social and cognitive domains. Collaborative learners in South Korea exhibit higher levels of motivation and a stronger sense of obligation to their peers [35].

Additionally, by encouraging students to take on leadership roles within their teams, this model aids in the development of leadership and teamwork abilities, two qualities that are essential for today's workforce. Furthermore, the Character Education Act [36] mandates that moral education, citizenship, and community involvement be at the forefront of South Korea's national curriculum. By incorporating these ideals into the curriculum, South Korea strives to prepare students for both academic performance and their roles as morally and responsibly responsible members of society.

4.3 China's Push for Innovation and Creativity

Given its rapidly expanding economy, China has recognized the need for educational institutions that transcend rote memorizing and standardized testing. Using project-based learning in classrooms to develop creativity and innovation, Chinese educational reforms in recent years have given these qualities great focus [37]. Driven by a need for economic modernization, Chinese educational reforms give critical thinking, teamwork, and practical problem-solving skills great weight. The early 2000s "New Curriculum Reform" specifically encourages schools to adopt multidisciplinary learning—in which students work on projects combining data from many topic areas. China's switch to PBL is helping students to be more adaptable and ready for a labor market getting more complex [38].

a. ***Singapore's "Thinking Schools, Learning Nation" Initiative***

Long regarded as one of the best systems of education worldwide, Singapore launched in the late 1990s, the nation's "Thinking Schools, Learning Nation" project which is a shining example of dedication to developing children with critical thinking, creativity, and problem-solving abilities. Combining active learning techniques including inquiry-based learning, group projects, and problem-based learning [39] this initiative promotes the evolution of a more student-centred approach. Under these circumstances, the teacher's job changes from that of a lecturer to that of a facilitator encouraging students' research and discovery. This strategy conforms with research and notes that student-centered pedagogies in Singapore concentrate on developing both intellectual and social skills, so preparing students for a sophisticated, globalized world [39].

b. ***Japan's Focus on Experiential Education***

In Japan's educational system, experiential learning—a technique that encourages to learn via activities and interactions rather than passively absorbing information—is highly valued. Most famously, the "Kyosei" approach emphasizes community involvement, personal accountability, and cooperation [31]. In order to apply their knowledge in practical situations, students frequently take part in field trips, internships, and community-based projects under this paradigm. In addition to Kyosei, Japan's integrated learning program encourages students to work on interdisciplinary projects, which allows them to explore real-world issues and generate innovative solutions. These programs give students the skills they need to succeed in a global market and foster a strong sense of social responsibility in them [28]. Japan's Whole Child Approach, which emphasizes the development of the whole child, integrates academic achievement with social-emotional learning (SEL), moral education, and empathy [40]. This approach, which is based on Confucian concepts, highlights the need of fostering students' emotional and ethical intelligence in order to help them develop not just their intellectual abilities but also their character and emotional resilience.

c. ***Bhutan's Gross National Happiness (GNH) Curriculum***

The GNH curriculum of Bhutan combines sustainability, mindfulness, and compassion into learning. It seeks to raise students who possess not only intellectual ability but also emotional intelligence and social awareness [41]. While promoting happiness and well-being as main benchmarks of success in education, the curriculum emphasizes on helping students to grasp sustainability—both socially and environmentally. These pedagogical approaches stress not only intellectual development but also the development of moral principles, emotional intelligence, and social consciousness.

They represent a change towards educational institutions that give students' emotional and ethical development top priority in addition to knowledge acquisition in a society fast changing.

Asian countries are reimagining the role of education in cultivating future leaders, innovators, and global citizens by emphasizing student-centered, project-based, and collaborative learning methodologies. Despite the persistence of issues, the evolving educational landscape offers opportunities for further reform and innovation.

5 AI as an Ally: Tools that Support Human-Centric Pedagogy

Artificial Intelligence (AI) possesses the capacity to transform education by enhancing human-centred teaching methods that emphasize personalized learning, student welfare, and comprehensive growth. Traditional educational systems frequently emphasize standardized learning experiences; however AI provides the capability to customize and modify instructional methods to address the varied requirements of pupils. Integrating AI-based tools in the classroom enables educators to cultivate environments that promote academic advancement while also facilitating emotional, cognitive, and social development—fundamental tenets of human-centric pedagogy.

5.1 Personalized Learning Through AI

AI significantly enhances human-centric teaching by facilitating tailored learning. AI tools may assess a student's learning behavior, preferences, and progress to provide customized information, ensuring that each student receives an experience suited to their individual needs and speed. This customization enhances student engagement and mitigates the sense of alienation sometimes experienced in conventional, uniform classrooms [42].

AI Tools:

- **Intelligent Tutoring Systems (ITS)**: These AI systems act as personalized tutors, providing real-time feedback and adapting to students' needs. For example, Carnegie Learning's MATHia system tailors mathematics instruction to each student's current understanding and pace [43].
- **AI-Powered Learning Management Systems (LMS)**: Platforms like Canvas or Google Classroom integrate AI to offer tailored recommendations, track progress, and allow for differentiated learning paths [44].

Personalized learning promotes student agency, ensuring that learners take ownership of their educational journey, a foundational aspect of human-centric pedagogy.

5.2 *Emotional and Mental Well-Being: AI for Social-Emotional Learning*

Human-centric pedagogy prioritizes the cultivation of emotional intelligence, self-awareness, and overall well-being. Artificial Intelligence can facilitate Social-Emotional Learning by offering tools that assess and improve students' emotional well-being, aiding in the management of stress, anxiety, and emotions. AI applications can aid educators in identifying students requiring supplementary emotional support.

AI Tools for Social-Emotional Learning:

- **Affective Computing**: AI systems that analyze facial expressions, voice tone, and body language to assess emotional states and provide feedback. Tools like **Empatica's Embrace** wristband track physiological markers of stress, helping both students and educators better understand emotional health [45].

- **Chatbots for Emotional Support**: AI-powered chatbots, such as **Woebot**, provide conversational support to students, helping them work through emotional challenges, manage stress, and practice self-reflection [46].

By integrating AI tools for SEL, educators can foster emotional well-being, which aligns with human-centric pedagogies that view education as an holistic process that nurtures the mind and spirit.

5.3 *Collaborative Learning and AI-Driven Peer Interaction*

Human-centric education emphasizes the significance of collaboration in the learning process. Artificial intelligence can augment collaborative learning environments by enabling peer interactions and fostering team-work. AI techniques can pair students with peers with analogous or complimentary learning styles, fostering dynamic groups that promote collaborative problem-solving and the enhancement of social skills.

AI Tools for Collaborative Learning:

- **AI in Group Formation**: Tools like **Socrative** use AI to group students based on their skills, preferences, and progress, creating balanced teams for cooperative activities [47]. **AI-Powered Collaboration Platforms**: Platforms such as **Miro** or **Trello** allow students to collaborate in real-time, offering features that facilitate task delegation, brainstorming, and sharing resources. AI can optimize collaboration by suggesting team roles, tasks, and resources based on individual contributions [48].

By supporting peer interactions, AI reinforces the **social development** aspect of human-centric pedagogy, ensuring that students not only excel academically but also grow socially and emotionally.

5.4 *Continuous Feedback and Formative Assessment*

AI facilitates immediate feedback, an essential component of human-centered education that emphasizes ongoing formative evaluation to support student development. Conventional assessments often take place at the conclusion of learning units, whereas AI-driven solutions offer immediate feedback that facilitates continuous learning, self-enhancement, and the cultivation of a growth mindset.

AI Tools for Continuous Feedback:

- **Automated Assessment Tools**: Systems like **Turnitin** and **Grammarly** provide students with instant feedback on assignments, helping them improve their writing and research skills [49].
- **Adaptive Learning Platforms**: Platforms like **DreamBox** and **Smart Sparrow** use AI to assess a student's responses and adjust the difficulty and content of learning materials accordingly, offering feedback that fosters continuous learning [50].

Real-time feedback ensures that students can address areas of weakness immediately, maintaining a flow of learning that prevents frustration and promotes deeper understanding.

5.5 *Supporting Teacher Professional Development*

Human-centric pedagogy also acknowledges the **well-being and growth of educators**. AI can help in this area by providing **personalized professional development** resources, feedback, and even **automating administrative tasks**, allowing educators more time to focus on student engagement and instructional quality.

AI Tools for Teacher Development:

- **AI-Powered Professional Learning Networks (PLNs)**: Platforms such as **Edmodo** and **Google for Education** use AI to recommend resources, training modules, and communities based on a teacher's teaching style, preferences, and needs.
- **AI-Assisted Lesson Planning**: Tools like **TeachFX** use AI to analyze classroom conversations, providing teachers with insights into student engagement, instructional effectiveness, and opportunities for improvement.

These AI tools help educators maintain their own well-being while enhancing their instructional effectiveness, aligning with the human-centric model that views teachers as integral to the educational ecosystem.

5.6 *Equity and Accessibility in Education*

AI tools can bridge educational gaps by promoting **equity and accessibility**. By tailoring learning experiences to individual needs, AI ensures that students with diverse learning abilities, language backgrounds, and disabilities have the support they need to succeed.

AI Tools for Accessibility:

- **Speech Recognition and Translation Tools**: **Google Translate** and **Microsoft Translator** use AI to break down language barriers, making learning accessible to students from different linguistic backgrounds.
- **AI for Special Education**: Tools like **Ghotit Real Writer** assist students with dyslexia and language-based learning disabilities by offering real-time spelling and grammar corrections in their writing [51].

These AI tools ensure that all students, regardless of their abilities or backgrounds, can participate in a human-centric learning environment that promotes **equity** and **inclusivity**. Intelligent systems, when ethically designed and deployed, can serve as powerful allies in promoting human-centric pedagogy. These tools enhance the learning experience by offering personalized feedback, accommodating diverse learning styles, and promoting emotional well-being.

These advanced tools facilitate inclusive and personalized learning environments, consistent with the principles of human-centric pedagogy by emphasizing student well-being, agency, and emotional development.

6 Challenges and Ethical Dilemmas

Despite the many benefits of integrating intelligent systems into education, several challenges and ethical dilemmas need to be addressed to ensure the equitable and ethical implementation of these technologies.

- **Digital Divides:** In many parts of Asia, rural and marginalized communities still lack access to the necessary technological infrastructure. Nearly 50% of rural students in countries like India, Nepal, and Cambodia do not have reliable internet access, creating significant barriers to educational equity. [52]
- **Loss of Teacher Autonomy:** As AI systems become more integrated into classrooms, there is a concern that teachers may become overly reliant on data-driven insights and lose their professional autonomy in decision-making. This could lead to a narrowing of pedagogical approaches and reduce the teacher's role as a critical thinking facilitator [5]. **Privacy and Surveillance:** The widespread use of AI in education raises significant concerns about surveillance and data privacy. The use of facial recognition and other monitoring technologies could lead to the over-surveillance of students, creating an environment where trust and psychological safety are compromised.
- **Bias in Algorithms:** AI systems trained on homogeneous datasets may inadvertently reinforce existing biases and inequalities, particularly regarding race, gender, and socio-economic status. For instance, studies have shown that facial recognition algorithms often perform poorly on individuals with darker skin tones, raising concerns about the equity of AI tools used in education [53].

To address these challenges, it is essential to adopt a human-centric approach to AI in education, one that prioritizes ethical design, transparency, and inclusivity.

7 Policy and Institutional Pathways Forward

Human-centered pedagogies, that focus on personalized instruction, social and emotional well-being, stand ready to guide the future of learning in this new industrial age. In this era of 'Industry 5.0', where the line between human and machine is blurred, this educational system should fundamentally change in a way that they shall prepare the students for the collaborative, ethical and adaptive skills that will be required. Finally, the support of human-centered pedagogies in the era of Industry 5.0, requires sound policy frameworks. These policies also need to promote cooperation among governments, educational institutions, and industry leaders to establish an enabling ethical and effective ecosystem for the integration of intelligent systems into education. Institutions play a key role in ensuring that educational systems are prepared for the challenges and opportunities posed by Industry 5.0. Universities, schools, and vocational training centers must reimagine their roles as providers of not only academic knowledge but also soft skills, emotional intelligence, and collaborative abilities necessary for the future workforce.

To ensure human centricity in the age of intelligent systems, the following steps are essential:

- **Collaboration with Industry**: Government and educational institutions must engage with industry leaders to ensure that educational curricula align with the evolving demands of Industry 5.0. Policies that promote **collaborative partnerships** between schools, universities, and tech companies will be essential in designing **real-world curricula** that incorporate the latest technologies [54].
- **Support for Educators**: Policymakers must allocate resources for **teacher training programs** that focus on using AI tools, fostering emotional intelligence, and **adapting to new technologies**. A curriculum that supports **lifelong learning** and **continuous professional development** will help educators navigate the rapidly changing educational landscape [55].
- **Digital Equity**: Ensuring equitable access to AI-powered educational tools is critical. Policymakers should prioritize access to digital infrastructure in **marginalized communities** to prevent the **digital divide** from exacerbating existing inequalities.

Ethical EdTech Standards:

- National policies should mandate transparency, fairness, and accountability in educational technology.
- **Community Engagement**: Parents, students, and local educators must co-design solutions to ensure relevance and trust.
- **Public Investment in Equity**: Bridge access gaps through subsidies, infrastructure, and inclusive content.
- **Curriculum Redesign**: Institutions need to overhaul curricula to include not only traditional academic subjects but also courses on **AI literacy**, **ethics in technology**, and **human–machine collaboration**. The aim should be to provide students with a balanced education that combines **technical expertise** with **humanistic education** [56].

- **Human-Centered AI Integration**: Institutions must integrate AI tools into classrooms in a way that complements human learning rather than replacing it. AI can help in **assessing learning progress**, **providing real-time feedback**, and **personalizing learning experiences**, but it should be used to enhance, not replace, human interaction and mentorship [57].

8 Conclusion: Towards a Compassionate Technological Future

Looking forward, human-centered teaching and learning will develop further and take on new forms, driven by more and more knowledge about how people actually learn. Going forward, the role of AI and analytics will become more and more integrated and the learning experience will become even more personalized. The core tenets of human-centric pedagogy—student agency, emotional development, and inclusive education—nevertheless will continue to underpin human-centric pedagogy's mission to provide an education that enables students in preparing for the complexities of our changing global context [54]. Asia finds itself in a unique crossroads of technological capabilities and rich cultural-philosophical heritage. The region has an opportunity to define globally how we educate with both machine intelligence and human wisdom. By embracing human-centric pedagogies, Asian education systems can ensure that technology amplifies—not diminishes—the values of care, curiosity, justice, and community.

Human-dominant pedagogy is the revolutionary differentiation in education; it puts student well-being, development and empowerment at its heart. Incorporating student-centered active learning, social and emotional learning, and technology in thoughtful, well-balanced ways, human-centric pedagogy offers a holistic approach to getting students ready for the rigors of the 21st century. In addressing the challenges of a globalized, high-tech world, human-centered pedagogies will be essential to making sure that all the learners—not just as students, but as people—succeed.

References

1. *AI in Education: Balancing Technology and Humanity to Create Equitable Learning*. https://www.linkedin.com/pulse/ai-education-balancing-technology-humanity-create-learning-toldson-zzo5e. Accessed 16 Apr. 2025.
2. Holmes, W., Bialik, M., & Fadel, C. (2019). *Artificial intelligence in education: Promises and implications for teaching and learning*. Center for Curriculum Redesign.
3. Cordeschi, Roberto. "AI TURNS FIFTY: REVISITING ITS ORIGINS." *Applied Artificial Intelligence*, vol. 21, no. 4–5, Apr. 2007, pp. 259–79. *DOI.org (Crossref)*, https://doi.org/10.1080/08839510701252304.
4. Luckin, R., Holmes, W., Griffiths, M., & Forcier, L. B. (2016). *Intelligence unleashed: An argument for AI in education*. Pearson Education.
5. Williamson, B., & Eynon, R. (2020). Historical threads, missing links, and future directions in AI in education. *Learning, Media and Technology*, 45(3), 223–235.
6. Pane, J. F., Steiner, E. D., Baird, M. D., & Hamilton, L. S. (2015). Continued Progress: Promising Evidence on Personalized Learning. RAND Corporation. https://www.rand.org/pubs/research_reports/RR1365.html.
7. Radianti, J., Majchrzak, T. A., Fromm, J., & Wohlgenannt, I. (2020). A systematic review of immersive virtual reality applications for higher education: Design elements, lessons learned, and research agenda. *Computers & Education*, 147, 103778. https://doi.org/10.1016/j.compedu.2019.103778.
8. Selwyn, N. (2016). Education and Technology: Key Issues and Debates. Bloomsbury Publishing.
9. Barker, R., & Searle, J. (2025). *Integrating AI in education: Human-centric pedagogies for Industry 5.0*. Journal of Education and Technology, 30(1), 21–34. https://doi.org/10.1007/s10758-025-0941-2.
10. Bishop, J. L., & Verleger, M. A. (2013). The Flipped Classroom: A Survey of the Research. *ASEE National Conference Proceedings*, Atlanta, GA.
11. Bell, S. (2010). Project-based learning for the 21st century: Skills for the future. *The Clearing House: A Journal of Educational Strategies, Issues, and Ideas, 83*(2), 39-43. https://doi.org/10.1080/00098650903505415.
12. Mitra, S. (2012). Beyond the Hole in the Wall: Discover the Power of Self-Organized Learning. TED Books.
13. Long, D. (2021). Education 5.0: Redefining Learning for a Sustainable Future. *Journal of Future Studies*, 26(1), 1–12.
14. UNESCO. (2021). *Reimagining our futures together: A new social contract for education*. https://unesdoc.unesco.org.
15. Biesta, G. (2010). *Good education in an age of measurement: Ethics, politics, democracy*. Routledge.

16. Deci, E. L., & Ryan, R. M. (2000). The "what" and "why" of goal pursuits: Human needs and the self-determination of behavior. *Psychological Inquiry, 11*(4), 227–268. https://doi.org/10.1207/S15327965PLI1104_01
17. Durlak, J. A., Weissberg, R. P., Dymnicki, A. B., Taylor, R. D., & Schellinger, K. B. (2011). The impact of enhancing students' social and emotional learning: A meta-analysis of school-based universal interventions. *Child Development, 82*(1), 405-432. https://doi.org/10.1111/j.1467-8624.2010.01564.x
18. Booth, T., & Ainscow, M. (2002). The Index for Inclusion: Developing Learning and Participation in Schools. Centre for Studies on Inclusive Education.
19. Fullan, M. (2013). The new pedagogy: Students and teachers as learning partners. *Learning and Leading with Technology, 40*(1), 30–32.
20. Tomlinson, C. A. (2001). *How to differentiate instruction in mixed-ability classrooms*. ASCD.
21. Black, P., & Wiliam, D. (2009). Developing the theory of formative assessment. *Educational Assessment, Evaluation and Accountability, 21*(1), 5–31. https://doi.org/10.1007/s11092-008-9068-5
22. Deysolong, Josephine. *Assessing the Benefits of Cooperative Learning or Group Work: Fostering Collaboration and Enhancing Learning Outcomes* 2023, p. 138386 Bytes. *DOI.org (Datacite)*, https://doi.org/10.6084/M9.FIGSHARE.23009159.
23. Schwab, K. (2016). *The fourth industrial revolution*. Crown Business.
24. Lasi, H., Fettke, P., Kemper, H. G., Feld, T., & Hoffmann, M. (2014). Industry 4.0. *Business & Information Systems Engineering, 6*(4), 239–242. https://doi.org/10.1007/s12599-014-0334-4.
25. Brynjolfsson, E., & McAfee, A. (2014). The second machine age: Work, progress, and prosperity in a time of brilliant technologies. W. W. Norton & Company.
26. European Commission. (2021). *Industry 5.0: Towards a sustainable, human-centric and resilient European industry*. Publications Office of the European Union. https://doi.org/10.2777/308407
27. Demir, K. A. (2022). Industry 5.0: A survey on enabling technologies and potential applications. *Journal of Intelligent Manufacturing, 33*(2), 359–387. https://doi.org/10.1007/s10845-021-01813-1
28. Zawacki-Richter, O., Marín, V. I., Bond, M., & Gouverneur, F. (2019). Systematic review of research on artificial intelligence in education. *International Journal of Educational Technology in Higher Education*, 16(1), 1–27.
29. Serholt, S. (2018). Child–robot interaction in education. In R. A. Sotillo (Ed.), *Emerging trends in education and AI* (pp. 112–132). Springer.

30. Singapore Ministry of Education. (2022). *EdTech Masterplan 2030*. https://www.moe.gov.sg.
31. Yamamoto, M. (2011). Kyosei as a model for experiential education: Bridging the gap between school and society in Japan. *Journal of Experiential Education, 34*(4), 283–300. https://doi.org/10.5193/JEE34.4.283.
32. Government of India. (2020). *National Education Policy 2020*. Ministry of Education. https://www.education.gov.in.
33. Seligman, M. (2019). *The science of well-being: A practical guide to emotional health*. Oxford University Press.
34. Sharma, A., & Dholakia, S. (2020). NEP 2020 and its impact on holistic education. *Indian Journal of Education Policy, 45*(3), 50-65. https://doi.org/10.1016/j.ijep.2020.04.001.
35. Kang, H. (2014). Collaborative learning in South Korean classrooms: The role of peer interaction in problem-solving. *Educational Studies, 41*(3), 352–366. https://doi.org/10.1080/03055698.2014.884249.
36. Park, M. (2017). Character education policy in South Korea: Moral values and civic engagement. *Asia Pacific Journal of Education*, 37(4), 562–576.
37. Zhao, Y. (2017). *What works may hurt: Side effects in education*. Teachers College Press.
38. Zhao, Y., Pugh, K., & Sheldon, S. (2020). AI and the teacher's role: A new approach to professional development. *Educational Technology Research and Development, 68*(2), 189-202. https://doi.org/10.1007/s11423-019-09735-4.
39. Tan, C. (2009). Thinking Schools, Learning Nation: The Singapore Education System. *International Journal of Educational Development, 29*(5), 553–562. https://doi.org/10.1016/j.ijedudev.2009.04.001.
40. Tsuneyoshi, R. (2014). The Japanese model of whole-child education. *International Journal of Educational Research*, 66, 95–104.
41. Thinley, J. Y. (2012). Educating for gross national happiness. *Journal of Bhutan Studies*, 26, 1–17.
42. Luckin, R. (2017). *Enhancing learning and teaching with technology: What the research says*. UCL Institute of Education Press.
43. Koedinger, K. R., McLaughlin, E. A., & Alibali, M. W. (2017). Intelligent tutoring systems: A learning analytics perspective. *Journal of Educational Data Mining, 9*(2), 15-30. https://doi.org/10.1080/03057328.2017.1324322.
44. Siemens, G. (2013). *Learning analytics: The emergence of a discipline*. Journal of Educational Technology, 13(2), 29-35. https://doi.org/10.2139/ssrn.2102863.
45. Picard, R. W. (2010). *Affective computing*. MIT Press.

46. Fitzpatrick, K., Darcy, A., & Vierhile, M. (2017). *Woebot: A conversational agent for mental health*. American Psychological Association. https://doi.org/10.1037/cpb0000102.
47. Graham, C. R., & Vo, S. (2016). Group formation strategies in learning environments: A review of research. *Computers & Education, 101*, 142-153. https://doi.org/10.1016/j.compedu.2016.07.002.
48. Sangwin, C. (2017). Artificial intelligence and collaborative learning. *Journal of Educational Technology & Society, 20*(4), 32-42. https://doi.org/10.1080/00461520.2017.1373762.
49. Baker, R. S. (2019). Formative assessment with AI: How machine learning tools are reshaping educational assessment. Journal of Educational Data Mining, 11(1), 5–20. https://doi.org/10.1155/2019/4324623.
50. Spector, J. M. (2016). *Foundations of educational technology: Integrative approaches and interdisciplinary perspectives*. Routledge.
51. Higgins, E., & Raskind, M. (2017). Supporting students with dyslexia using AI. *Journal of Learning Disabilities, 50*(3), 213–221. https://doi.org/10.1177/0022219416665140
52. International Telecommunication Union (ITU). (2020). *Measuring digital development: Facts and figures 2020*. https://www.itu.int.
53. Eubanks, V. (2018). *Automating inequality: How high-tech tools profile, police, and punish the poor*. St. Martin's Press.
54. Brynjolfsson, E., & McAfee, A. (2014). *The second machine age: Work, progress, and prosperity in a time of brilliant technologies*. W.W. Norton & Company.
55. Darling-Hammond, L., Hyler, M. E., & Gardner, M. (2017). *Effective teacher professional development. Palo Alto: Learning Policy Institute*.
56. Koller, D., Parisi, D., & Regan, R. (2018). *The evolution of education: Aligning curriculum with Industry 5.0. Educational Technology, 58*(4).
57. Kerr, M. (2019). AI in education: A holistic human-centered approach. *Technology in Education Journal, 29*(3), 57–72. https://doi.org/10.1007/s10758-019-09445-w.

Digital Banking Transformation in Asia: Fintech, Inclusion, and Future of Industry 5.0

Ritu Wadhwa, Purwa Srivastava, Rushina Singhi, and Kiran Jindal

1 Introduction

Technological Development has brought the world closer, wherein everything is just a click away. However, the concept of "Digital Banking" is not new; its history traces back to the 1990s when ICICI Bank introduced the first of its kind Automated Tellers Machines (ATMs) [1]. ATM, which is also phrased as Any-Time-Money Machines due to the

R. Wadhwa
Amity Business School, Amity University, Uttar Pradesh, Noida, India

P. Srivastava
Jaypee Institute of Information Technology, Uttar Pradesh, Noida, India

R. Singhi
Nilkamal School of Mathematics, Applied Statistics and Analytics, SVKMs NMIMS, Mumbai, India

K. Jindal (✉)
Mehr Chand Mahajan DAV College for Women, Chandigarh, India
e-mail: jindalkiran@gmail.com

© The Author(s), under exclusive license to Springer Nature Singapore Pte Ltd. 2025

P. Agarwal et al. (eds.), *Building a Human-Centred Infrastructure for Sustainable Industry 5.0 in Asia*,
https://doi.org/10.1007/978-981-95-0417-6_5

convenience offered to the users in cash withdrawal from bank accounts using their respective Debit Cards. The advancement of technology has made it possible for us to establish a banking system built on principles but also enhances customer service, lowers societal risk, and increases shareholder profits [2]. Online banking, also known as virtual banking, is defined as the use of telecommunication networks and the Internet through a website or system run by banks themselves or other financial entities to provide a wide range of financial services and products to consumers at any time, any place. Even words like Artificial Intelligence (AI) or 'chat pods' aren't new to the banks and financial technological (fintech) industries but have gotten on the tongue of corporates during the COVID-19 pandemic due to digitization of this industry [3].

In the realm of credit and banking, digitization lowers the cost of delivering pertinent services and boosts operational security for banks and their clients [4]. Digitization reduces human error and thus leads to building the customer locality. Digitization focuses on a human-centered approach and increases operational savings. Automation and smart technologies also improve job happiness, provide staff with chances for upskilling, and foster customer engagement through service design that is driven by empathy. There is a continuous bank facility available through the means of online banking. Also, customers need not physically visit the branch for their day-to-day operations, which decreases the operating costs for the banks too [5].

Gradual technological improvements and the introduction of artificial intelligence (AI) and machine learning (ML) have made data processing and maintenance convenient. Therefore, the banking industry has also realized the need for digitization. Due to this, traditional banks like State Bank of India (SBI) are either approaching Fin-Tech platforms or creating their own such as Yono to provide the best user experience through innovative services. Digitization, AI and ML development in the financial sector has increased the awareness and convenience to users than what it had before in the financial sector. Now all types of services are just a click away for the consumers which is very easy and hassle-free [6]. It has also enabled organizations to operate cost-effectively as it has reduced the errors made by employees as individuals. The banking sector has undergone a profound transformation in recent years, propelled by the relentless advancement of digital technologies. This paradigm shift has not only revolutionized the way financial institutions operate but has also fundamentally altered the roles they play in the broader economic landscape. The shock of COVID-19 has turned digitization into a strategic problem that demands a swift overhaul of numerous bank business operations, including partnerships, customer connections, communication channels, resource allocation, and financing. Moreover, it has promoted value proposition redefinition and digital platform collaboration/interaction across all financial institutions [7]. However, clients have not fully exploited these services because of a lack of awareness and expertise [8].

Digital banking is poised to continue and evolve, bringing about a myriad of transformative changes that will reshape the financial landscape. The relentless pace of technological innovation, coupled with shifting consumer expectations, is expected to drive digital banking toward even greater prominence and influence. Prior research in the field of digital banking mostly examined consumer attitudes and antecedent characteristics that are important to consumers when they use digital banking channels or factors influencing consumers' intentions to utilize contemporary banking channels [9]. Research shows that a 1% increase in the value of National Electronic Fund Transactions (NEFT) and Real-Time Gross Settlement (RTGS) increases business per employee by 0.08% and 0.03%, respectively [10]. The CASA to Deposit ratios of 0.016 and 0.0078% are further explained by changes in RTGS and NEFT transactions. Additionally, a shift in RTGS has a noticeable impact on the advancements (0.7%). The cost of cash has been significantly influenced by credit card transactions at POS and ATMs. Our research suggests two real-world applications: RTGS-based transaction promotion must first pick up speed; this will improve the bank's performance. As the digital banking landscape evolves, regulatory frameworks will also play a crucial role in shaping its future. Governments and regulatory bodies are likely to adapt and establish policies that balance innovation with the need for consumer protection, data security, and overall financial stability. Striking this delicate balance will be imperative for fostering an environment where digital banking can thrive responsibly. The potential of digital banking is enormous. It aims to create a more technologically sophisticated, individualized, and inclusive financial environment. The potential advantages for financial institutions and individuals point to a future where digital banking will continue to redefine and improve how we connect with and manage our funds, even while issues like cybersecurity and regulatory concerns remain. The continued expansion of ATM financial services and the use of Debit/Credit Cards are crucial for the survival and profitability of commercial banks. This is especially true when utilizing point-of-sale money transfers, which are common in supermarkets, shops, and other retail establishments. It has been shown that banks must employ debit cards in conjunction with efficient monitoring programs to cut back on needless manpower and operational expenses. Governments ought to support commercial banks in their fight against cybercrimes, which not only undermine the financial system but also other industries, which in turn affects the banking sector. The financial sector is experiencing needs due to the emergence of new technologies and rising consumer expectations; digital transformation is essential to boosting consumers. Advances in financial technology are expected to result in significant transformations in the financial services and commercial sectors [11]. Fintech has the potential to significantly improve the system experience for banks, catering to various fund types and geographical locations. Meanwhile, investors stand to gain from the shortened transaction processing times [12]. Fintech is about orchestrating the symphony of various digital harmonies to transform the procedures, operations, and business blueprints of the financial sector. This paper aims to provide knowledge regarding the benefits of using digital banking and the role of various fintech practices in Digital Banking.

2 Review of Literature

The consequences and prospects of digitizing banking and financial industries have been extensively researched in the literature. Some of the most well-known studies have been discussed as follows:

Gupta and Xia [2] analyze how AI used to power a chatbot for customer support has improved accessibility and efficiency to a great extent within businesses. The study's conclusions show that ChatGPT offers several noticeable benefits for women entrepreneurs by improving operational effectiveness. ChatGPT can assist companies in improving customer satisfaction, optimizing business processes, conserving resources and time, and promoting collaboration in customer service, advertising and marketing, and internal oversight.

Based on previous trends in the digitization of the banking industry it can be concluded that digitization of banking is not even in all regions. The use of digital technologies in the banks has increased market efficiency and at the same time has created a systematic risk to financial stability [13]. Differences in the culture of the organisations, lack of trained and qualified personnel, increased fraud because of use of digital means in the banking transactions are various challenges being faced for digital transformation [14]. Nguyen et al. [15] concluded that digitalization is a rivalry driver that establishes banks' competitive advantages and produces additional prospects to develop their customer base and range of services.

Yıldırım and Erdil [7], discussed the immediate transformation across various facets of banking enterprises. This encompasses alterations in customer relationships, communication channels, resource allocation, partnerships, and financing. Additionally, it instigates a re-evaluation of the value proposition and encourages collaborative interactions among financial institutions, facilitated by digital platforms.

Pavithra and Geetha [16] highlighted how the use of Digital banking has become an integral part of our lives and how it has become an effective and the most viable tool for creating customer value. The purpose of this article is to determine the variables influencing consumers' perceptions of digital banking services, as well as their degree of satisfaction and preference for them. The result showed that Customers are happy with digital banking services since they find them to be omnipresent, handy, and quick when transferring money.

Ajmera and Bhatt [17] drives the impact of variables like convenience, versatile environment, saw responsiveness, picture of the bank, security, risk, execution benefits, social impact, and indulgent inspiration towards mobile banking. This study made understanding the idea of relationships between different elements that are both, directly and indirectly, relevant to mobile payment applications easier.

Prasanth and Sudhamathi [18] discussed customer satisfaction and customer relevance towards E-banking. This study discovered that students' perceptions of banking services are influenced by the banks they use. The researcher employed a proportionate stratified random sampling technique, which is a more accurate way to choose respondents.

Malali and Gopalakrishnan [19] discussed the role of AI-powered technologies in reducing the chances of human errors and transforming the roles of financial service providers to a new Fin-Tech industry offering a higher customized service with utmost customer satisfaction. This article looked at some of the major unresolved issues in this field of business to study the dynamics of AI ecosystems in the banking and finance industry and how they are quickly becoming major disruptors.

Yue et al. [20], examined the fintech industry's taxonomy and presented the data from an economic standpoint. They offered a bird's eye perspective of the advancements in fintech research. The report mostly drew from a survey of the literature on fintech services. According to their findings, classical ideas will still be relevant in the current fintech environment. However, a technologically advanced environment can help with financial decision-making and increase the likelihood of fraud detection.

Kaur et al. [8] highlight the evolution of Fin-tech industries in India and how it changed the economy with its introduction. Increased operational effectiveness, lower costs, disruption of long-standing industry structures, blurring of industry boundaries, facilitating strategic disintermediation, creating new entry points for entrepreneurship, and democratizing access to financial services are some of the advantages of technology in the financial sector.

Yeremenko and Rudskaya [21] the researchers looked at the banking industry's advances in Russia in a conceptual study. They developed the notion of digital banking, that is, advancements in banking, and payment methods from cards to digital banking. This research has looked at everything from mobile banking to digital banking. Banks, according to the study, should employ cutting-edge technology, deliver services at a reasonable cost, and improve the environment.

Berndt et al. [22], the research focussed on analyzing the readiness of banking technologies in developing countries. The research used the Technology Readiness Index (TRI) as a major quantitative tool to assess the technology readiness in South Africa a developing economy. This study found that the reluctance of consumers to adopt technology should be considered by banks when developing new products and allocating resources to boost customer happiness. It is demonstrated that characteristics like optimism and innovation are essential drivers for customers' technology readiness index, while factors like discomfort and insecurity are inhibitors, and that the majority of respondents are embracing and accepting modern technology. De Angeli et al. [23] presented a method and results of an ethnographic study to build an understanding of Automatic Teller Machine (ATM) adoption in Mumbai, India. The study combined field observations and semi-structured interviews of early ATM adopters, bank customers who do not use ATMs, and people who used the ATM for the first time as part of the research. Moro-Visconti et al. [24] emphasise that FinTechs promise to disrupt and reshape the financial industry by cutting costs, improving the quality of financial services, and creating a more diverse and stabler financial landscape. Sharing, the circular economy, favourable regulation, and information technology drive their existence. Taherdoost [25] emphasizes the influence of digital baking on financial inclusion which opens up hope for marginalized people. To keep the fintech services Up and running many significant dangers need to be addressed malware complications, Phishing attacks, and data breaches. Cybersecurity services like encryption, multifactor authentication, and compliance with the laws can create strict defensive measures. Mehdiabadi et al. [26] discussed that technology is one of the key forces influencing banking's future, along with political and economic considerations. In order to make strategic decisions, effectively predict the future, and take advantage of current opportunities, banking managers urgently need to be aware of technological trends. The goal of contemporary banking is Industry 5.0, which is built on tactics for breaking into the market in a whole new way.

3 Research Objectives

The research was carried out to investigate the following objectives:

1. To assess various factors in the banking industry's digitalization.
2. To Examine the pros and cons of Digital Banking.
3. To investigate Fintech methods used in the banking sector, such as ML and AI.
4. To examine the hurdles to implementing full dependence on digitization in the banking sector.

4 Discussion

To assess various factors in the banking industry's digitalization.

Various factors affecting the digitization of the Banking and Financial Services Sector are as follows.

- Technical literacy and digital awareness—The digitalization of the banking industry is a positive trend driven by customer demand, technological advancements, competition, and regulatory changes. The impact of emerging technical elements, such as artificial intelligence, big data analytics, and visualization, on the macro-level digital transformation of business models remains relatively small [27]. Digital transformation happens for a variety of reasons, including providing services to remote locations without physical offices, standing out from rivals, or cutting expenses [28]. In a country like India, raising digital consciousness and strengthening the functions of digital media connection are essential to digitizing any sector of the economy. Customers should be made aware of how convenient it is to work with digital banking services and how easily they can access them at any time [29].

- Internet Accessibility—In rural areas, inadequate internet connectivity discourages the use of digital work tools and keeps people from learning about and employing new technologies. Artificial intelligence and other intelligent technologies used in remote learning must be strengthened to promote individualized, inclusive, and interactive online learning experiences [30]. More than one billion people utilize the internet in China than any other nation worldwide. India came in second place with almost 933 million people using any kind of gadget to access the internet. After all, the United States has about 307 million Internet users [31].

The nation has the second-largest internet user base in the world. It also offers the most reasonably priced mobile data plans on the market. Despite this, there are Indian citizens living in rural areas that lack internet connection for every internet customer. A substantial section of the population lives in places with poor internet access, considering that 66% of people live in rural regions.

- Data Security and encryptions—Security is one of the key elements driving digitalization in this field. This industry handles a great volume of sensitive data, which needs to be always protected, particularly in light of the rising number of cybercrimes. Numerous studies have been carried out to assess that data security is regarded as a serious concern in rural homes owing to a lack of technology understanding.

To Examine the pros and cons of Digital Banking.

India has the most internet users in the world. Users' accessibility and convenience have greatly increased because of FinTech and digital banking. Customers may use digital platforms to easily manage their accounts, transfer payments, and pay bills since they have the flexibility to do it whenever and wherever they want. As a result, there is no longer a need for physical branches, and underprivileged groups may now access financial services.

Fintech companies have used cutting-edge technologies like blockchain, artificial intelligence, and data analytics to enable frictionless financial transactions [32]. These services have sparked innovation in financial services and products. These technologies provide consumers with an extensive array of alternatives customized to meet their individual needs, ranging from sophisticated budgeting tools to personalized investing platforms. The time and effort needed for various financial tasks have decreased due to the automated and simplified procedures, which have also produced faster and more efficient transactions. Imagine the world economy as a ship navigating choppy waters in 2024. Overall, it's charting a 3.0% growth course, but advanced economies are like anchors, dragging it down with their sluggish 1.4% pace. However, digital transformation needs to go beyond simple technological advancements in the framework of Industry 5.0, which emphasizes the harmonic fusion of human intelligence and technological growth.

Pros: A revolutionary period in the financial sector has been brought about by the emergence of digital banking and financial technology, or fintech. These innovations provide a plethora of benefits that have completely redefined old banking processes. The benefits are summarised as follows:

1. Easy Access: Digital banking makes it feasible for banks to serve customers who live in remote locations or who are unable to visit traditional facilities during an emergency. In addition, individuals may use financial services whenever they choose [33], which is 24 hours a day, 7 days a week [34–36], even on holidays and at odd hours [37].

2. Quick process: Digital banking enables speedy operations, such as bill payments, loan applications, rapid cash transfers, and customers do not need to physically visit the branch to utilise any of these services [35].
3. Cost cutting: Digital banking helps banks reduce the overhead cost associated with physical branches. It has resulted into charging lesser fees for the services provided to various customers and better interest rates in deposits [33, 38, 39].
4. Enhanced Security: Advanced security features like multi-factor authentication, encryption, and real-time fraud detection are frequently included in digital banking, providing a high level of safety for sustainable data.
5. Personalized Services: Banks may utilize data analytics to provide personalized user experiences, customized products, and financial advice based on the unique interests and behaviour of each client.
6. Financial Management Tools: To assist consumers in managing their money more skillfully, several online banking platforms include integrated financial management tools that offer investment services, cost trackers, and budgeting applications [40].
7. Real-time Monitoring: Users may keep an eye on the activities on their accounts in real-time and receive rapid alerts for any transactions. This feature makes it easier to manage funds and quickly identify any unauthorized activity [41].
8. Innovation and Integration: To improve the user experience overall, digital banking promotes ongoing innovation, which includes integrating with other financial services and technologies like blockchain, mobile wallets, and fintech apps.
9. Sustainability and Ethics: Industry 5.0 encourages green banking, socially conscious innovation for faster adaptations to coustmer demands and market changes.

Cons: Digital banking and financial technology (fintech) have many benefits, but their widespread acceptance is not without notable obstacles and disadvantages. The major issues are:

1. Security Issues: Hackers use digital banking services as easy targets when they want to steal money or private data. Consumers may become targets of phishing schemes, in which dishonest parties

deceive them into divulging personal information or login credentials. Massive data breaches have the potential to reveal the financial and personal details of millions of people, which might result in identity theft and financial damage [42].

2. Technical issues: There may be disruptions or outages on banks' digital systems due to slow internet or bad weather making it difficult for users to access their accounts or complete transactions [33]. Apart from this, all the customers especially in remote areas might not have the access to internet or digital competence to utilize the online banking services. Inaccurate account balances, transaction mistakes, and other faults may also result in glitches and bugs in banking apps or websites. Certain banking applications might not work with every device or could need regular upgrades that some users would find difficult to handle.
3. Lack of Personal Interaction: When it comes to addressing complicated problems or receiving individual care, some people prefer in-person encounters over digital ones. Some client complaints may not be sufficiently addressed by chatbots and automated systems, which might irritate them [39].
4. Data Privacy: Banks gather and retain a lot of personal data, which raises questions about how this data is utilized and safeguarded. The degree of data collecting and monitoring associated with digital banking may cause unease among certain clients as these systems are vulnerable to fraud, cyber-attacks, and data breaches. Additionally, the obtained data is typically shared with internal or external marketing agencies, which annoys customers even more.
5. Dependence on technology: In digital banking, the operations rely completely on technology. Even with human-centred goals, there's a risk of dehumanizing customer service if AI and automation aren't used thoughtfully.
6. Energy and Environmental Impact: Digital banking requires a lot of infrastructure, including enough bandwidth, technological tools, internet access, web-based applications, etc. Because of its high energy use, it raises environmental concerns.
7. Potential for Over-Spending: As digital banking is so convenient, people may find it simpler to overspend or handle their money improperly because transactions only require a few clicks.
8. Regulatory Issues: Cross-border digital banking services may encounter difficult legal and regulatory frameworks. In a digital

environment, ensuring adherence to diverse financial rules and standards may pose greater complexity.

Understanding these cons is essential for both consumers and financial institutions to navigate the digital banking landscape effectively, ensuring that the benefits are maximized while the risks are mitigated.

To investigate Fintech methods used in the banking sector, such as ML and AI

Quick technological advancements are enabling new approaches to handle many financial operations, such as sending extremely quick trading strategies and onboarding bank clients. The application of AI ensures a balanced client-computer interface with help from computer-generated assistants and their management that the clients consistently approve [43]. Cashless cards, mobile wallets, and QR codes are just a few of the new payment structure elements that are gradually being integrated into our daily lives [44].

The history of using Artificial Intelligence (AI) and Machine Learning (ML) in finance is still quite new. One of the earliest examples was in 1961 when Arthur Samuel wrote a program that could play checkers. This led to a long string of advancements in how we use AI and ML to understand data and to make predictions based on that data. India has the most growth potential, ranking 15th out of the top 25 AI nations (Gupta 2023). A transformational age has begun in the banking and financial services sector with the integration of Artificial Intelligence (AI) and Machine Learning (ML), which is revolutionizing established procedures and improving overall operational efficiency. Financial organizations may now make better judgments by utilizing ML and AI technology to analyze large datasets and extract insightful data. Big data, fintech AI, and blockchain technology will all be used more often in the future to enhance technology and avoid cybercrimes, cyberattacks, and data breaches across all banking services and goods [45].

One widely recognized application of ML and AI in banking is to enhance fraud detection and prevention systems. These systems can quickly identify anomalies, identify possibly fraudulent activities, and assess transaction data patterns. Because ML and AI can adapt to shifting patterns and learn from them, they are vital for protecting financial institutions and their consumers and staying ahead of sophisticated fraudulent schemes. Innovations in the Indian banking and financial services sector that are most used include machine learning (ML) and artificial intelligence (AI). Machine learning (ML) and artificial intelligence (AI) are frequently used in the fields of increased customer assistance, client behavioural prediction, detection, and customization of the client experience. In addition, fraud detection, credit underwriting, loan processing, intelligent document processing, and KYC norm resolution are among the applications of AI and ML [46]. These technologies reduce human error by automating processes and increase operational efficiency by minimizing human interaction. Due to investors' faith in fintech businesses' capacity to upend established business models through inventive technological solutions, these companies have also been able to raise substantial sums of money in a short amount of time. With policies, the Indian government promotes fintech. In the future, the advancement in AI can provide relevant customer data to banks which will give way to provide more customized services for bank customers. AI can provide banking applications and interfaces the power to integrate many activities like booking tickets and booking cabs giving customers a smarter experience [47]. Banks can employ AI technologies to integrate personalized, real-time insights into their digital platforms, aiding customers in managing their finances effectively. AI can facilitate tailored notifications, delivered at optimal times and locations within the digital interface. Establishing a systematic framework for personalization entails considering customer aspirations and enabling the co-creation of products, fostering user-driven innovation. Furthermore, AI is transforming risk management methodologies through advancements in credit assessment, fraud detection, and regulatory adherence. Organizations can utilize machine learning algorithms to instantly scrutinize extensive datasets, pinpointing fraudulent behavior, evaluating creditworthiness, and guaranteeing regulatory compliance. Consequently, this mitigates risks and bolsters financial stability [48].

To examine the hurdles to implementing full dependence on digitization in the banking sector.

Even while digitization can completely change the banking and financial industry, several important obstacles prevent total reliance on this technological change. The ongoing digital gap across various demographic groups is one of the main challenges. Access to digital devices, dependable internet connectivity, and the requisite abilities to operate digital platforms are not universally available. This discrepancy can result in financial exclusion, depriving some groups of appropriate access to basic banking services, especially the elderly and those living in underserved regions.

Security issues provide yet another difficult obstacle. There is a greater chance of identity theft, data breaches, and cyber dangers as financial transactions become more and more digital. A major concern when implementing a completely digitized banking and financing sector is the likelihood of hacking [39]. Many banks grapple with outdated, incompatible systems that hinder the seamless integration of new digital technologies. Migrating to modernized platforms is costly and complex, often requiring extensive system overhauls. Digitization exposes banks to heightened cyber threats, demanding robust security measures to protect sensitive customer data and financial transactions. Building and maintaining such defences requires continuous investment and proactive adaptation to evolving security landscapes.

5 Conclusion

The Banking Sector in India has observed a drastic change evolving right from the introduction of Debit cards and Automated Teller Machines to organizations like Paytm, PhonePe, BharatPe, etc. as well as the introduction of various governmental payment platforms like NPCI, BHIM UPI affected by various factors like Digital awareness and technical literacy, Internet Connectivity, Data security and encryptions and more. The BFSI sector alone can't overcome the digital gap that digitizes the sector completely, Artificial Intelligence (AI), Augmented Reality (AR), and Machine Learning (ML) are gradually becoming a reality in the finance sector but have both pros and cons which should be thoroughly considered by the government or industrial experts while implementing it in the respective sector. In place of providing customised services using AI and ML, industrialists must focus on how to provide data secure and encrypted services keeping in view the risk of data leak or data loss from the servers. The banking industry has tremendous prospects for expansion and diversification in the future. But overcoming the obstacles posed by the digital revolution, shifting legal requirements, and shifting consumer expectations will need a strong sense of flexibility, clever alliances, and an unwavering dedication to innovation. Leveraging technology while tackling cybersecurity, inclusivity, and ethical issues will be essential to realizing the full potential of a financial sector that is future-proof. The banking industry has obstacles relating to cybersecurity, the digital divide, regulatory frameworks, client trust, and operational difficulties when it fully relies on digitalization. To overcome these challenges and ensure a seamless and inclusive shift to a digitally driven financial sector, a comprehensive strategy combining technology breakthroughs, regulatory flexibility, and coordinated efforts to close accessibility and security gaps is needed.

Indian banks are putting more of an emphasis on technology to enhance their financial services. Financial institutions are incorporating ethical frameworks that place a higher priority on consumer trust, data protection, and equal access as they transition from traditional digitization to intelligent automation and hyper-personalized banking services. These banks have made these services available on mobile devices around the clock, allowing customers to access their account information and make payments whenever they want. Fintech businesses are streamlining their processes and establishing standards for the banking industry. All of this has led many banks in India to partner with fintech startups to offer similar services without having to invest as much money upfront indicating a brighter and more successful future for BFSI Sector collaborating with advanced technological changes. This human-centric methodology ensures that the digital evolution of banking serves people first, establishing a more reasonable and sustainable financial future for all.

References

1. Shrotriya, V., & Yadav, P. S. (2019). Impact Of Technology In Banking And Financial Services Sector–A Critical Analysis. *Think India Journal*, *22*(14), 8002–8014.
2. Gupta, A., & Xia, C. (2018). A paradigm shift in banking: Unfolding asia's fintech adventures. In *International Symposia in Economic Theory and Econometrics* (Vol. 25, pp. 215–254). Emerald Group Publishing Ltd. https://doi.org/10.1108/S1571-038620180000025010.
3. Yadav, H., Kar, A. K., & Kashiramka, S. (2022). Artificial intelligence adoption for fintech industries - An exploratory study about the disruptions, antecedents and consequences. In *Lecture Notes in Computer Science* (pp. 3–12). Springer International Publishing. https://doi.org/10.1007/978-3-031-15342-6_1.

4. Toropova, I., Mingaleva, A., & Knyazev, P. (2019). Macroeconomic model of banking digitization process. In *Lecture Notes in Networks and Systems* (pp. 82–90). Springer International Publishing. https://doi.org/10.1007/978-3-030-22493-6_9.
5. Criollo Hidalgo, V., De Bracamonte Morales, P. J., De La Cruz Cortegana, K. W., García Zare, E. J., Huamán Almonacid, G. S., Maurtua Gurmendi, L. G., & Soto Abanto, S. E. (2023). Digitalización bancaria: Alternativa para optimizar los procesos operativos de una institución financiera. *Proceedings of the 3rd LACCEI International Multiconference on Entrepreneurship, Innovation and Regional Development (LEIRD 2023): "Igniting the Spark of Innovation: Emerging Trends, Disruptive Technologies, and Innovative Models for Business Success."* https://doi.org/10.18687/leird2023.1.1.239.
6. Martínez-Peláez, R., Ochoa-Brust, A., Rivera, S., Félix, V. G., Ostos, R., Brito, H., Félix, R. A., & Mena, L. J. (2023). Role of Digital Transformation for Achieving Sustainability: Mediated Role of Stakeholders, Key Capabilities, and Technology. *Sustainability (Switzerland)*, *15*(14). https://doi.org/10.3390/su151411221.
7. Yıldırım, A. C., & Erdil, E. (2023). The effect of Covid-19 on digital banking explored under business model approach. *Qualitative Research in Financial Markets*, *16*(1), 87–107. https://doi.org/10.1108/qrfm-08-2021-0142.
8. Kaur, S. J., Ali, L., Hassan, M. K., & Al-Emran, M. (2021). Adoption of digital banking channels in an emerging economy: exploring the role of in-branch efforts. *Journal of Financial Services Marketing*, *26*(2), 107–121. https://doi.org/10.1057/s41264-020-00082-w.
9. Montazemi, A. R., & Qahri-Saremi, H. (2015). Factors affecting adoption of online banking: A meta-analytic structural equation modeling study. *Information and Management*, *52*(2), 210–226. https://doi.org/10.1016/j.im.2014.11.002.
10. Shaikh, I., & Anwar, M. (2023). Digital bank transactions and performance of the Indian banking sector. *Applied Economics*, *55*(8), 839–852. https://doi.org/10.1080/00036846.2022.2094880.
11. Kumari, A., & Devi, N. C. (2022). The impact of fintech and blockchain technologies on banking and financial services. *Technology Innovation Management Review*, *12*(1/2). https://doi.org/10.22215/timreview/1481.
12. Vivek Dubey. (2019). FinTech Innovations in Digital Banking. *International Journal of Engineering Research And*, *V8*(10). https://doi.org/10.17577/IJERTV8IS100285.
13. Shkodina, I., Derid, I., & Zelenko, O. (2019). Digital transformation of global banking: Challenges and prospects. *Financial and credit activity: problems of theory and practice*, *3*(30), 45-51.

14. Zhao, J., Li, X., Yu, C.H., Chen, S. and Lee, C.C. (2022), "Riding the FinTech innovation wave: FinTech, patents and bank performance", Journal of International Money and Finance, Vol. 122, p. 102552.
15. Nguyen, Q.T.T., Ho, L.T.H. and Nguyen, D.T. (2023), "Digitalization and bank profitability: evidence from an emerging country", International Journal of Bank Marketing, Vol. 41 No. 7, pp. 1847–1871.
16. Pavitra, C. B., & Geetha, K. (2021). Factors Affecting Customers' Perception Towards Digital Banking Services. *Turkish Journal of Computer and Mathematics Education (TURCOMAT)*, *12*(11), 1608–1614. https://doi.org/10.17762/turcomat.v12i11.6091.
17. Ajmera, H., & BHATT, D. V. (2021). *A Study on Factors Affecting Consumer Attitude and Intention Towards the Mobile Payment Applications in Gujarat* (Doctoral dissertation, Thesis for Ph. D. Gujarat Technological University, India). https://doi.org/10.13140/RG.2.2.33648.58883.
18. Prasanth, S., & Sudhamathi, S. (2021). Analysis of Indian Bank Customer's Attitude towards E-Banking. *Shanlax International Journal of Management*, *8*(4), 82–89. https://doi.org/10.34293/management.v8i4.3661.
19. Malali, A. B., & Gopalakrishnan, S. (2020). Application of Artificial Intelligence and Its Powered Technologies in the Indian Banking and Financial Industry: An Overview. *IOSR Journal Of Humanities And Social Science (IOSR-JHSS*, *25*(6), 55–60. https://doi.org/10.9790/0837-2504065560.
20. Yue, Z., Wang, K., & Ye, M. (2023). The impact of fintech on corporate innovation: Mediating role of entrepreneurship. *International Entrepreneurship and Management Journal*, *20*(1), 231–252. https://doi.org/10.1007/s11365-023-00911-z.
21. Yeremenko, I., & Rudskaya, E. (2016). International Journal of Economics and Financial Issues Banking Business Innovations: Conceptual Foundations of Modern Economy Development. *International Journal of Economics and Financial Issues* |, *6*(S8), 361–369. http:www.econjournals.com.
22. Berndt, A. D., Saunders, S. G., & Petzer, D. J. (2010). Readiness for banking technologies in developing countries. *Southern African business review*, *14*(3).
23. De Angeli, A., Athavankar, U., Joshi, A., Coventry, L., & Johnson, G. I. (2004). Introducing ATMs in India: A contextual inquiry. *Interacting with Computers*, *16*(1), 29–44. https://doi.org/10.1016/j.intcom.2003.11.003.
24. Moro-Visconti, R., Cruz Rambaud, S., & López Pascual, J. (2020). Sustainability in fintechs: An explanation through business model scalability and market valuation. *Sustainability*, *12*(24), 10316. https://doi.org/10.3390/su122410316.
25. Taherdoost, H. (2023). Fintech: Emerging trends and the future of finance. In *Financial Innovation and Technology* (pp. 29–39). Springer International Publishing. https://doi.org/10.1007/978-3-031-17998-3_2.

26. Mehdiabadi, A., Shahabi, V., Shamsinejad, S., Amiri, M., Spulbar, C., & Birau, R. (2022). Investigating industry 5.0 And its impact on the banking industry: Requirements, approaches and communications. *Applied Sciences*, *12*(10), 5126. https://doi.org/10.3390/app12105126.
27. Werth, O., Schwarzbach, C., Rodríguez Cardona, D., Breitner, M. H., & Graf von der Schulenburg, J. M. (2020). Influencing factors for the digital transformation in the financial services sector. *Zeitschrift Fur Die Gesamte Versicherungswissenschaft*, *109*(2–4), 155–179. https://doi.org/10.1007/s12297-020-00486-6.
28. Kitsios, F., Giatsidis, I., & Kamariotou, M. (2021). Digital transformation and strategy in the banking sector: Evaluating the acceptance rate of e-services. *Journal of Open Innovation: Technology, Market, and Complexity*, *7*(3), 204. https://doi.org/10.3390/joitmc7030204.
29. Hanedar, E., Alonso, C., Uña, G., Prihardini, D., Bhojwani, T., & Zhabska, K. (2023). Stacking up the Benefits: Lessons from India's digital journey. *IMF Working Papers*, *2023*(078), 1. https://doi.org/10.5089/9798400240416.001.
30. Ferri, F., Grifoni, P., & Guzzo, T. (2020). Online learning and emergency remote teaching: Opportunities and challenges in emergency situations. *Societies*, *10*(4), 86. https://doi.org/10.3390/soc10040086.
31. *Number of internet users worldwide 2023*. (2023). Statista. https://www.statista.com/statistics/273018/number-of-internet-users-worldwide/
32. Tomer, P. (2024). Financial technology revolution in India: An appraisal. *RESEARCH REVIEW International Journal of Multidisciplinary*, *9*(4), 177–191. https://doi.org/10.31305/rrijm.2024.v09.n04.021.
33. Drigă, I. & Isac, C. (2014). E-banking services - features, challenges and benefits. *Annals of the University of Petrosani, Economics*. 14(1): 49–58.
34. Koskosas, I. (2011). The pros and cons of internet banking: a short review. *Business excellence and management*, *1*(1), 49–58.
35. Nedumaran, G. & Baladevi, M. (2018). Pros and cons of online banking services. *Bodhi International Journal of Research in Humanities, Arts and Science*. 2(13): 106–109.
36. Rammaiya, M. V., & Prakash, G. (2019). KAP study of e-banking in Indore. *Amity Journal of Management*, *7*(1), 13–21.
37. Kataria, M. (2019). Digital banking in India: Recent trends, advantages and disadvantages. Inspira-Journal of Commerce. *Economics & Computer Science*, *5*(3), 301–304.
38. SaranyaPriyadarshini, C. (2018). A study on significance of digitization in banking services. *International Journal of Application or Innovation in Engineering & Management (IJAIEM)*, *7*(3), 65–68.
39. Vesić, T., Lazović, C., & Petronijević, D. (2020). *The Necessity of Digitalization of the Banking System - A Chance or a Threat to the Development*

of the Banking Market? 125–130. https://doi.org/10.15308/finiz-2020-125-130.

40. Kalyani, P. (2016). An empirical study of the effects of demonetization in india in the year 2016 and analyzing shifting trends in marketing/purchasing to the alternative options. *Journal of Management Engineering and Information Technology*, *3*(6), 20–34.
41. Kemp, S. (2023, February 13). Digital 2023: India — datareportal – global digital insights. *DataReportal – Global Digital Insights*. https://datareportal.com/reports/digital-2023-india
42. Khan, H. F. (2021). E-Banking system benefits and issues. In *Insights into Economics and Management Vol. 11* (pp. 40–48). Book Publisher International (a part of SCIENCEDOMAIN International). https://doi.org/10.9734/bpi/ieam/v11/9085d.
43. Srivastava, A., & Kumar, A. (2023). Reshaping banking with digital technologies. *Fintech and Cryptocurrency*, 35–57. https://doi.org/10.1002/9781119905028.ch3.
44. Agarwal, S., & Zhang, J. (2020). FinTech, lending and payment innovation: A review. *Asia-Pacific Journal of Financial Studies*, *49*(3), 353–367. https://doi.org/10.1111/ajfs.12294.
45. Wewege, L., Lee, J., & Thomsett, M. C. (2020). Disruptions and digital banking trends. *Journal of Applied Finance and Banking*, *10*(6), 15–56. https://www.researchgate.net/publication/343050625.
46. Mytnyk, B., Tkachyk, O., Shakhovska, N., Fedushko, S., & Syerov, Y. (2023). Application of Artificial Intelligence for Fraudulent Banking Operations Recognition. *Big Data and Cognitive Computing*, *7*(2), 93. https://doi.org/10.3390/bdcc7020093.
47. Murinde, V., Rizopoulos, E., & Zachariadis, M. (2022). The impact of the FinTech revolution on the future of banking: Opportunities and risks. *International Review of Financial Analysis*, *81*. https://doi.org/10.1016/j.irfa.2022.102103.
48. Agrawal, S. S., Rose, N., & Prabhu Sahai, K. (2024). The fintech revolution: AI'S role in disrupting traditional banking and financial services. *Decision Making: Applications in Management and Engineering*, *7*(1), 243-256.

Banking Outreach and Usage Pattern of Banking Services in Bihar

Ritesh Ravi, Vandana Kumari, and Vivekanand Pandey

1 Introduction

The literature available on banking outreach in India concentrates on three main areas. The first is to evaluate the status of financial inclusion and measure its progress [1]. The second is to identify the reasons behind financial exclusion [2–4]. Third, it aims to evaluate the impact of banking outreach on other economic indicators [5, 6]. Among the socioeconomic indicators, banking outreach has been shown to have a positive impact on poverty reduction [7–9], the growth of micro and small-scale businesses [10], and the production and employment potential of people [11–14]. Despite this recognised contribution of financial inclusion, developing countries have been unable to attain the desired level of banking outreach

R. Ravi (✉)
Bihar Institute of Public Administration and Rural Development, Gaya, Bihar, India
e-mail: ritesh.ravi2@gmail.com

V. Kumari
Department of LSW and PMIR, A N College, Patna, Bihar, India

V. Pandey
Amity University, Patna, Bihar, India

© The Author(s), under exclusive license to Springer Nature Singapore Pte Ltd. 2025

P. Agarwal et al. (eds.), *Building a Human-Centred Infrastructure for Sustainable Industry 5.0 in Asia*,
https://doi.org/10.1007/978-981-95-0417-6_6

and continue to struggle in this regard. According to the [15], 39% of the world's population is financially excluded from banking services in 183 countries. One of the significant aspects of the status of financial inclusion is credit outreach, which has been studied extensively [16–18]. Barik and Sharma [19] stated that it is only credit outreach that can result in maximum benefits of financial inclusion, such in terms of economic development and poverty reduction. While investigating why credit outreach is a major issue, [20] found that education and skill plays a significant role in credit worthiness from formal lending sources to farmers. References [21, 22] added that higher income, better education, being a man, and being older are associated with greater use of formal accounts and formal credit. According to [23], age, education, financial literacy, income, and internet connectivity are positively related to financial inclusion. And on the other hand, the documentation required to open bank accounts and the distance to the nearest access point are negatively related to financial inclusion.

The digital age has brought about a shift towards online banking and self-service kiosks (SSKs), with traditional branch banking losing ground. However, while this may seem like progress towards financial inclusion, it presents a new set of challenges. A study by [24] in India found that only 13% of respondents had used phone banking, 47% knew what SSKs were, and more than 78% had used ATMs. These figures are less than satisfactory, especially considering that over 85% of the population in India use smartphones. Another study by [25] revealed that most respondents had significant experience with ATMs, but the study only covered computer-literate individuals. Given that a large portion of the population in India is still computer illiterate, this presents a limitation. Meanwhile, [26] conducted a study in a specific city to gauge perceptions of ATM services.

India, one of the world's fastest-growing economies, still struggles to provide basic banking services to all households despite government initiatives like the Pradhan Mantri Jan Dhan Yojna. While having a bank account is almost accomplished, credit outreach remains a major issue, especially in rural areas like Bihar. This study aims to examine the usage pattern of loans, branch banking, interactive kiosks, and Internet banking among households, identify factors that influence banking decisions, and assess consumer satisfaction with various banking services. The study proposes to make two contributions to the literature by focusing on the accessibility and usability dimensions of banking outreach and using primary data to analyse consumer behaviour and satisfaction. Additionally, this study is among the few that attempt banking analysis at the state level in India. The paper is organized into five sections: literature review, theoretical framework, methodological framework, results, discussion, and conclusion.

2 Literature Review

2.1 Financial Inclusion and Its Approaches

The topic of financial inclusion has two main perspectives: one emphasizes the inclusion of economically and culturally disadvantaged groups, while the other advocates for the inclusion of all individuals using financial services, irrespective of social status or geographic location [27–29]. This study aligns with the latter perspective.

Analyzing efforts to enhance banking outreach can be approached through three methods, considering factors that assess the coverage of financial inclusion. In India, discussions on banking outreach predominantly revolve around two approaches: one focusing on supply and demand factors [30, 31], and the other considering accessibility, availability, and usability dimensions [32, 33]. However, [29] comprehensive third approach, based on five types of financial exclusion, is rarely utilized in Indian banking literature.

This study endeavors to incorporate primarily unavailable data from secondary sources, especially concerning the usage patterns of basic banking services and qualitative information regarding challenges faced and satisfaction levels. Through this approach, a more thorough evaluation of banking outreach can be achieved.

2.2 Status of Financial Inclusion

The existing literature extensively covers the status of banking outreach, often relying on secondary data across various geographic levels. At a global scale, [34] highlighted that 1.7 billion adults lack access to financial services, with developing countries facing greater challenges. This study focuses on one of India's less urbanized states. While [19] note significant progress in Indian financial inclusion due to Pradhan Mantri Jan Dhan Yojna (PMJDY), universal financial inclusion, especially in credit outreach and digital banking, remains incomplete. Kazi and Shemim [35] found inadequate financial inclusion in Assam, with notable district-wide disparities. Credit outreach is critical for inclusive growth, particularly in rural economies [36, 37]. Formal financial systems favor high-income groups, leading to the emergence of informal credit sources in countries like India [38]. Regional disparities persist, with higher credit penetration in the southern and western regions compared to the eastern area [39]. In terms of digital banking, [40] observed low penetration of ATM and online banking in India. Despite the push for a cashless economy, digital banking adoption remains uneven, with certain demographic groups using it less frequently [19].

2.3 Determining Factors of Financial Inclusion

Demographic factors significantly influence financial inclusion, with age, gender, education, income, and urbanization playing pivotal roles, as studied in Peru by [41]. Sarigul [42] highlights a strong correlation between urbanization rates and financial inclusion in Turkey, indicating improved accessibility and broader product usage with increased urbanization. Kumar Vaid et al. [43] emphasize that banking service penetration, technology, trust, and income levels are key contributors to financial inclusion. In businesses, formality and education are crucial. Bhanot et al. [2] study in the northeast region of India identifies income, education, access to financial information, awareness of self-help groups, proximity to post office banks, terrain, government benefits, and recipients in plain areas as vital factors. Kumar [22] reveals that regional socioeconomic and environmental factors shape consumer habits, with the number of factories and employees influencing banking penetration. Barik and Sharma [19] recommend enhancing digital infrastructure, establishing financial literacy centers, and extending credit to marginalized groups to achieve India's financial inclusion goals. Leeladhar [17] suggests a holistic approach, including awareness campaigns, promotion of no-frills accounts, ATM modifications for literacy challenges, and collaboration with various resources, including technology, expertise, and NGOs, to address financial exclusion.

3 Theoretical Model

The theoretical model of this research aims to investigate the usage patterns of banking services among households and identify determinants influencing these patterns. It also seeks to assess consumer satisfaction with various banking services. This model is designed to contribute to literature in three main dimensions:

3.1 Usage Patterns Dimension

This dimension focuses on the modes of banking, including branch banking, ATM usage, and online banking, as well as sources of loans, such as banks, Non-banking Finance companies (NBFCs), money lenders, friends, relatives, and other sources of credit. The study examines households' choices in opting for or not opting for these banking modes and loan sources.

3.2 Determinants Dimension

This dimension explores the factors that influence households' choices in modes of banking and sources of loans. These factors encompass demographic characteristics and geographical areas of households.

3.3 Consumer Satisfaction Dimension

The model also includes an assessment of consumer satisfaction with various banking services to gauge the quality of their experiences.

By integrating these dimensions and employing primary data analysis, this research aims to provide insights into the factors influencing banking choices and consumer satisfaction, particularly at the state level in India. This approach is in line with the study's unique contributions to literature.

4 Data and Analysis

4.1 Study Area

Bihar is India's third-largest state, with a population comparable to that of Japan.[1] It has been one of India's fastest growing states with least urbanisation. Its economy is primarily based on the service sector with 61% of GDP and agriculture with 20% (Bihar Budget Analysis 20-2, 2020). In addition, most of the banking outreach indicators are extremely low in Bihar especially when compared to the penetration of credit of other Indian states and union territories [3].

4.2 Study Variables and Data Collection Tools

Primary data was collected from households in Bihar's Patna and Madhepura districts using a self-administered semi-structured interview schedule comprising 96 questions. The Banking Service Outreach Index (BSOI) ranked Patna highest and Madhepura lowest, providing a comprehensive view from opposing ends [3]. The survey, involving 300 respondents, included 150 from Patna (36 villages and urban areas) and an equal number from Madhepura (six villages/urban areas). Additionally, qualitative insights were gathered through Focused Group Discussions (FGDs) to explore subjective factors influencing banking outreach [44].

4.3 Description of a Sample

Households, selected to represent diverse demographic groups based on rural/urban status, religion, social categories, annual income, and land holdings, were evenly distributed between urban and rural areas in both districts. Hindus constituted 82%, and Muslims 18% of respondents, with variation in proportions across Patna and Madhepura. Social category distribution included OBC (46%), SC (22%), General (18%), and EBC (13%). In Patna, 37.3% identified as SC or OBC, while Madhepura had 55.3% from the OBC category. Income distribution revealed 68% below the poverty line, with 77% in Madhepura earning less than one lakh rupees annually, compared to 59.4% in Patna. The majority fell into the 1–2 Lacks and 2–5 Lacks income groups. The term "household having asset"

[1] https://statisticstimes.com/demographics/india/indian-states-population.php.

(HHA) served as a poverty indicator, with only 7% labeled as "having no assets." Patna and Madhepura had 3.3 and 10.7% households not falling into the HHA category, respectively.

4.4 *Determinant of Banking Outreach*

This section deals with the identification of determinants for banking outreach where two constructs i.e., Modes of banking and Sources of Loan have been taken. Modes of banking further includes opting Branch banking, ATM, and online banking as dependent variables. Similarly, Sources of Loans includes opting banks, Non-banking Finance companies (NBFC's), Money lenders, Friends and Relatives and other sources of credit as dependent variables. The dichotomous responses, taken from the households, indicate '1' as opting and '0' as not opting. Independent or explanatory variables consist of demographic characteristics and geographical area of households. As the explanatory variables are categorical, n-category of variable, (n − 1) dummies are taken, and one category is arbitrarily taken as reference category. The explanatory variables along with their coding is described in Table 1.

For modes of banking, X1, X2, X3, X4, X5, X6, X7, X9, X10, and X11 are proposed explanatory variables, whereas for sources of loan, X1, X2, X3, X4, X5, X6, X7, X9, X10, and X11 are proposed explanatory variables.

Since the dependent variables are categorical, the binary logistics regression model is applied to identify the explanatory variables, which are expressed in discrete numbers or categorical scales [45]. The Logit regression function (Li) is represented by.

$$L_i = \left(\frac{P_i}{1 - P_i}\right) - \alpha + \sum\nolimits_{j=1}^{j=k} \beta_j X_j + \in_j$$

where, Odd ratio is ratio of probability of happening and not happening an event. Odd ratio in equation form can be represented as follows.

$$\frac{P_i}{1 - P_i} = e^{\alpha + \sum_{j=1}^{j=k} \beta_j X_j}, i = 1, 2, \ldots\ldots, k$$

Table 1 Details of dependent and independent variables

S No.	*Constructs/dependent variables*	*Independent variables and their categories*
1	**Modes of banking** 1.1 Branch banking 1.2 ATM 1.3 Online banking	X1-Location (rural-0, urban-1), X2-Household size (1–2 members-1, 3–5 members -2, 6–8 members-3, more than 8–9),
2	**Sources of loan** 2.1 Bank 2.2 NBFC 2.3 Money lender 2.4 Friends and relatives Others	X3-Religion (Hinduism-1, Muslim-2, others-9) X4-Social category (scheduled tribe-1, scheduled caste-2, other backward class-3, extreme backward caste-4, general-9), X5-Bank (public sector bank-1, private banks-2, foreign banks-3, regional rural bank-4, others-9), X6-Education level (not literate-01, literate-02, secondary-3, higher secondary-4, graduate-5, post graduate and above-9), X7-Profession (farmer-1, casual labour-2, self-employed-3, and others-9), X8-Computer literacy (Yes-1, No-0), X9-Migrated member (Yes-1, No-0), X10-Household income (<30 K annually-1, >30 to <50 K annually-2, >50 K to <75 K-3, >75 K to <1 Lack annually-4, 1 to 2 Lack-5, 2–5 Lack-6, 5 Lack and above-9) and X11-Household having asset (Yes-1, No-0)

The Probability of happening an event (Y = 1) is given by following equation

$$P\,(Y = 1|\;X1,\;X2,\ldots..,\;X3) = \frac{1}{1 + e^{-\alpha - \sum_{j=1}^{j=k} \beta_j X_j}}$$

To determine the combined effect of independent variables on dependent variables in logistic regression, likelihood ratios, Score, and Wald are analyzed. According to [46] these test statistics follow Chi-square distribution and likelihood ratio is the most appropriate statistic for small sample size.

4.5 *Satisfaction Measurement of Consumers*

The questionnaire evaluated household satisfaction on diverse banking issues using a 5-point Likert scale, encompassing aspects like banking service ease, employee attitude, loan disbursement, information dissemination, encouragement for electronic banking, grievance handling, timely services, functional ATMs, and availability of cash. Open-ended responses were included to delve deeper into issues and identify potential banking service problems. Descriptive statistics were employed to analyze the collected responses, providing a comprehensive overview of household sentiments on various banking aspects.

5 Result and Analysis

This section is divided into four subsections: usage patterns of different banking modes, the status of credit outreach, determinants of banking outreach, and individual household satisfaction with basic banking services. The first part details household usage of branch banking, ATMs, online banking, and loans. The second section explores factors influencing preferences for various banking modes and loan sources. The third part evaluates household satisfaction using Likert scales and summarizes responses regarding encountered problems with banking services. Content analysis is employed to present key observations from the collected data.

5.1 *Usage Pattern of Different Modes of Banking*

The shift from traditional brick-and-mortar banking to interactive kiosk/ATM banking and online banking due to technological advancements reflects changes in banking service usage habits. This transition is explored through factors such as the mode of use, distance from the banking outlet, frequency of use, and the number of bank accounts, which are discussed in this section.

Modes of Banking Opted by Households

At household level branch banking is used by 98.7% of the households. However, only 56.7% use ATMs and 26% of total households use online banking. Moreover, 40% belong to rural households and 73.3% to urban households in using ATM. Usage of ATM in Patna district (53.3%) is less than Madhepura (60%), Whereas in urban Patna it is quite higher (82.7%). Usage of online banking is more than twice in urban areas compared to rural areas. 31.3% of households of Patna districts are using online banking and 15.3% in Madhepura.

Distance and Frequency of Usage of Different Modes of Banking

Eighty percent of bank branches and ninety percent of ATMs are within one kilometer of where household live, with the longest distance being five kilometers. In terms of frequency of use, two-thirds of households use branch banking occasionally. In urban areas, branch banking is used less frequently than in rural areas. Although 17.8% of rural households use branch banking frequently, there is no household in the sample that uses branch banking frequently. The use of ATMs in rural areas is higher than in urban areas. In rural areas, 58.7% of households use ATMs on a regular basis, compared to 34.7% in urban areas.

Households Having Bank A/Cs in Different Types of Banks

As reported earlier 98.7% of the households have bank A/Cs. When it comes to banking sector ownership, public sector banks (87.2%) play a significant role, with 87.2% of households having bank accounts in those banks. In urban areas, 95.9% of households have bank accounts with PSBs, while in rural areas this number is 78.4%. In total, private sector banks and RRBs serve 2.7 and 10.1% of households, respectively. In rural Bihar, RRBs provide services to 20% of households.

Number of Different Types of Bank Accounts in a Household

In Bihar, the average number of local bank accounts per household is four. Whereas Patna districts have more local bank accounts and remittance accounts per household than Madhepura. In total, 7 of the 10 households have PMJDY accounts, and 1 of the 4 households have remittance accounts.

5.2 *Status of Credit Outreach*

This section compares credit penetration between banking institutions and non-banking financial companies (NBFCs), money lenders, friends, family, and other lending sources. It delves into loan characteristics such as Incidence of Indebtedness (IOI), loan sources, purpose, Time to Avail Loan (TAL), Amount of Debt (AOD), Rate of Interest (ROI), and repayment and installment periods to gain a comprehensive understanding of how households utilize loans.

Incidence of Indebtedness (IOI) and Sources of Loan

Findings reveal diverse sources of household borrowing, with 61.7% borrowing from banks, and moneylenders serving one-fifth of households. The banking system accounts for 48.5%, while NBFCs, friends, relatives, and other sources contribute 13.1, 10.6, and 6.6%, respectively. Rural areas see higher moneylender usage (23.8%) than urban areas (16.7%). Notably, Patna district has lower banking penetration (29.8%) than Madhepura (65.4%) in loan disbursement. Patna (22.3%) surpasses Madhepura (0%) in receiving financial help from friends and relatives. Rural areas favor NBFCs more (10.7%) compared to urban areas (4.5%), while friends and relatives' reliance is higher in urban settings (16.7 vs. 8.2%). Rural households notably utilize alternative sources like Contractors, Jeevika, Mandi, Rani Saria, and SHGs.Top of Form.

IOI and Banking Sector

Public sector banks play a significant role in loan disbursement in Bihar, constituting 44.7%, followed by private sector banks at 31.9%. In rural areas, private sector banks contribute more (33.3%) compared to urban areas (30.0%), while public sector banks show the opposite trend (27.8% in rural, 67.8% in urban). Regional Rural Banks (RRB) rank third, with a 37% penetration in rural areas and an overall contribution of 21.3% to loan disbursement. Small Finance Banks (SFB) have a limited impact, lending to only 2.1% of total households due to their nascent stage. Patna exhibits better private sector bank performance than Madhepura, where RRB stands out in loan disbursement.

Purpose of Loan

A significant portion of total loans is allocated to medical treatment (23%) and initiating new businesses (20%). Daughter's marriage (14%) and household expenses (14%) also hold considerable shares, while home and vehicle loan each account for 10%. Urban areas dominate in home loans, education loans, and vehicle loans, whereas rural areas lead in medical treatment, daughter's marriage, starting a new business, and household expenses. Other expenses encompass farming, festivals, land purchase, investment in business, and events like parent and brother demise, and son's marriage.

Time to Avail Loan

In the majority of cases, money lenders (80%) and friends and relatives (43%) offer instant loans. NBFCs surpass banks in loan disbursement speed, with over three-fourths of households receiving NBFC loans within 15 days, while half of bank loans take over a month. Rural areas generally experience longer loan processing times than urban areas.

Amount of Debt (AOD)

Banking institutions dominate in disbursing the amount of debt (74.4%), whereas NBFCs and money lenders contribute 8.2 and 12.2%, respectively. Friends and relatives provide a modest 3.2%, while other sources contribute only 2%. The minimum AOD varies, with banks offering ₹18,000 and NBFCs ₹15,000. Banks provide the highest loan amounts.

Rate of Interest (ROI)

Banks and NBFCs charge interest rates ranging from 7–24% and 10–36%, respectively. Money lenders charge higher rates, ranging from 24–120%. Friends and relatives in urban areas generally don't charge interest, while in rural areas, they may act as money lenders. Most households opt for 10–13.5% ROI from banks. Rural households generally experience higher

ROIs. Moneylenders typically charge 60–120% ROI, while home loans in Patna see 7–10% ROI for 50% of households.

Repay Period and Instalment Period

Money lenders have flexible or unlimited repayment periods, focusing more on interest rates. Banks offer a maximum repayment period of 10–20 years, usually opting for three-year periods. NBFCs have a 12–36 months repayment window. Friends and family loans typically have a one-year repayment period unless specified. Banks and money lenders charge monthly installments, while NBFCs and others may have weekly, bi-monthly, or monthly schedules. Repayment periods for friends and relatives are generally unspecified.

5.3 *Determinant of Banking Outreach*

This section tries to find the decisive factors of opting for different modes of banking in first sub-section and credit options in the second sub-section.

Modes of Banking: ATM and Online Banking Service

As previously stated in this study, nearly all households use branch banking, so logistical regression analysis is not required to explain it. As a result, logistic regression analysis is used to identify the explanatory variables underlying ATM and online banking use. Model significance test statistic and summary for usage of ATM and online banking reports that the p-value for likelihood ratio test is significant for both the model. Other test statistics are significant as well. Here ATM and Online banking services are dependent variables and Location, Religion, Social category, Education Level, Profession, Computer Literacy and Household Income, Household having asset are explanatory variables.

Table 2 shows that opting/using an ATM is influenced by a household's location, social group, occupation, income, and computer literacy, whereas opting online banking is influenced by religion, social group, occupation, income, and computer literacy (Tables 3 and 4).

The impact of household location (Rural/Urban) on ATM usage is confirmed by cross-tabulation, indicating that 73.3% of urban households use ATMs, while only 40% of rural households do. Logistic regression,

Table 2 Logistic regression model for significance of independent variables for usage of ATM and Online banking services

Modes of banking	*ATM*			*Online banking*		
Effects of explanatory variables	*Wald Chi square*	*Df*	*Sig.*	*Wald Chi square*	*Df*	*Sig.*
Location	8.126	1	0.004***	0.903	1	0.342
Religion	1.126	1	0.289	5.964	1	0.015**
Social group	19.058	4	0.001***	31.169	4	0.00***
Education	3.342	5	0.647	7.847	5	0.165
Occupation	7.056	3	0.070**	8.520	3	0.036**
Household income	2.715	4	0.607	9.588	4	0.048**
Computer literacy	18.830	1	0.00***	10.399	1	0.001***

Source Author calculation
Note ***denotes significance at 1%, ** denotes significance at 5%, * denotes significance at 10%

comparing the actual probability of categories to a reference category, reveals that urban households are 3.309 times more likely than rural households to use ATMs. OBC and SC households are less likely than the General/Unreserved category to use ATMs, with odds ratios of 0.157 and 0.084, respectively.

For internet banking adoption, household religion plays a role, with Muslim families less likely to use online banking compared to Hindus (14.8% vs. 30.9%). Muslim households have an odds ratio of 0.205, indicating lower likelihood. SC, OBC, and EBC categories have negative impacts on online banking use, with odds ratios of 0.028, 0.083, and 0.010, respectively. EBC households are the least likely to use online banking among social groups. Computer-literate households are 6.58 times more likely to use internet banking, highlighting the significance of computer literacy in determining usage.

Sources of Loan: All lending sources, Banks, NBFC, Moneylender, Friends/Relatives and Other Sources of Loan

The p-value of the likelihood ratio test, as per the model significance test statistics in Tables 5 and 6, is less than equal to 0.012 for all models. This

Table 3 Logistics regression model parameter estimates and Odds ratio for usage of ATM services

S No.	Description of variables	ATM			Online banking		
		Parameter estimates	*Sig.*	*Odds ratio*	*Parameter estimates*	*Sig.*	*Odds ratio*
	Intercept	−1.578	0.375	0.206	−37.410	0.998	0.000
1	Location (rural as reference)						
	Urban	1.197	0.001***	3.309	0.192	0.708	1.212
2	Religion (Hinduism as reference)						
	Muslim	−0.019	0.971	0.981	−1.587	0.035**	0.205
3	Social group (general as reference)						
	OBC	16.681	1.000	1.7E + 7	−26.277	0.999	0.000
	EBC	−2.472	0.001***	0.084	−3.586	0.000***	0.028
	SC	−1.850	0.003***	0.157	−2.488	0.000***	0.083
	ST	−0.343	0.655	0.710	−4.654	0.000***	0.010
4	Education level (not literate as reference)						
	Literate	0.163	0.803	1.177	−0.163	0.892	0.850
	secondary	−0.611	0.407	0.543	−0.647	0.611	0.524
	Senior secondary	−1.167	0.184	0.311	0.561	0.678	1.752
	Graduate	−0.411	0.617	0.663	−1.361	0.342	0.257
	Postgraduate or above	−0.521	0.666	0.594	−1.267	0.424	0.282
5	Occupation (farmer as reference)						
	Casual labour	−0.549	0.512	0.578	20.666	0.999	9.4E + 8
	Self employed	-1.386	0.142	0.250	18.940	0.999	1.6E + 8
	Others	−0.015	0.987	0.985	20.484	0.999	7.8E + 8
6	Household income (<50 thousand as reference)						
	50 thousand-1 Lack	1.920	0.143	6.822	18.388	0.999	9.6E + 7
	1–2 Lack	1.582	0.243	4.867	19.523	0.998	3.0E11
	2–5 Lack	2.567	0.062	13.030	19.298	0.998	2.4E + 9
	5 Lack and above	2.519	0.083	12.418	18.402	0.999	9.8E + 6
7	Computer literacy (No as reference)						
	Yes	2.153	0.000***	8.607	Yes	2.153	0.000***

Source Author calculation
Note *** denotes significance at 1%, ** denotes significance at 5%, * denotes significance at 10%

Table 4 Logistic regression model for significance of independent variables for different sources of loan

	All sources			*Bank*			*NBFC*		
Explanatory variables	*Wald Chi square*	*Df*	*Sig.*	*Wald Chi square*	*Df*	*Sig.*	*Wald Chi square*	*Df*	*Sig.*
Location	5.433	1	0.020**	0.143	1	0.705	1.778	1	0.182
Religion	1.842	1	0.175	0.020	1	0.886	1.020	1	0.312
Social group	6.489	4	0.165	27.027	3	0.000***	2.600	3	0.457
Education level	13.226	5	0.021**	8.240	5	0.144	1.266	5	0.938
Occupation	0.995	3	0.803	9.529	3	0.023**	2.851	3	0.415
Migrtion	0.171	1	0.679	0.811	1	0.368	1.809	1	0.179
Household income	4.558	4	0.336	2.922	4	0.571	0.114	4	0.998

Source Author calculation
Note *** denotes significance at 1%, ** denotes significance at 5%, * denotes significance at 10%

indicates the significance and meaningfulness of all five models for further discussion. The results of other tests are also statistically significant. The model considers the adoption of various credit sources by households as dependent variables, with proposed explanatory variables including Location (Rural/Urban), Religion, Social Group, Education, Occupation, Migration, and Household Income. Findings indicate that the urbanization of the block where households reside, and the highest education level of household members influence their choice of a lending source. Social groups and household occupation also impact the decision to opt for the banking system as a loan source. Additionally, religion, social category, and occupation significantly contribute to selecting moneylenders as a source of loans. The migration of household members explains other lending sources. However, the variables examined in this analysis are unable to account for debt from NBFC loans and loans from friends/relatives.

According to Table 4, rural households are twice as likely as urban households (reference category) to have loans, with 76.3% of rural households borrowing compared to 47.3% of urban households. The highest education level among household members significantly influences loan decisions, as households with secondary education as the highest level are three and a half times more likely to require loans than those with other

Table 5 Logistic regression model for significance of independent variables for moneylender, friends/relatives and other lending sources

	Money lender			*Friends/relatives*			*Other sources*		
Explanatory variables	*Wald Chi square*	*Df*	*Sig.*	*Wald Chi square*	*Df*	*Sig.*	*Wald Chi square*	*Df*	*Sig.*
Location	0.263	1	0.608	0.010	1	0.921	1.841	1	0.175
Religion	4.901	1	0.027**	1.383	1	0.240	0.000	1	0.997
Social group	14.343	3	0.002***	4.067	3	0.254	0.168	3	0.983
Education level	4.530	5	0.476	6.997	5	0.221	1.916	5	0.861
Occupation	17.225	3	0.001***	1.050	3	0.789	1.121	3	0.772
Migration	1.492	1	0.222	0.049	1	0.825	3.129	1	0.077*
Household income	3.978	4	0.409	3.213	4	0.523	3.298	4	0.509

Source Author calculation
Note *** denotes significance at 1%, ** denotes significance at 5%, * denotes significance at 10%

education levels. Cross-tabulation reveals varying borrowing percentages among education groups, with the lowest for graduates (33.3%) and the highest for secondary-level households (84%). Secondary education emerges as the most favorable qualification for loan approval.

The odds ratio for EBC is 4.996, indicating EBC households are five times more likely to have bank loans, while SC households are six times less likely. The borrowing pattern differs among social categories, with 60% of general, 62.1% of OBC, 72.2% of EBC, and 15.9% of SC households taking loans from banks. Self-employed and others (businessmen and employees) are four times and seven and a half times more likely than farmers' households to receive bank loans, respectively. Loan uptake varies across occupations, with 37.5% of farmers, 43.6% of casual workers, 69% of self-employed individuals, and 59% of households with other income sources taking bank loans.

Muslim households are 4.7 times more likely to borrow from moneylenders compared to Hindu households, while OBC and EBC households are 10 and 50 times more likely to take loans from moneylenders, respectively, compared to general category households. The likelihood of loans is highest in farming-based households and lowest in self-employed and other occupational means households.

Table 6 Logistics regression model parameter estimates and odds ratio for taking a loan from all sources, banks, and moneylender

S No.	Description of variables	*All sources*			*Bank*			*Money lender*		
		Parameter estimates	*Sig.*	*Odds ratio*	*Parameter estimates*	*Sig.*	*Odds ratio*	*Parameter estimates*	*Sig.*	*Odds ratio*
	Intercept	−0.467	0.588	0.627	−0.907	0.455	0.404	2.712	0.047	15.054
1	Urbanisation (Rural as reference)									
	Urban	−0.743	0.020**	0.476	−0.161	0.705	0.852	0.271	0.608	1.311
2	Religion (Hindu as reference)									
	Muslim	0.601	0.175	1.823	−0.070	0.886	0.933	1.551	0.027**	4.718
3	Social Group (General as reference)									
	OBC	0.951	0.016	2.589	1.181	0.116	3.258	−2.382	0.018**	0.092
	EBC	0.310	0.541	1.363	1.609	0.066*	4.996	−3.768	0.043**	0.023
	SC	0.660	0.170	1.935	−1.818	0.021**	0.162	0.123	0.889	1.131
	ST	−21.134	1.000	0.000						
4	Education Level (Not Literate as reference)									
	Literate	0.521	0.387	1.684	−0.696	0.378	0.498	0.018	0.980	1.018
	Secondary	1.261	0.070**	3.529	0.135	0.881	1.144	−0.874	0.313	0.417
	Senior Secondary	0.161	0.835	1.174	−1.677	0.094	0.187	−1.537	0.246	0.215
	Graduate	−0.334	0.619	0.716	−0.969	0.312	0.380	0.308	0.758	1.361
	Postgraduate or above	−0.623	0.434	0.536	0.100	0.942	1.105	−18.704	0.998	0.000
5	Occupation (Farmer as reference)									
	Casual Labour	0.352	0.540	1.422	0.742	0.297	2.100	−2.730	0.002***	0.065
	Self Employed	0.561	0.354	1.752	1.364	0.070*	3.911	−3.228	0.002***	0.040
	Others	0.240	0.665	1.271	2.006	0.006**	7.436	−3.725	0.000***	0.024
6	Migration (No as a reference)									
	Yes	0.170	0.679	1.185	0.497	0.368	1.644	−0.986	0.222	0.373
7	Household Income (<50 thousand as reference)									
	50 thousand-1 Lac	0.414	0.262	1.513	-0.279	0.520	0.757	0.318	0.523	1.374
	1-2 Lack	−0.562	0.336	0.570	−1.114	0.191	0.328	1.422	0.205	4.144

(continued)

Table 6 (continued)

S No.	Description of variables	*All sources* Parameter estimates	Sig.	Odds ratio	*Bank* Parameter estimates	Sig.	Odds ratio	*Money lender* Parameter estimates	Sig.	Odds ratio
	2–5 Lack	0.570	0.364	1.768	0.285	0.778	1.330	−1.430	0.304	0.239
	5 Lack and above	0.287	0.644	1.333	0.498	0.664	1.646	−1.272	0.463	0.280

Source Author's calculation

5.4 *Level of Satisfaction, Suggestion, and Problems with Various Banking Services*

Suggestions collected at the household level and satisfaction with various banking services are divided into four broad categories below.

Attitude of Banking Personnel Towards Customers

Banking employees, especially in rural branches, exhibit a negative attitude towards poor, illiterate, or less educated customers, particularly during transactions and complaint resolution. Private sector banks generally offer better customer service, but rural branches, both public and private, display similar employee attitudes. Urban customers, however, seem indifferent to employee attitudes, and known complaints are promptly addressed.

Loan

Obtaining a bank loan poses significant challenges due to the lengthy and intricate loan disbursement process. The study reveals malpractices, especially in rural areas, leading to dissatisfaction among both rural and urban households regarding loan services.

ATM

Customers in rural areas express dissatisfaction with ATM services, while urban customers are generally content. Common ATM-related issues reported include link failures and cash shortages.

Other Banking Issues

Customers highlight various concerns such as long queues, time-consuming services, the need for a loan guarantor, cleanliness of bank branches, lack of seating arrangements, insufficient facilities, absence of separate queues for elderly individuals, non-acceptance of coins, minimum balance problems, and complicated check deposit procedures. They also mention unclear information dissemination through Short Message Service (SMS) and discuss challenges faced during the demonetization period.

6 Discussion

6.1 *Implications for Theories*

The study validates the efficacy of government-led financial inclusion initiatives, exemplified by PMJDY, supporting the premise that well-crafted policies enhance financial inclusion rates [47]. It emphasizes the growing significance of digital financial inclusion, aligning with previous studies [48–51] and technology adoption theories like [52]. The study reaffirms the role of literacy, infrastructure, and socio-economic factors in banking outreach [53], stressing the need for targeted financial literacy initiatives. It also highlights income and asset levels' influence on securing loans, aligning with existing economic theories.

6.2 *Implications for Practice and Policy Making*

The study underscores the importance of measures to enhance financial inclusion and address disparities. Initiatives like PMJDY positively impact households, necessitating expanded banking infrastructure and outreach for inclusivity. Despite progress, a significant number of households avoid ATMs and online banking, emphasizing the imperative shift to digital banking recommended by RBI (2019). Bridging the credit gap requires strengthening microfinance institutions, expanding small finance banks, and supporting self-help groups, especially in rural areas. Tailoring financial products to regional needs, introducing specialized savings for significant life events, promoting health insurance, and enhancing financial literacy are crucial for inclusive financial policies. Policymakers should prioritize financial literacy initiatives, disseminate information widely, and ensure equitable access to banking services for all social groups.

7 Conclusion

The government's goal of achieving universal access to bank accounts in Bihar has almost been accomplished, but digital banking remains a major concern, particularly in rural areas. To increase acceptance of digital banking practices, the government should prioritize computer literacy programs for all citizens. However, urbanisation, social and religious groups, and the attitude of bankers also play a decisive role in the adoption and use of digital banking. Despite government efforts, money lenders continue to play a significant role in loan disbursement, particularly in rural India, which remains a policy concern. Moneylenders are more likely to provide loans to Muslim, OBC, farmer, and impoverished households. The attitude of bankers is also a major concern, particularly for impoverished households who are hesitant to use the banking system as a source of loans. Affluent households are more likely to take out loans from banks, and RRBs play an important role in loan disbursement in rural areas. Finally, households often turn to moneylenders, friends, and relatives because they offer longer repayment periods, instant loans, and a simple loan disbursement process, which traditional financial institutions do not have.

Acknowledgements This paper is based on a chapter of my Ph.D. thesis (Ritesh Ravi). As a result, I'd like to thank Dr. Abhijit Ghosh, my guide, and Dr. Neetu Choudhary, my teacher, as well as my institution, the A N Sinha Institute of Social Studies in Patna, Bihar, India, and the Indian Council for Social Science Research in New Delhi, for providing me with fellowship during that time.

References

1. Kumar, S.: Banking Sector reforms and Outreach of Scheduled Commercial Banks in the Northern Region in India. *Man & Development* 32(1), 1–16 (2010).
2. Bhanot, D., Bapat, V., Bera, S.: Studying financial inclusion in north-east India. *International Journal of Bank Marketing* 30(6), 465–484 (2012).
3. Ravi, R., Ghosh, A.: Problems of Banking Outreach in Bihar: A District Level Study. *Man and Development* 40(2), 57–76 (2018).

4. Ghosh, A.: *Managing Risks in Commercial and Retail Banking*. John Wiley & Sons, Hoboken (2012).
5. Sharma, S.: A detailed comparative study on e-banking VS traditional banking. *International Journal of Advanced Research* 2, 302–307 (2016).
6. Ghosh, S.: A simple index of banking fragility: Application to Indian data. *The Journal of Risk Finance* 12(2), 112–120 (2011).
7. Biswanger, H.P., Khandekar, S.R.: (Reference cited but full details missing – Please verify and complete.)
8. Levine, R.: Africa's growth tragedy: Policies and ethnic divisions. *The Quarterly Journal of Economics* 112(4), 1203–1250 (1997).
9. Burgess, R., Pande, R.: Do rural banks matter? Evidence from the Indian social banking experiment. (Working Paper, 2003).
10. Eastwood, R., Kohli, R.: Directed credit and investment in small-scale industry in India: Evidence from firm-level data 1965–78. *The Journal of Development Studies* 35(4), 42–63 (1999).
11. Aghion, P., Bolton, P.: A theory of trickle-down growth and development. *The Review of Economic Studies* 64(2), 151–172 (1997).
12. Banerjee, A., Singh, S.K. (eds.): *Banking and Financial Sector Reforms in India*. Deep & Deep Publications, New Delhi (2001).
13. Banerjee, A.V., Newman, A.F.: Occupational choice and the process of development. *Journal of Political Economy* 101(2), 274–298 (1993).
14. Yunus, M.: The Grameen Bank. *Scientific American* 281(5), 114–119 (1999).
15. World Bank: Global Financial Development Report 2017. World Bank, Washington DC (2017). (Assumed reference; full title incomplete.)
16. Dev, S.M.: Financial Inclusion: Issues and Challenges. *Economic and Political Weekly* 41(41), 4310–4313 (2006).
17. Leeladhar, V.: Taking Banking Services to the Common Man - Financial Inclusion. *Reserve Bank of India Bulletin* 59(10), 73–77 (2005).
18. Dufhues, T., Buchenrieder, G.: (Reference incomplete; kindly check.)
19. Barik, S., Sharma, P.: Progress of Financial Inclusion in India: A State Level Analysis. *Journal of Public Affairs* 19(3), e1877 (2019).
20. Bai, C., Du, Y., Hu, J.: Financial Literacy, Credit Constraints and Household Investment. *China Economic Review* 51, 1–17 (2018).
21. Fungáčová, Z., Weill, L.: Understanding financial inclusion in China. *China Economic Review* 34, 196–206 (2015).
22. Kumar, C.S.: Financial Inclusion in India: A Case Study of West Bengal. *RBI Working Paper Series* WPS(DEPR):8/2011 (2011).
23. Abel, S., Mutandwa, L., Le Roux, P.: A review of financial inclusion for inclusive growth in Zimbabwe. *African Journal of Economic and Management Studies* 9(2), 190–208 (2018).

24. Kaushik, A.K., Rahman, Z.: An empirical study of Indian consumers' channel choice behavior in a multi-channel environment. *Journal of Retailing and Consumer Services* 26, 1–12 (2015).
25. Hota, S., Mishra, D.: Financial Inclusion and Economic Growth in India. *International Journal of Management Studies* 5(3), 1–8 (2018).
26. Sahi, G.K., Gupta, M.: A study of customers' perception towards ATM services in Dehradun city. *International Journal of Marketing and Technology* 8(2), 1–13 (2018).
27. Leyshon, A., Thrift, N.: The restructuring of the UK financial services industry and the rise of financial exclusion. *Environment and Planning A* 25(10), 1355–1377 (1993).
28. Ford, J., Rowlingson, K.: Low Income and Early Exit from Owner Occupation. Joseph Rowntree Foundation, York (1996).
29. Kempson, E., Whyley, C.: Access to Current Accounts: A Report to the British Bankers' Association. British Bankers' Association, London (1998).
30. Yangdol, R., Sarma, M.: Demand-side factors for financial inclusion: A cross-country empirical analysis. *International Studies* 56(2-3), 163–185 (2019).
31. Kumar, C., Mishra, S.: Banking outreach and household level access: Analyzing financial inclusion in India. In: 13th Annual Conference on Money and Finance in the Indian Economy, Mumbai (2011).
32. Pesqué-Cela, V., Tian, L., Luo, D., Tobin, D., Kling, G.: Defining and measuring financial inclusion: A systematic review and confirmatory factor analysis. *Journal of International Development* 33(2), 316–341 (2021).
33. Chakrabarty, K.C.: Financial Inclusion. In: RBI Speeches (2012).
34. Demirguc-Kunt, A., Klapper, L., Singer, D., Ansar, S., Hess, J.: The Global Findex Database 2017: Measuring Financial Inclusion and the Fintech Revolution. World Bank, Washington DC (2018).
35. Kazi, M.R., Shemim, A.: A District Level Analysis of the Status of Financial Inclusion in Assam, India. *The International Journal of Community and Social Development* 5(3), 245–265 (2023).
36. Linh, T.N., Long, H.T., Chi, L.V., Tam, L.T., Lebailly, P.: Access to rural credit markets in developing countries: The case of Vietnam. *Sustainability* 11(5), 1468 (2019).
37. Ray, S.: Challenges and changes in Indian rural credit market: A review. *Agricultural Finance Review* 79(3), 338–352 (2019).
38. Sinha, A., Pandey, V.: Financial Inclusion in India: Challenges and Opportunities. *Economic Affairs* 64(1), 81–88 (2019).
39. Rajesh, R., Das, P.: Determinants of Credit Penetration in India. *The Journal of Developing Areas* 53(2), 1–13 (2019).
40. Ravi, R., Gaurav, K.: Digital Banking Adoption in India. *International Journal of Financial Studies* 7(2), 30 (2019).

41. Izquierdo, M., Tuesta, D.: Factors that Matter for Financial Inclusion: Evidence from Peru. *Emerging Markets Review* 20, 75–86 (2014).
42. Sarigul, H.: The Determining Factors of Financial Inclusion in Turkey. *Journal of Economics Finance and Accounting* 7(3), 223–235 (2020).
43. Kumar Vaid, Y., Singh, V., Sethi, M.: Determinants of Successful Financial Inclusion in Low-Income Rural Population. *The Indian Economic Journal* 68(1), 82–100 (2020).
44. Wilkinson, S.: Focus Group Research. In: Silverman, D. (ed.) *Qualitative Research: Theory, Method and Practice*, pp. 177–199. Sage, London (2004).
45. Menard, S.: Coefficients of determination for multiple logistic regression analysis. *The American Statistician* 54(1), 17–24 (2000).
46. Hosmer, D.W., Lemeshow, S., Sturdivant, R.X.: *Applied Logistic Regression.* 2nd edn. Wiley, New York (1989).
47. Cull, Robert, Asli Demirgüç-Kunt, and Jonathan Morduch.: *The microfinance business model: Enduring subsidy and modest profit. The World Bank Economic Review* 32(2), 221–244 (2018).
48. Ali, K., Jianguo, D., Kirikkaleli, D., Mentel, G., Altuntaş, M.: Testing the role of digital financial inclusion in energy transition and diversification towards COP26 targets and sustainable development goals. *Gondwana Research* (2023). https://www.sciencedirect.com/science/article/pii/S1342937X23001387.
49. Saxena, A., Mandal, A., Mittal, P.: Financial literacy and digital product use for financial inclusion: A GETU model to develop financial literacy. In: *2022 8th International Conference on Advanced Computing and Communication Systems (ICACCS). IEEE (2022).* https://ieeexplore.ieee.org/document/9784962.
50. Mohapatra, S., Mishra, A.K.: The evolving financial landscape in emerging markets and developing economies. In: *The Financial Landscape of Emerging Markets and Developing Economies, Springer, Cham* (2020). https://link.springer.com/chapter/https://doi.org/10.1007/978-3-030-60008-2_1.
51. Nagpal, A., Jain, M., Jain, A.: Determining the role of digital technology, governance and institutions in advancing financial inclusion in BRICS nations using probit regression analysis. *Journal of Social and Economic Development* 22, 52–74 (2020). https://link.springer.com/article/https://doi.org/10.1007/s40847-020-00112-2.
52. Rogers, E.M.: *Diffusion of Innovations, 5th edn. Free Press, New York* (2003).
53. Ghosh, S.: Financial inclusion and financial fragility: Evidence from India. *Emerging Markets Review* 13(4), 429–439 (2012). https://doi.org/10.1016/j.ememar.2012.09.003.

Indian Rupee: An Emerging Trading Currency of Asia and Across in Industry 5.0

Ritesh Dwivedi, Vikas Batra, and Preeti Singh

1 Introduction

The de-dollarization of the global economy, in which it is moving toward a reduced dependency on the US dollar for international trade, is triggering initiatives to increase the use of the Indian rupee in international transactions in terms of invoicing, payment, and settlement and internationalize the rupee. The recent appreciation of the Indian rupee, coupled with the country's strong economic performance, has

R. Dwivedi (✉)
Symbiosis Institute of Business Management, Noida, India
e-mail: ritesh.dwivedi@sibmnoida.siu.edu.in

Symbiosis International (Deemed University), Pune, India

V. Batra
Department of Economics, Indira Gandhi University, Meerpur, Rewari, Haryana, India
e-mail: vikasbatra7@gmail.com

P. Singh
Daulat Ram College, University of Delhi, New Delhi, India
e-mail: pspreeti91@gmail.com

© The Author(s), under exclusive license to Springer Nature Singapore Pte Ltd. 2025
P. Agarwal et al. (eds.), *Building a Human-Centred Infrastructure for Sustainable Industry 5.0 in Asia*,
https://doi.org/10.1007/978-981-95-0417-6_7

led to a debate about its internationalization. According to the Tarapore Committee on Fuller Capital Account Convertibility (CFAC), an "international currency" is widely used for international transactions, such as the US dollar, Euro, British Pound, Swiss Franc, and Japanese Yen. Internationalization" of a currency means the external credibility in which the economy is integrating as well as the usage of the currency for invoicing and settlement of cross-border transactions, freedom of non-residents to hold financial assets/liabilities in that currency, and freedom of non-residents to hold tradable balances in that currency at an offshore location. A certain amount of internationalization may even accompany capital controls. In recent years, the Indian Rupee has gained significant importance as a trading currency due to several key factors:

- Trading Volume: The Indian Rupee is one of the most actively traded currencies in the world. It has a daily turnover of over $100 billion in the foreign exchange market.
- SDR Basket Inclusion: Indian Rupee is part of the SDR basket since 2015. That says something about its rising significance as a reserve asset, widely used by the world's central banks.
- Settlement Currency: Indian Rupee is increasingly being used as a settlement currency in international trade transactions, supported by the rising use of Rupee-denominated instruments such as offshore Rupee bonds and currency futures contracts.
- Foreign Exchange Regulations liberalized: Indian government has implemented measures to liberalize the foreign exchange regulations in the country. For example, RBI relaxed the restrictions that were imposed on the use of Rupee-denominated instruments by foreign investors in order to allow them to easily invest in India.
- Offshore Market Development: The development of offshore Rupee markets, including the Non-Deliverable Forward (NDF) market, has given investors more flexibility in managing their Rupee exposure, thus increasing the currency's liquidity and popularity as a trading currency.

Promoting the Indian Rupee as an international currency would reduce the Indian economy's vulnerability to external shocks and lessen its dependence on foreign currency. However, for the Indian Rupee to be recognized as an international currency, its foreign exchange turnover must rise to equal the share of non-US, non-Euro currencies. Currently, the Indian Rupee accounts for only 1.6% of global forex turnover. Nevertheless, Indian banks have opened vostro rupee accounts with banks of other nations to operationalize the rupee trade arrangement. The recent framework introduced by the Reserve Bank of India could be a step towards establishing the INR as an international currency and could have significant long-term benefits for the Indian economy [1, 2] (*ET*). While there is limited official information on the actual trades conducted this far, policymakers are eager to promote this policy.

2 Literature Review

The literature underscores the necessity for increased long-term investment in the Indian rupee markets to bolster its internationalization [3]. Institutional investors, including pension funds and sovereign wealth funds, are seen as key players in providing the patient capital essential for the development of rupee markets, as argued by the author. This patient capital is crucial for fostering India's economic growth and realizing its full potential on the global stage.

Force studies that explain the determinants of Indian Rupee's regional currency status for South Asia have also been carried out. As pointed out by [4], the increasing demand for the Rupee as an exchange or trade currency has been fuelled by the rapid growth of Indian economy, politically stable environment and more interdependent regional economy. Chakrabarty [5] has equally noted the Internationalization of Indian currency challenges and prospects as well. He underscored that 'for India to be able to facilitate on the growth of the Rupee as an exchange currency, India has to significantly invest on financial infrastructure, facilitate on more financial integration and remove regulatory bottlenecks. India in that is concentrated on.' However, the Indian Rupee could be an international currency unit if India were to address the structural aspects of inflation, fiscal deficits and financial sector reforms—although it will face these challenges [6]. Even India's economic reforms, liberalisation of capital markets, and increasing volumes of trade have also facilitated the growth of the Rupee as a trading currency. Rajan [7] also argues that Indian policies such as economic reforms, liberalization of capital markets and increase in trade volumes have greatly assisted the Rupee to rise up as an exchange currency.

In the case of India, despite the success in popularizing the rupee as a currency, there are still issues related to capital controls, foreign exchange and currency exchange [8]. Ize [9] has examined the factors that have led to the growth of the Indian rupee as a new currency in the global economy. The authors say that India's economic growth, trade liberalization, financial reforms and deepening trade are the main factors that have supported the promotion of the rupee as a trading currency. After all, it is the latest business of the Forex market. These include the London Stock Exchange, the Tokyo Mercantile Exchange and the Chicago Mercantile Exchange. The value of the Indian rupee depends largely on economic factors such as supply and demand, inflation, trade and commerce in India and around the world.

Although the Indian rupee is not yet recognized as a private currency, the Indian government has taken a number of measures to support the rupee's international market. Major one is allowing Indian companies to issue rupee-denominated bonds in foreign trade and encouraging the use of the rupee in international trade settlement. However, there are still certain complexities that needs to be understood but once the process gets started, solutions will be negotiated with like-minded nations. There certain main drivers behind the rise of the Indian rupee as a trading currency, including its unique growth-inducing characteristics and the impact of the Indian government's policies and actions. Another important development is India's consistent growing economy which generates confidence around the impact of the Indian rupee as a trading currency on international trade and investment. There is also great need to assess the effectiveness of government policies and procedures that support the use of the Indian rupee as a trading currency and its impact on domestic and international financial markets.

3 Methodology

The analytical discussion has been structured along the following lines, which should help in doing a systematic examination of the topic and using critical thinking to ensure a comprehensive evaluation. The secondary sources of research information were derived from the internet, which is credible, with publications from prominent organizations such as the IMF, RBI, WTO, MCI, GOI, and journals such as ET and Mint. The objectives of the research are as follows:

- To discuss challenges and opportunities of the internationalization of the Indian Rupee as a trading currency
- To outline the ongoing developments towards making Indian Rupee as a trading currency.
- Assess the effectiveness of government policies and regulatory frameworks in promoting the Indian Rupee as a trading currency.
- Analyse the influence of the Indian Rupee on other developing economies and assess its effect on international trade and investment flows and its implications.

4 Discussion

4.1 Challenges and Opportunities

It is very important to understand the risks and opportunities associated with the global market for the Indian rupee as a trading currency and consider the strategy to reduce risks and achieve optimal benefits. The influence of the Indian rupee on other emerging economies has also been necessary to assess the seminal role it plays in supporting financial markets and boosting economic growth. This gives both an opportunity and a challenge for the Indian economy.

Babu [10] provides a detailed analysis of the benefits and the challenges faced during this process. He stressed that the benefits of a low exchange rate include making Indian companies competitive in the international market. However, the paper also addresses India's fundamental challenges in supporting the rupee: limited depth in the rupee market and pollution and regulatory concerns. Arora [11] also looked at the current state and obstacles encountered in the process of internationalizing the Indian rupee. To this end, the paper also recognizes various reforms undertaken by India, including the development of an offshore rupee market and the offering of masala bonds to support the rupee, which forms parts of the overall philosophy supporting currency union. However, despite such achievements, the paper also identifies several challenges, including these fluctuating values, that necessitate a more robust and domestically focused market. Capital shortages, fiscal reforms, and currency controls remain some of the challenges India faces in promoting the rupee as a viable trading currency [12].

India must enhance its financial infrastructure and promote financial integration to market the rupee as a global currency [13]. India has to tackle currency volatility, inflation, and fiscal reforms before the rupee can be turned into a market currency [14]. The impact could potentially affect the competitiveness of the economy and foreign investment, making it less appealing for businesses to invest outside the country.

Nevertheless, it is crucial to establish clear regulations regarding exchange rates, taxes, and capital controls to encourage international trade in the rupee, particularly in cross-border transactions. A robust currency could make the rupee less valuable when compared to other foreign currencies, making Indian goods and services more appealing to foreign buyers. India's global economic impact. This could potentially strengthen India's role as a trading nation and grant it more influence in the region. It will also reduce reliance on other traditional reserves, such as the US dollar, and foster international trade. This leads to the exchange of the Indian rupee with international trade, fostering competition and implementing effective rules and regulations to guarantee favorable outcomes. Of the company. The internationalization of the Indian rupee presents both opportunities and challenges, as discussed in the Journal of International Business, economics, and Politics (2017) and the Reserve Bank of India (2014).

4.2 *Strategies to Maximize the Benefits of Indian Rupee Internationalisation*

India should actively market the rupee as a trading currency and establish good trade relations with other countries to support its development [15]. The best way to promote international trade, where the Indian rupee functions as a trading currency, is to deepen and work on foreign trade. The government can further improve the exchange rate by participating more in bilateral agreements. Monetary policy must be more transparent, adequately regulate the economy and support economic development.

The government should maintain low interest rates, financial stability and sound fiscal policy to maintain confidence in the rupee. Review agreements, promote regional agreements and participate in international conferences to enhance the role of the rupee in the world economy (Internationalization of Indian Rupee: Project) (Reserve Bank of India (RBI)).

4.3 The Economic and Political Factors

Economic reforms and economic relations are a few factors supporting the growth of the rupee as a trading currency. Gupta [16] studies this research in the context of challenges and opportunities related to the internationalization of the rupee. It provides policy recommendations to policymakers and stakeholders on implementing international laws. Inflation and interest rates and institutions such as governance and trade also impact the global market of the Indian rupee. The study finds the macroeconomic environment and domestic support crucial for the growth of the rupee as a trading currency, according to Shukla [17].

India needs to build a stable economy, improve its fiscal position, and resolve administrative issues to facilitate the growth of the rupee as a trading currency [18]. Dash's [19] study builds on previous research by focusing on areas such as trade and investment that support the rupee as a trading currency.

The internationalization of the rupee requires major changes in the financial market through liberalization of the rupee market and creation of foreign exchange markets. This is also supported by the gravity model study by Tandon [20] which shows that the order of the rupee used in the market (such as bilateral trade and distance) plays a significant role in the choice of currency for rupee transactions.

India has been one of the fastest growing economies with an average GDP growth of around 7% per annum over the last decade. This growth has attracted foreign investment, increasing the demand for the Indian rupee. Liberalization of FDI policy, simplification of tax policy and changes in sectoral liberalization are examples of reforms introduced to attract foreign investors and increase ease of doing business, thereby increasing demand for the rupee. A stable democratic governance increases investor confidence. This political environment reduces the risk of sudden deterioration or instability in policies that may affect foreign trade. Be quick to resolve the issue of rupee exchange to manage international trade (Internationalization of Indian rupee by the Reserve Bank of India) (Reserve Bank of India, World Bank Report).

4.4 *Usage Trends and Patterns of the Indian Rupee as a Trading Currency*

As the Indian economy continues to expand, the Indian Rupee has gained significant footing in the global financial market, with several trends and patterns arising about its use as a trading currency:

- Cross-border transactions: The use of the Indian Rupee in cross-border transactions is increasing. Main areas of trade use include Nepal, Bhutan, and Bangladesh. Bilateral payment arrangements between India and these countries have promoted this trend.
- Increased Rupee-denominated bonds: Indian companies are issuing more Rupee-denominated bonds in foreign markets, boosting the use of the Rupee in international transactions. Such bonds are appealing to foreign investors who seek to gain exposure to India's high-growth economy and hedge against currency risks.
- Commodity trade using Rupee: The Rupee is increasingly used in commodity trade, mainly for oil imports. Several countries producing oil accept Rupees for payment. One such country is Iran, and the other is Venezuela.
- Increasing share of Rupee in global currency reserves: The Rupee has gradually increased its share of global currency reserves, even though it is not a reserve currency. According to the International Monetary Fund (IMF), the Rupee's share of global currency reserves increased from 0.6% in 2015 to 2.1% in 2020.
- Growth of offshore Rupee markets: Offshore Rupee markets, such as the Non-Deliverable Forward (NDF) market, have expanded significantly. These markets allow investors to hedge their exposure to the Rupee without holding the currency, increasing the Rupee's usage in international transactions (International Monetary Fund (IMF).

4.5 *Government Policies and Regulatory Frameworks*

India had enacted policies that encouraged the adoption of the Rupee as an international trading currency. This would include, inter alia, liberalization in certain areas of the Foreign Exchange As foreign exchange transaction policy was relaxed for a variety of foreign exchange purposes, the requirement for funds also got liberalized. It increased their ease to fund them through rupee-denominated bonds, amongst many other financial tools. The government introduced Rupee-denominated oil contracts in 2018, where Indian companies were allowed to purchase crude oil from Iran using Rupees, thus reducing the need for foreign exchange transactions and promoting the use of the Indian Rupee in international trade.

Another factor is that the government encouraged the offshore rupee markets such as the NDF market in which investors were able to enter the rupee contracts outside of India. In so doing, this improved the depth and liquidity in the Rupee markets while making easier the access of the foreign investors towards Rupee-denominated assets. The Bharat QR code is another initiative where a QR-based payment system enables digital payments using mobile phones, thereby increasing the use of digital payment systems in India and making it easier for businesses to accept payments in Rupees. The Reserve Bank of India has also entered into currency swap agreements with other central banks in Japan, UAE, and SAARC countries. These agreements would allow the bilateral exchange of central banks' currency. Overall, such policies coupled with the regulating framework have so far made Indian rupee, as a tradable currency accessible through cost reduction enhancements in liquidity coupled with increased accesses to assets denominated in rupee.

4.6 *Effectiveness of Policy Frameworks Towards of Indian Rupee*

Policy and regulatory measures support the foundation for the use of the Indian rupee as a trading currency, but there is still room for improvement. Increasing the depth and efficiency of financial markets will strengthen the use of the Indian rupee as a trading currency. This can be done by creating greater awareness about the rupee, signing more foreign exchange agreements, reducing trade and encouraging Indian companies to use the rupee in the broader economy. In addition, the Indian government should also focus on effective business management and investor protection, monitoring of business and maintenance, and creating effective investor management through common law. Also, establishing good relations with other countries and regions will increase the use of the Indian rupee in the international market. India should pay more attention to bilateral and multilateral trade agreements, encourage cross-border trade and joint ventures, and encourage multilateral commercial cooperation in the region. Another way to encourage the use of the

Indian rupee as a business currency is to promote rupee financial products and services. India can encourage the creation of rupee-denominated derivatives such as futures and options, and increase the availability of rupee-denominated products such as mutual funds and exchange-traded funds (ETFs) (Reserve Bank of India).

The Reserve Bank of India recently significantly promoted the direct rupee settlement process with its trading partners. In August of last year, 2024, the RBI requested banks in India to import goods from the UAE and settle the transactions directly in Indian rupees in relation to dirhams. This step would decrease dependence on the U.S. Dollar and strengthen the rupee-dirham market, in view of the UAE being India's third largest trading partner, with trade worth nearly $83 billion annually in the financial year 2023–2024 [21]. In a similar manner, the RBI has resumed discussions with the Central Bank of Russia to establish a framework for expanding the trade of local currency. This is in response to payment issues that emerged when bilateral trade increased following the Ukraine conflict in 2022. The objective is to create a benchmark rate between the Indian rupee and the Russian Ruble, eliminating the need for the U.S. Dollar to facilitate smoother trade transactions.

In July 2023, the Reserve Bank of India released a report outlining the roadmap for the internationalization of the Indian rupee. As a collective, they acknowledged that these would involve a greater fluctuation in exchange rates globally and some potential effects on domestic monetary policy, often referred to as the Triffin dilemma. But the benefits far outweigh these challenges, as pointed out by the IDG, where limited risk of an exchange rate, low capital costs because of better access to international financial markets, higher seigniorage benefits, and reduced foreign exchange reserve requirements exist [22].

4.7 *Influence of Indian Rupee on Developing Economies Across Asia and World*

Jaishankar [23] focussed attention on the challenges faced by the Indian Rupee in competing with the US Dollar as a global reserve currency. Wherein the author contends that India must tackle issues such as high inflation, fiscal deficits, and corruption to bolster the Rupee's position as a trading currency.

India's strong economy, growing economy and favourable location have made it a valuable international currency [24]. A study examines the role of the Indian rupee in the world economy. The author believes India needs to address issues such as inflation, financial inequality, and financial reforms to support the growth of the rupee as a trading currency [24]. The growth of the Indian rupee as a trading currency will have an impact on trade relations and economic growth. With the adoption of the Indian rupee as a trading currency, India's trade volume with other developing economies will also reach the same level. This means that imports and exports and trade between the two countries will increase. This makes the business more efficient and thus increases the profit of the entire business. This will help different economies in handling trade situations more practically and reduce dependence on a single benefit. Entry into the Indian market will also be very easy and other nations will be able to participate in India's new initiatives on manufacturing and trade.

4.8 The Impact of the Indian Rupee on Asian and Global Financial Markets

The Indian Rupee impact aspects on global financial markets can be discussed in below mentioned:

- Exchange rate: The movement in the Indian Rupee's rate of exchange versus other major world currencies can, in turn, affect global financial markets. In a certain time period, rising trends of Rupee may affect hegemony of the US dollar definitely.
- Commodity prices: For decades, India is heavily dependent on commodity imports, relating with oil and gold, priced in US dollars. Here, a new-found balance in the Rupee-US dollar exchange rate will reduce the burden on Indian side while purchasing the global commodity.
- Investment Flows: Investment Inflows are vital for any economy right now and its very crucial in the case of India's economy. The investor sentiment that shifts to favor India affects the global capital inflows. Favorable investor sentiment may promote increased India-bound investment flows and, in turn, possible Rupee appreciation.
- Reserve currency status: If the Indian Rupee becomes a more widely accepted trading currency, this can challenge the hegemony of other major currencies, such as the US dollar and the euro, which would have serious implications for the global financial system and the international balance of power among nations.

- Bond markets: The Indian government and corporate bond markets are increasing, and Rupee usage is also rising. Consequently, fluctuations in the value of the Rupee will impact emerging markets, such as global bond markets ("The Indian Rupee's Impact on Global Markets." Investopedia) (Investopedia, 30 Aug. 2021) [25].

4.9 *Broader Economic Trends and Implications*

The internationalization of the Indian rupee has also led to numerous significant economic trends and implications that are responsible for sustainable growth and the development of the economy. It includes:

- Recent developments have shown the trends of increased global acceptance of the Rupee. Internationalizing the Indian Rupee has increased its international acceptance as one of the biggest currencies while reducing reliance on major reserve currencies, including the US dollar, the euro, or the yen [26].
- Internationalization of the Indian Rupee has facilitated access by Indian firms to international capital markets by giving the latter opportunities to issue Rupee-denominated bonds and other forms of security.
- The internationalization of the Indian rupee has increased regional cooperation among India and its neighbouring South Asian countries.
- The visible effect of internationalization of the Indian rupee will reflect in increased the credibility of the Indian economy and financial markets [27], indicating India's renewed efforts to work with other countries on economic front.

Increased economic integration and collaboration between India and other countries on diverse categories of products will also get support from the internationalization of the Indian rupee to some extent while minimizing the risks and expenses involved in such cross-border transactions. Indeed, the new world order is poised in such a way that suites to India's economic interests [28]. Recent geopolitical developments have played a significant role in fostering a more stable and diverse global economy [29].

5 Conclusion

The internationalization of the Indian rupee is very much required for having enhanced economic sovereignty and reducing India's dependence on global currencies. Our economy has shown the resilience in last few years and other economies are taking lot of interest in working with us. In order to reap the benefits at maximum, it is crucial to have global standard products for foreign markets and strengthening India's financial system to support the sustained growth of economy. International cooperation is core necessity for having more acceptance for Rupee as trade currency. The rise in the value of the rupee will be propelled by more reforms, political and economic stability, and the capacity to export goods. Government policies and more specific interventions will be required towards improving exchange rate and foreign exchange management under the current volatile situations [30]. Improving governance and strengthening financial markets has been the key area of focus while ensuring international cooperation and solidarity. Bilateral agreements with more nations and continuously adjusting policies in line with changing economic scenario is very necessary to enhance confidence in the rupee trade.

The government has tried to reduce the exchange rate and increase the asset accessibility to support the Rupee further. With an increasing appreciation of the rupee, trade increases, transaction costs are reduced, currency diversity is increased, and access to Indian markets is improved. Rupee value holds greater significance across the world markets in terms of affecting exchange rates, commodity value, stock value, foreign exchange reserves, and financial markets [31]. Internationalization of Rupee will pave the way for more closer economic integration and growth while expanding India's collaboration among different regions and boosting confidence in the Indian economy.

References

1. Singh, R. (2021, March 19). Indian Rupee: A growing force in the global forex market. *The Economic Times*.
2. Survey. (2023, January 31). Promoting international trade in rupee to help reduce creency volatility. *The Economic Times*.
3. Seshachellam, P. (2020). *Indian Rupee Internationalisation: A case for Pateint Capital* .
4. Dhar, B. &. (2016). *Emergence of the Indian Rupee as a Regional Currency.*

5. Chakrabarty, K. (2015). *The Internationalisation of the Indian Rupee: Issues and Prospects.*
6. Subramanian, A. &. (2014). *The Indian Rupee as an International Currency.*
7. Rajan, R. (2013). *Emerging Economies and the Internationalisation of their Currencies: The Case of the Indian Rupee.*
8. Singh, A. &. (2018). " *Internationalization of Indian Rupee: A Progress Report".*
9. Ize, A. &. (2015). *Emerging Currencies: The Rise of the Indian Rupee.*
10. Babu, M. (2019). *Opportunities and Challenges for the Internationalization of the Indian Rupee.*
11. Arora, R. &. (2017). *Internationalization of Indian Rupee: Status and Challenges .*
12. Thingalaya, N. &. (2015). *The Internationalisation of the Indian Rupee: Issues, Challenges and Prospects.*
13. Venkatesh, H. (2014). *Internationalisation of the Indian Rupee: Emerging Challenges and Opportunities".*
14. Rajan, R. (2012). *Emerging Market Currencies and the International Monetary System: Challenges and Opportunities for the Indian Rupee .*
15. Kulkarni, K. &. (2014). *The Emergence of the Indian Rupee in International Trade: Some Strategic Issues".*
16. Gupta, P. a. (2020). *Recent developments and Prospects for the Internationalisation of the Indian Rupee.*
17. Shukla, J. &. (2019). "*Determinants of Internationalisation of Indian Rupee.".*
18. Ray, P. M. (2013). *Internationalization of the Indian Rupee: Determinants and Prospects.*
19. Dash, M. (2017). *Internationalization of Indian Rupee: A Macro Perspective.*
20. Tandon, A. &. (2017). *The Internationalization of the Indian Rupee: An Empirical Study.*
21. Vora, N. & Kalra, J. (2024), *India central bank asks banks to push direct rupee-dirham settlement*, retrived from https://www.reuters.com/markets/rates-bonds/india-central-bank-asks-banks-push-direct-rupee-dirham-settlement-sources-say-2024-08-16/?utm_source=chatgpt.com.
22. The Hindu (2023), *Internationalisation of rupee can cause excess exchange rate volatility, says RBI group*, Retrived from Internationalisation of rupee can cause excess exchange rate volatility, says RBI group - The Hindu.
23. Jaishankar, D. (2012). " *India's Currency Conundrum: Can the Rupee Compete with the Dollar?".*
24. Gangopadhyay, S. (2012). *The Emergence of the Indian Rupee as a Global Currency .*
25. "The Indian Rupee's Impact on Global Markets." Investopedia, I. 3. (n.d.). *The Impact of the Indian Rupee on global financial markets.*

26. Fund, T. R. (n.d.). *Broader Economic trends and Implications associated with the internationalization of the Indian Rupee.*
27. Gangopadhyay, S. (2012). *The Indian Rupee in the Global Currency System*
.
28. Internationalization of the Indian Rupee" by RBI, t. W. (n.d.). *The Economic and Political factors that have driven to the rise of the Indian Rupee as a trading currency.*
29. RBI, F. T. (n.d.). *Current Position of the Indian Rupee in the global financial market.*
30. The Economist, T. F. (n.d.). *Impact of rise of the Indian Rupee as a trading currency in trade relationships and economic growth of other developing economies.*
31. RBI, T. E. (n.d.). *Government Policies and regulatory frameworks that aim to promote the use of the Indian Rupee as a trading currency.*

Role of the Finance Sector in Building a Human-Centered Infrastructure for Sustainable Industry 5.0 in Asia

Alka Chaudhary and Shweta Anand

1 Introduction

Industry 5.0 represents a paradigm shift that harmonizes human creativity and advanced technologies such as Artificial Intelligence (AI), robotics, and the Internet of Things (IoT) [1]. This shift emphasizes sustainability, resilience, and human-centric approaches, contrasting with Industry 4.0's focus on automation and efficiency [2]. Asia, as a hub of industrial growth, must align its financial strategies with this transformative vision. The finance sector acts as the backbone, facilitating investments and fostering innovation to support sustainable, human-centered infrastructure [3].

Global trends in sustainable finance further underscore the urgency of this transition. Initiatives like the European Union's Green Deal

A. Chaudhary (✉)
Amity Business School, Amity University Uttar Pradesh, Noida Campus, India
e-mail: alkachaudhary22@gmail.com

S. Anand
School of Management, Gautam Buddha University, Greater Noida, UP, India
e-mail: shweta.anand7@gmail.com

© The Author(s), under exclusive license to Springer Nature Singapore Pte Ltd. 2025

P. Agarwal et al. (eds.), *Building a Human-Centred Infrastructure for Sustainable Industry 5.0 in Asia*,
https://doi.org/10.1007/978-981-95-0417-6_8

and the global commitment to achieving net-zero emissions by 2050 highlight the growing momentum toward integrating sustainability into economic systems [4]. The EU Green Deal aims to mobilize over €1 trillion in sustainable investments, setting a benchmark for regions worldwide [4]. Similarly, global frameworks such as the Paris Agreement have catalyzed efforts to align financial flows with low-carbon and climate-resilient development [5]. These initiatives underscore the pivotal role of the finance sector in bridging the gap between ambitious climate goals and actionable projects. For Asia, these global trends present both a challenge and an opportunity. Rapid industrialization and a wealth of natural resources position Asian economies at the forefront of this transformation [6]. By leveraging sustainable finance, Asia can drive inclusive growth while addressing environmental and social challenges, demonstrating its leadership in the global transition to Industry 5.0 [7].

This chapter delves into the critical role of the finance sector in driving Asia's transition toward Industry 5.0, with examples, case studies, and visualizations to elucidate its impact.

2 The Finance Sector: A Catalyst for Sustainable Growth

The finance sector—encompassing banks, investment firms, insurance companies, and development institutions—plays an instrumental role in enabling Industry 5.0. By steering resources toward innovative and inclusive projects, financial institutions help industries embrace sustainability and resilience [7, 8] (Fig. 1).

2.1 Key Functions of the Finance Sector

1. **Capital Mobilization** Capital mobilization is a fundamental function of the finance sector, enabling the allocation of resources toward transformative technologies and green infrastructure projects. Financial institutions play a critical role in directing funds to initiatives that drive innovation and sustainability [6, 9]. A notable example is the issuance of green bonds by Asian financial entities, which have been instrumental in financing renewable energy projects. These include large-scale solar parks in India and expansive wind farms in China, contributing significantly to the region's transition toward clean and sustainable energy solutions [10].

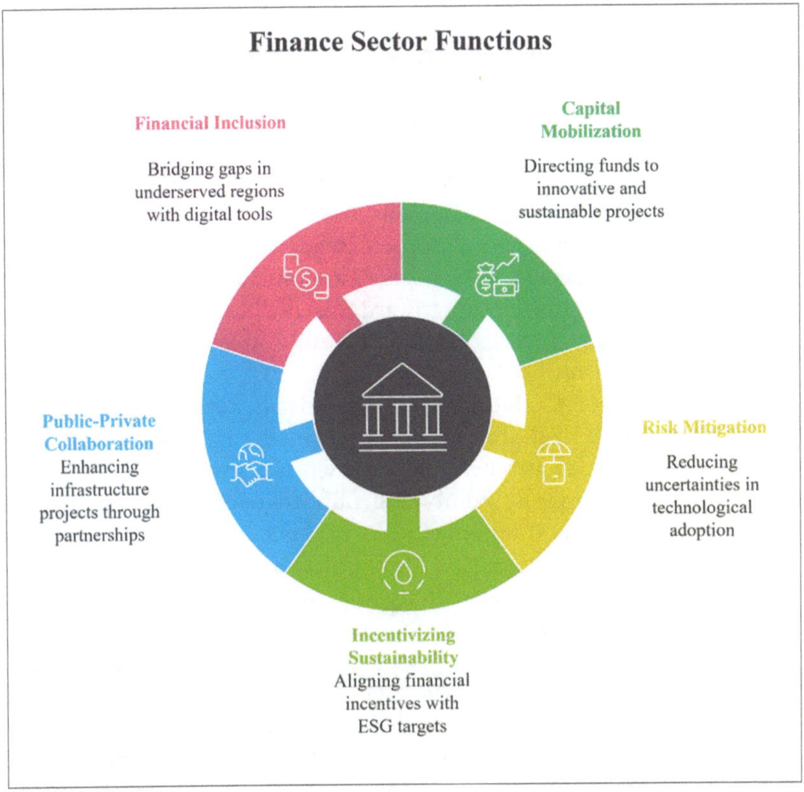

Fig. 1 Key functions of the finance sector

2. **Risk Mitigation** Advanced financial products, such as catastrophe bonds and climate risk insurance, are pivotal in reducing uncertainties associated with adopting new technologies. These instruments provide a safety net against potential losses, enabling businesses to innovate without fear of significant financial setbacks [11, 12]. For instance, Japan's insurance sector has developed tailored risk mitigation solutions specifically designed for AI-driven manufacturing systems. These solutions ensure that businesses can integrate advanced technologies while safeguarding against operational disruptions and unforeseen challenges, thereby fostering confidence and resilience in technological adoption [13].

3. **Incentivizing Sustainability** Incentivizing sustainability is a key focus of the finance sector, achieved through mechanisms like sustainability-linked loans that motivate industries to adopt environmentally friendly practices. These loans align financial incentives with measurable environmental, social, and governance (ESG) targets, fostering a culture of accountability and green innovation [14, 15]. A prime example is Singapore's Sustainability-Linked Loan Grant Scheme, which provides financial incentives to companies meeting specific ESG goals. This initiative not only supports businesses in transitioning toward sustainable operations but also strengthens the broader push for responsible and eco-conscious economic growth [16].
4. **Public–Private Collaboration for Infrastructure** Public–private partnerships (PPPs) are crucial for advancing large-scale infrastructure projects such as renewable energy parks, smart grids, and transportation systems. By combining public governance with private-sector expertise and funding, PPPs enhance efficiency, reduce risks, and drive innovation [14, 15]. Vietnam's solar energy expansion, achieved through collaborations with local banks and international climate funds, is a prime example, transforming the country into a regional leader in renewables while attracting significant foreign investment [6]. Similarly, smart grid initiatives in India, supported by international financial institutions, integrate renewable energy sources with advanced technology to optimize energy distribution and reduce inefficiencies [17]. As Industry 5.0 emphasizes sustainability and inclusivity, PPPs will remain vital for creating resilient and human-centered infrastructure [18].
5. **Financial Inclusion and Digital Ecosystems** Microfinance and fintech platforms are transforming financial inclusion by bridging gaps in underserved regions through scalable and efficient digital ecosystems. In India, Paytm has enabled millions in remote areas to access digital payments, microloans, and insurance services while integrating seamlessly with government schemes to promote financial literacy and inclusion [19, 20]. Similarly, GCash in the Philippines empowers rural communities by providing mobile-based savings accounts, loans, and payment options through collaborations with local and international partners [6, 21]. These platforms align with the human-centric principles of Industry 5.0 by fostering entrepreneurship, strengthening economic resilience, and

promoting inclusive financial systems that empower marginalized populations [7].

3 Interplay Between Finance and Technology in Industry 5.0

The convergence of finance and technology (fintech) is pivotal in shaping the future of Industry 5.0, where human-centric and sustainable practices define industrial progress. This interplay is enabling scalable and inclusive projects by transforming how resources are allocated, risks are managed, and inclusivity is fostered in financial ecosystems [1, 7]. Fintech innovations such as AI-driven credit scoring, blockchain-based green financing, decentralized finance (DeFi), and IoT-enabled supply chain financing are revolutionizing traditional financial systems to align with the goals of Industry 5.0 [10, 22].

4 AI-Driven Credit Scoring

AI-driven credit scoring utilizes machine learning algorithms to evaluate borrowers' creditworthiness by analyzing diverse data sources, including transaction histories, social media activity, and mobile payment records. This innovative approach enhances access to financing, particularly for underserved communities and small and medium-sized enterprises (SMEs), empowering them to adopt Industry 5.0 technologies such as automation and green solutions [1, 15].

In India, platforms like CredAvenue have revolutionized the SME financing ecosystem by providing real-time credit assessments. These assessments enable faster loan approvals, allowing SMEs to invest in automation and sustainable technologies to remain competitive in a rapidly evolving industrial landscape [19]. Similarly, in China, Ant Group's AI-based credit scoring system, integrated within its Alipay platform, has successfully extended loans to rural businesses and individuals who lack traditional credit histories. These funds are often used to drive digitization efforts, such as integrating IoT in agricultural practices [23].

The impact of AI-driven credit scoring on Industry 5.0 is significant. It expands financing opportunities for businesses in emerging markets, reducing the time and cost associated with traditional credit assessments [10]. Furthermore, its scalability supports a larger pool of borrowers, accelerating the regional adoption of advanced technologies and fostering inclusivity in the global financial landscape [7].

5 Blockchain-Based Green Financing

Blockchain technology is transforming green financing initiatives by providing a transparent and secure mechanism to track the flow of funds, ensuring they are utilized for their intended purposes. By incorporating smart contracts, blockchain automates processes, reduces inefficiencies, and enhances investor confidence, making it a vital tool in promoting sustainability [10, 22].

For example, in Southeast Asia, the Asian Development Bank (ADB) has partnered with blockchain firms to establish a transparent framework for green bond issuance. This initiative supports renewable energy projects, such as wind energy farms in Vietnam, by attracting sustainable investments [5]. Similarly, in Singapore, the Climate Impact X (CIX) platform leverages blockchain to tokenize carbon credits, facilitating the trading of emissions offsets. This not only enables industries to meet regulatory requirements but also funds sustainability projects [24].

The integration of blockchain in green financing aligns seamlessly with Industry 5.0 by fostering transparency, which builds investor trust and ensures accountability. It also directs financial resources toward environmentally friendly technologies, thereby encouraging innovation in manufacturing and energy sectors. Through this, blockchain drives sustainable development while accelerating the adoption of green technologies [7].

6 Decentralized Finance (DeFi) for Project Funding

Decentralized Finance (DeFi) utilizes blockchain to provide lending, borrowing, and investment opportunities independent of traditional financial institutions. This model is particularly beneficial for funding Industry 5.0 projects, offering accessible and flexible financial solutions to a broader audience [10, 25].

In the Philippines, DeFi platforms have empowered renewable energy startups like Kilusang Pagbabago to crowdfund solar energy installations in off-grid areas, promoting decentralized energy production and enhancing energy accessibility [5]. Similarly, in South Korea, DeFi platforms are bridging funding gaps by enabling SMEs to adopt AI and robotics in their operations, supporting the country's push toward smart manufacturing [26].

DeFi's contribution to Industry 5.0 is transformative. It democratizes access to funding, ensuring inclusivity for small and medium enterprises (SMEs). The speed of financing through decentralized systems enables timely execution of critical projects, while reduced reliance on centralized institutions enhances resilience in financial ecosystems. Together, these factors position DeFi as a key enabler of Industry 5.0 advancements [7].

7 IoT-Integrated Supply Chain Financing

The integration of IoT into supply chain financing is reshaping the financial landscape for manufacturers and logistics providers by enhancing visibility and reducing risks. By enabling real-time tracking of goods, IoT solutions provide financial institutions with reliable data, facilitating better lending terms and optimized credit lines [7, 10].

In China, Alibaba's fintech arm has implemented IoT sensors and AI analytics to dynamically assess suppliers' creditworthiness based on real-time inventory and shipment data. This innovation has streamlined supply chain operations, ensuring that financing aligns with actual performance metrics [27]. In Indonesia, platforms like Tanihub utilize IoT technology to monitor crop health and market trends, enabling microloans for farmers. This not only improves agricultural productivity but also aligns financing with real-time agricultural needs [28].

IoT-integrated supply chain financing contributes significantly to Industry 5.0 by optimizing resource allocation across complex supply chains, fostering trust through real-time insights, and promoting sustainability by encouraging efficient resource usage and waste reduction. These advancements position IoT as a critical enabler in modernizing supply chain ecosystems [2].

8 AI-Powered ESG Assessment Tools

AI-powered ESG (Environmental, Social, and Governance) assessment tools are revolutionizing sustainable investing by analyzing large datasets to evaluate companies' ESG performance. These tools enable investors to identify and prioritize projects that align with Industry 5.0 objectives, fostering a sustainable and data-driven approach to investment [7, 10].

In Japan, firms like MS&AD Insurance utilize AI platforms to evaluate ESG risks and opportunities, directing investments toward green manufacturing projects that align with the country's sustainability goals [29]. Similarly, in Malaysia, AI-driven tools are helping identify sustainable palm oil producers, ensuring that financing is allocated to initiatives that uphold ESG principles [30].

The precision offered by AI in ESG assessments ensures that investments are channeled into high-impact projects, fostering greater accountability through data transparency. Additionally, the scalability of these tools attracts global investors to regional sustainable projects, amplifying their impact and supporting the widespread adoption of Industry 5.0 technologies. Through these innovations, AI-powered ESG tools play a pivotal role in shaping a sustainable industrial future [3].

9 The Evolution of Industrial Revolutions

The progression of industrial revolutions from Industry 1.0 to Industry 5.0 demonstrates how well humanity has been able to use technology to advance. Each phase introduced groundbreaking innovations supported by corresponding financial advancements [31, 32] (Fig. 2).

1. **Industry 1.0 (Late 18th Century): The Age of Mechanization** The first industrial revolution, which began in the late eighteenth century, marked the age of mechanization. During this period, mechanized production powered by water and steam transformed agriculture and manufacturing, significantly improving efficiency and productivity. Financial advancements, such as the rise of investment banks and joint-stock companies, played a crucial role in supporting this transformation by funding the development of large factories and transportation infrastructure [33]. In Asia, India's cotton textile mills, financed by both British and local investors in the late nineteenth century, laid the foundation for industrial growth and modernization in the region [34].
2. **Industry 2.0 (Late 19th Century): The Age of Electrification** The late nineteenth century brought the second industrial revolution, characterized by the widespread use of electricity and the introduction of assembly lines, which revolutionized production processes by increasing efficiency and reducing costs. This era also

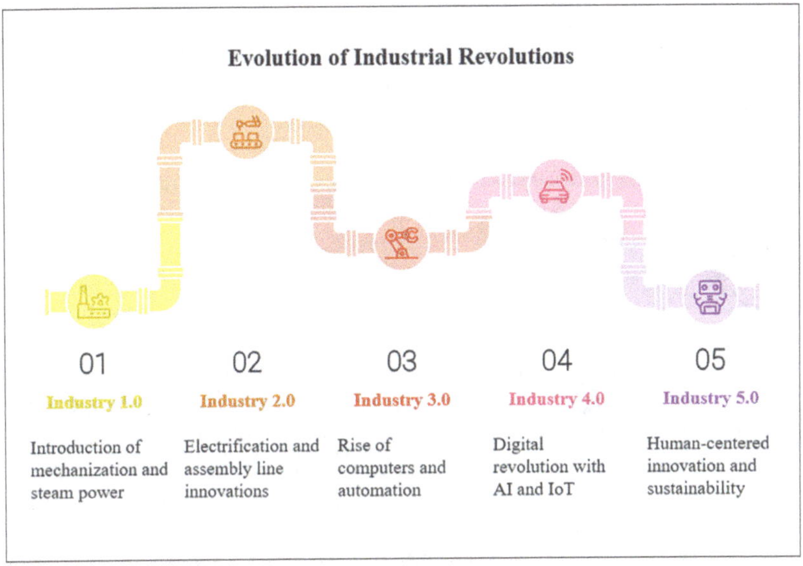

Fig. 2 The evolution of industrial revolutions

saw significant improvements in connectivity through the development of telegraphs and railroads. Financially, industrial banks played a pivotal role by providing the necessary funding for the expansion of railroads and electrical grids [35]. In Asia, Japan's Meiji Restoration was a notable example of this transformation, with the establishment of industrial banks that financed rapid modernization efforts, including the development of factory systems and infrastructure projects [36].

3. **Industry 3.0 (Mid-20th Century): The Age of Computers and Automation** The third industrial revolution, which emerged in the mid-twentieth century, was marked by the introduction of computers, automation, and early robotics. These technological advancements revolutionized manufacturing and services by streamlining processes and increasing efficiency. Financially, this era saw the rise of venture capital as a critical driver of technological innovation, providing funding for ground breaking developments [37]. In Asia, South Korea exemplified this revolution by collaborating with

banks to develop export-oriented industries. By leveraging automation, South Korea transformed into a global manufacturing hub, driving economic growth and technological leadership in the region [38].

4. **Industry 4.0 (Early 21st Century): The Digital Revolution** The fourth industrial revolution, emerging in the early twenty-first century, introduced transformative technologies such as Artificial Intelligence (AI), the Internet of Things (IoT), and big data. These innovations enabled the development of smart factories and seamless digital connectivity, revolutionizing how industries operate and interact [32]. Financially, this period was marked by the rapid growth of startups and tech enterprises, fueled by venture capital, private equity, and fintech solutions. In Asia, China's robust fintech ecosystem played a pivotal role in this transformation, supporting startups like Alibaba and Tencent. These companies spearheaded digital advancements across industries, driving innovation and economic growth [39].
5. **Industry 5.0 (Present): The Human-Centered Revolution** Industry 5.0 marks a transformative era where technology and human ingenuity converge to create sustainable and inclusive progress. Unlike its predecessor, Industry 4.0, which emphasized automation and data exchange, Industry 5.0 focuses on human-centric innovation. One of its hallmarks is the collaboration between artificial intelligence (AI) and human creativity to address complex challenges and enhance decision-making [9]. Green technologies, such as renewable energy systems, circular manufacturing, and carbon capture, underscore the importance of environmental stewardship in modern industrial practices [40].

In the financial domain, Industry 5.0 is driving a paradigm shift toward integrating profitability with social and environmental objectives. Instruments like green bonds, which fund projects with clear environmental benefits, and sustainability-linked loans, which incentivize companies to meet ESG (Environmental, Social, and Governance) targets, are gaining prominence [11]. Impact investing, where financial returns align with measurable societal benefits, is reshaping investment strategies globally.

Asia exemplifies these principles, with Singapore emerging as a green finance hub. The city-state integrates cutting-edge technologies with ESG frameworks to attract investments in clean energy, sustainable infrastructure, and inclusive growth initiatives [16]. Beyond Singapore, Japan has championed renewable energy innovations, particularly in solar technology, while India's green banking initiatives have spurred investments in sustainable agriculture and affordable housing [5]. South Korea, through its "Green New Deal," promotes smart grids and electric mobility, showcasing the regional commitment to blending technology and sustainability [41].

These examples underscore Industry 5.0's potential to harmonize technological advancement with human-centric values, paving the way for a more resilient and inclusive global economy.

10 Building Human-Centered Infrastructure

Human-centered infrastructure is a transformative approach to development that places individual well-being, inclusivity, and environmental stewardship at the core of planning and implementation. It recognizes that infrastructure is not just about physical structures but also about creating systems and environments that empower people, reduce inequalities, and promote sustainable development [12]. This concept aligns closely with the United Nations Sustainable Development Goals (SDGs), particularly those aimed at reducing inequalities (Goal 10), ensuring decent work and economic growth (Goal 8), and fostering resilient and sustainable industrialization (Goal 9) [18].

A human-centered infrastructure focuses on inclusivity by addressing the needs of marginalized and underserved populations, ensuring that everyone has access to basic amenities such as clean water, reliable energy, and affordable housing [15]. It also emphasizes creating employment opportunities that prioritize safety, fairness, and dignity for workers, thus contributing to economic stability and growth [42]. In the context of environmental stewardship, human-centered infrastructure incorporates green technologies, renewable energy, and sustainable practices to minimize ecological impact and combat climate change [11].

For instance, urban development projects designed under this framework often integrate smart technologies to improve efficiency, such as energy-saving building designs, intelligent transportation systems, and waste-to-energy solutions. These initiatives not only enhance the quality of life for residents but also promote long-term environmental sustainability [2].

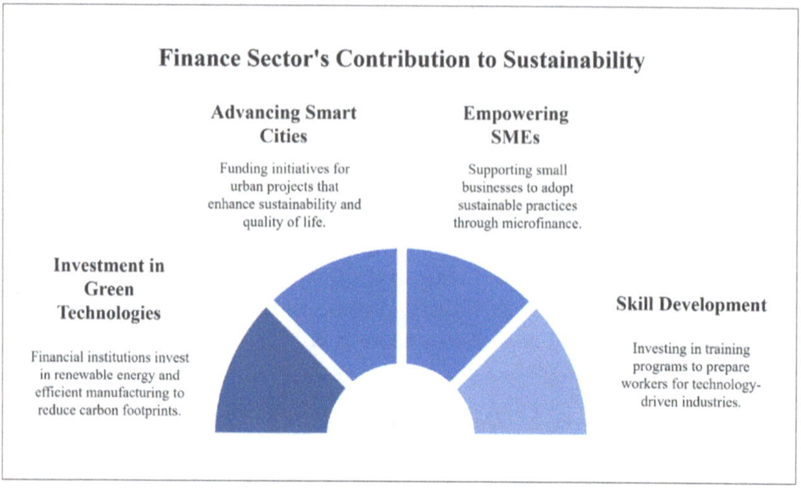

Fig. 3 Finance sector' contribution

Additionally, human-centered infrastructure promotes equitable access to education and healthcare, ensuring communities can thrive socially and economically. By addressing systemic inequalities and environmental challenges simultaneously, this approach supports holistic development and strengthens societal resilience [12]. This paradigm shift in infrastructure development fosters a world where progress benefits all individuals, aligning infrastructure investments with broader global goals for a sustainable and inclusive future [40] (Fig. 3).

10.1 Finance Sector's Contribution

1. **Investment in Green Technologies** The finance sector is at the forefront of driving investments in green technologies, focusing on projects that prioritize sustainability and environmental stewardship. Financial institutions in Asia are channeling significant resources into renewable energy projects, energy-efficient manufacturing processes, and innovative waste management solutions [11]. These investments not only reduce the carbon footprint of industries but also foster long-term economic growth. For instance, China's Industrial and Commercial Bank (ICBC) has played a crucial role in financing

smart grid projects, which integrate renewable energy sources into industrial operations. These grids enhance energy efficiency, reduce dependency on fossil fuels, and promote cleaner industrial processes, aligning with global sustainability goals [43].

2. **Advancing Smart Cities** The development of smart cities is another area where the finance sector plays a pivotal role by funding initiatives that incorporate efficient transportation, clean energy, and advanced data management systems. Financial institutions provide the necessary capital for large-scale urban projects that enhance the quality of life for residents while promoting sustainability [5]. The Asian Development Bank (ADB), for example, has supported numerous digital connectivity initiatives in Southeast Asia. These projects enable smart urban planning by leveraging technology to optimize resources, improve infrastructure, and address urban challenges like congestion and pollution, paving the way for sustainable and resilient cities [5].
3. **Empowering Small and Medium Enterprises (SMEs)** Small and medium enterprises (SMEs) are the backbone of Asia's economy, and their transformation into more innovative and sustainable operations is vital for regional growth. Financial institutions support SMEs through funding that enables them to adopt cutting-edge and environmentally friendly technologies [15]. Microfinance initiatives in countries like Bangladesh have been instrumental in this regard. These programs provide SMEs with access to capital, allowing them to transition to digital platforms and implement green operational practices [44]. By empowering SMEs, the finance sector not only promotes economic inclusivity but also strengthens the adoption of sustainable business models across the region.
4. **Skill Development and Workforce Resilience** As industries increasingly integrate advanced technologies, the finance sector contributes to building workforce resilience through investments in skill development and vocational training. Banks and investment funds sponsor training programs designed to prepare workers for technology-driven industries, ensuring they remain competitive in the evolving job market [42]. South Korea's KB Financial Group exemplifies this effort by collaborating with technical institutions to upskill workers for AI-integrated industries [45]. These initiatives enhance employability, reduce the risk of workforce displacement,

and ensure that industrial growth remains inclusive and human-centered, reinforcing the principles of sustainable development.

11 Human-Centric Innovations: Reshaping Industries

In the evolving landscape of Industry 5.0, human-centric design is redefining the relationship between technology and the workforce. Prioritizing human well-being, creativity, and inclusivity, industries are transforming traditional workspaces through the integration of ergonomics, advanced automation, and sustainability. These innovations are not only enhancing productivity but also ensuring that workers' physical and mental health remain at the forefront of industrial advancement [9, 32]. The following examples highlight how human-centric innovations are reshaping industries.

11.1 Ergonomic Automation in Manufacturing

One of the most significant advancements in human-centric design is the implementation of collaborative robots, or cobots. Unlike traditional industrial robots, cobots are engineered to work alongside humans, assisting with repetitive and physically demanding tasks while minimizing physical strain. For instance, in the automotive sector, Toyota in Japan utilizes cobots to support workers in assembling vehicles. These robots handle tasks such as heavy lifting and precision assembly, reducing the risk of workplace injuries and allowing employees to focus on creative problem-solving [46]. Similarly, Foxconn in Taiwan has integrated cobots into its electronics manufacturing processes, where they assemble smartphones while adhering to ergonomic standards to ensure worker safety [47]. These applications have led to tangible benefits, including enhanced job satisfaction, lower injury rates, and increased productivity.

11.2 Smart Factories with Worker-Centric Designs

Smart factories are embracing AI-powered workstations to create worker-centric environments. These adaptive systems analyze workers' movements and postures in real time, providing immediate feedback to prevent fatigue and injury [2]. Companies like Siemens have implemented these innovations in their Chinese manufacturing facilities, offering adjustable tools and ergonomics coaching tailored to each worker [48]. In the textile industry across South Asia, motion-sensor chairs and AI-driven lighting systems are improving physical comfort and efficiency. These technologies contribute to better health outcomes, fostering an inclusive workplace that supports diverse worker needs.

11.3 Augmented Reality (AR) in Training and Operations

Augmented Reality (AR) has emerged as a transformative tool for training and operational efficiency, offering immersive and interactive experiences. In Singapore's aerospace industry, ST Engineering uses AR glasses to guide technicians during complex aircraft maintenance tasks, improving precision and minimizing errors [49]. In India's healthcare sector, AR is used to train medical professionals on performing surgeries and using advanced medical devices, effectively bridging skill gaps [50]. These innovations have resulted in higher skill retention, fewer operational errors, and enhanced workplace safety.

11.4 Sustainability and Employee Well-Being in Design

Green factory designs are redefining the industrial workspace by prioritizing sustainability and employee well-being. Hyundai's Ulsan plant in South Korea incorporates natural lighting, indoor gardens, and air filtration systems to create a healthier and more productive environment [51]. Similarly, Taiwan Semiconductor Manufacturing Company (TSMC) has integrated renewable energy systems and noise-reduction technologies in their facilities, fostering mental and physical well-being among workers [52]. These initiatives not only enhance employee satisfaction and retention but also align with environmental sustainability goals.

11.5 Workforce Inclusion Through Assistive Technologies

Human-centric design also extends to inclusivity, with industries developing assistive technologies to empower differently-abled workers. Robotic exoskeletons by Panasonic in Japan enable workers with limited mobility to perform physical tasks, while adaptive precision farming tools in China allow elderly and disabled workers to contribute effectively to agriculture [53].

11.6 Human-Centered Artificial Intelligence (AI)

Human-centered AI is increasingly being utilized to monitor and improve mental health in workplaces. For example, Infosys in India employs AI platforms to analyze communication patterns and assess employee stress levels, offering tailored wellness programs to support their workforce [54]. Similarly, banks in Singapore use AI systems to monitor workload balance and detect burnout risks, creating a supportive and proactive work culture [55]. These initiatives enhance mental health outcomes, reduce workplace stress, and promote overall well-being.

12 A Broader Perspective Across Asia

12.1 Japan: Financing Smart Manufacturing

Japan's financial institutions, such as Mitsubishi UFJ Financial Group (MUFG), play a key role in supporting the adoption of Industry 5.0 technologies in smart manufacturing. Industry 5.0 focuses on human-centered innovation, where advanced technologies like AI and collaborative robots (cobots) work alongside human workers to enhance productivity and creativity [32]. MUFG has financed projects that integrate cobots and AI-driven systems into manufacturing processes, optimizing operations while keeping human workers central [56].

12.2 India: Scaling Renewable Energy

India's Green Energy Corridor, supported by the State Bank of India (SBI) and international climate funds, exemplifies the finance sector's role in advancing renewable energy in line with Industry 5.0 principles. Industry 5.0 emphasizes the collaboration between humans and advanced technologies to drive sustainable and innovative growth [15]. The Green Energy Corridor integrates renewable energy sources like wind and solar with smart grid technology, creating a seamless, AI-driven infrastructure that optimizes energy distribution [57]. This collaboration between human expertise, advanced AI systems, and renewable technologies aligns with Industry 5.0's focus on enhancing productivity while prioritizing environmental sustainability. The finance sector's investment in this initiative not only reduces India's dependency on fossil fuels but also demonstrates how human-centered, technology-driven systems can lead the way toward a greener, more sustainable future.

12.3 ASEAN: Bridging Digital Divides

The Asian Development Bank (ADB) has been instrumental in addressing regional disparities in Southeast Asia through its digital connectivity projects, particularly in rural areas. By expanding internet access and digital infrastructure, these initiatives bring marginalized communities online, enabling them to participate in the broader digital economy [5]. This inclusivity is a key component of Industry 5.0, which prioritizes human-centered development and the integration of all individuals into the technological landscape. ADB's efforts to bridge the digital divide allow rural communities to leverage Industry 5.0 technologies, such as AI, smart devices, and automated systems, fostering greater economic participation, enhancing local industries, and contributing to a more inclusive, sustainable future.

12.4 Sustainable Development and Digital Connectivity in Central Asia

Kazakhstan is accelerating its renewable energy transformation through initiatives focused on expanding wind and solar energy capacity. Supported by over $500 million in financing from the European Bank for Reconstruction and Development (EBRD), these projects align with the nation's commitment to achieving carbon neutrality by 2050 [58]. Key projects like the Burnoye Solar Plant and Yereymentau Wind Farm significantly reduce reliance on fossil fuels, promoting clean energy use and sustainability. By integrating advanced technologies for efficient energy management, these initiatives reflect the principles of Industry 5.0, which emphasize human-centered, technology-driven solutions for environmental and economic progress.

In neighboring Uzbekistan, strides are being made in digital connectivity to support the nation's readiness for Industry 5.0. A major initiative focuses on expanding broadband internet access and improving ICT infrastructure across the country. This endeavor has been supported by a $100 million funding initiative from the Asian Infrastructure Investment Bank (AIIB), which underscores the importance of connectivity in driving economic and social progress [59]. The enhanced internet infrastructure has significantly improved access to digital tools for local businesses and educational institutions. As a result, businesses have been able to adopt modern technologies, while educational institutions have expanded digital learning opportunities, fostering inclusivity and building workforce capabilities. These advancements collectively contribute to Central Asia's evolving role in global economic and technological landscapes.

13 Smart City Development and Renewable Energy in the Middle East

13.1 Saudi Arabia: NEOM Project

In Saudi Arabia, the ambitious NEOM project is redefining the concept of urban development through its focus on sustainability, advanced technology, and green energy. Valued at $500 billion, NEOM is envisioned as a futuristic smart city that integrates artificial intelligence and renewable energy to create a sustainable, human-centered living environment. The project is funded through a combination of public and private investments, with significant contributions from the Saudi Public Investment Fund (PIF) and international partnerships [60]. NEOM's innovative design and infrastructure aim to set new global benchmarks for urban development, offering a blueprint for cities of the future. By incorporating cutting-edge technology and prioritizing environmental sustainability, the project aligns with Saudi Arabia's Vision 2030 [61].

13.2 United Arab Emirates: Renewable Energy Initiatives

In the United Arab Emirates (UAE), renewable energy initiatives are playing a pivotal role in shaping a sustainable future. A key component of the UAE's dedication to renewable energy is the Mohammed bin Rashid Al Maktoum Solar Park, one of the biggest solar farms in the world. This project has garnered over $2.5 billion in funding from a mix of international and local banks, including green loans that underscore its eco-friendly objectives [62]. The UAE's Energy Strategy 2050, which seeks to attain a 50% share of renewable energy in the nation's energy mix, benefits greatly from the solar park.

By harnessing solar power at such a massive scale, the project not only reduces carbon emissions but also supports the UAE's leadership in global sustainability efforts.

14 Digital Financial Inclusion and Renewable Energy in South Asia

14.1 Pakistan: Digital Financial Inclusion

In Pakistan, efforts to promote digital financial inclusion have revolutionized access to formal banking for rural populations. The deployment of innovative fintech platforms has been at the heart of this initiative, addressing the financial exclusion that has historically hindered economic growth in underserved areas. A standout achievement is the development of the Raast digital payment system, a collaborative effort led by the State Bank of Pakistan with support from international partners such as the Bill & Melinda Gates Foundation [63]. This state-of-the-art payment platform has enabled millions of individuals to access secure, efficient, and low-cost banking services. By integrating rural communities into the formal financial ecosystem, the initiative has laid a robust foundation for inclusive economic growth, empowering individuals and small businesses to thrive in the digital economy.

14.2 Nepal: Hydropower Development

In Nepal, the Upper Tamakoshi Hydropower Project has emerged as a transformative development in the country's energy sector. As the largest hydropower plant in Nepal, this project exemplifies a milestone in achieving energy self-sufficiency. It has been realized through a diverse financing mechanism that includes contributions from domestic banks, international development agencies, and the Nepal Electricity Authority [64]. The hydropower plant has significantly increased the nation's electricity generation capacity, reducing dependence on energy imports and supporting industrial growth. This development not only strengthens Nepal's energy security but also enhances its ability to foster sustainable economic development.

15 Advancing Sustainability and Inclusion in Southeast Asia

15.1 Philippines: Microgrid Deployment

In the Philippines, the deployment of microgrids on remote islands has transformed access to reliable electricity, ensuring energy inclusivity for underserved communities. This initiative aims to address the challenges faced by geographically isolated regions that are often disconnected from the national power grid. Through a financing mechanism supported by the World Bank and private equity firms, these projects exemplify the effectiveness of public–private partnerships in driving sustainable development [14]. The introduction of microgrids has provided affordable and stable energy to these communities, significantly improving quality of life. Reliable electricity has empowered local enterprises to grow, facilitated modern educational tools in schools, and fostered overall socio-economic progress.

15.2 Indonesia: Circular Economy Initiatives

In Indonesia, the push for a circular economy has taken center stage through initiatives focused on waste-to-energy plants and advanced recycling infrastructure. These projects aim to address the dual challenges of urban waste accumulation and the need for sustainable energy solutions. A key aspect of their success is the innovative financing mechanism involving green bonds issued by Indonesian financial institutions [65]. These bonds have attracted investments that support the construction of facilities capable of converting waste into energy while promoting recycling. Urban centers like Jakarta have particularly benefited from these efforts, with reduced landfill dependency and increased adoption of clean energy practices. This initiative not only mitigates environmental concerns but also aligns with Indonesia's commitment to sustainability, offering a replicable model for other nations facing similar challenges.

16 Innovative Advancements in East Asia

16.1 South Korea: Advancing a Hydrogen Economy

South Korea is at the forefront of embracing a hydrogen economy as part of its ambitious efforts to decarbonize industrial processes and transition to cleaner energy solutions. This initiative is heavily supported by a robust financial mechanism that combines public funding under the Korean New Deal and significant contributions from private banks such as KB Financial Group [66]. These investments have facilitated the establishment of hydrogen-powered industrial complexes and the development of hydrogen-fueled vehicles, marking a transformative shift in the nation's energy and industrial landscape. By prioritizing hydrogen energy, South Korea is setting a global standard for sustainable industrial practices and advancing its commitment to carbon neutrality [67].

16.2 Taiwan: AI in Semiconductor Manufacturing

In Taiwan, the integration of artificial intelligence (AI) into semiconductor manufacturing is revolutionizing the industry and optimizing production capabilities. Supported by government-backed loans and venture capital investments, this initiative underscores Taiwan's dedication to innovation in high-tech industries [68]. The Taiwan Semiconductor Manufacturing Company (TSMC), a global leader in semiconductor production, has been at the helm of this transformation, utilizing AI technologies to enhance precision, efficiency, and scalability in manufacturing processes. This AI-driven approach not only strengthens TSMC's position as an industry leader but also highlights Taiwan's critical role in shaping the future of smart manufacturing on a global scale [69].

16.3 Asia's Industry 5.0 Potential

Asia stands at the crossroads of tremendous opportunity and significant challenges as it embraces Industry 5.0. On one hand, the region's diverse economies—ranging from advanced markets like Japan and Singapore to emerging ones like Vietnam, India, and Bangladesh—provide fertile ground for technological adoption, financial innovation, and sustainable growth. The abundance of natural resources, rapid urbanization, and expanding digital ecosystems offer an unparalleled opportunity to drive human-centered industrial development [7]. At the same time, Asia's cultural diversity, socioeconomic disparities, and fragmented regulatory environments present hurdles that must be addressed to unlock its full potential [14] (Fig. 4).

Opportunities in Industry 5.0 Transition

1. **Unified ESG Frameworks** Creating a region-wide ESG framework can attract cross-border investments and streamline sustainability efforts. Asia can become a leader in green finance by leveraging unified green taxonomies to standardize reporting practices [5]. Unified ESG frameworks will ensure consistency in sustainability reporting and compliance, boosting investor confidence and fostering collaborative green initiatives.
2. **Financial Innovations for Sustainability** Financial tools like green bonds, sustainability-linked loans, and climate risk insurance offer opportunities to fund renewable energy, smart grids, and circular economies. Innovations in blockchain-based green financing can

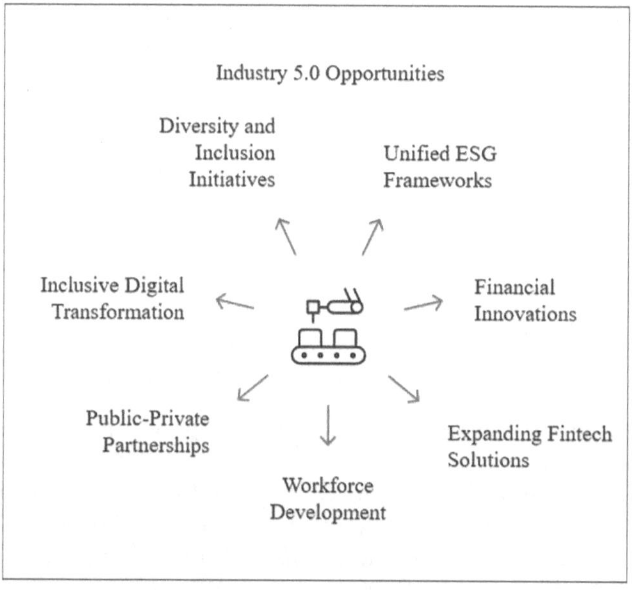

Fig. 4 Opportunities in Industry 5.0

enhance transparency and investor confidence [14]. For instance, Indonesia's issuance of green bonds has successfully funded waste-to-energy projects, demonstrating the potential for financial innovation in advancing sustainability goals.

3. **Expanding Fintech Solutions** Fintech platforms can bridge gaps in financial inclusion by offering AI-driven credit assessments, mobile-based microloans, and payment systems [28]. Regions like Southeast Asia and Central Asia can use fintech to empower SMEs and marginalized communities. Programs like Pakistan's Raast payment system illustrate how digital platforms can revolutionize access to formal financial services, particularly in underserved areas [56].
4. **Technology for Workforce Development** Industry 5.0 offers opportunities for upskilling programs and workforce training tailored to advanced technologies like AI, IoT, and automation. Governments and businesses can collaborate to provide education and training that ensures workforce readiness [15]. For example, South Korea's New Deal initiatives include targeted vocational training programs to equip workers with skills relevant to hydrogen energy and AI-integrated industries [66].
5. **Public–Private Partnerships (PPPs)** Strengthening PPPs offers a strategic approach to funding large-scale infrastructure projects such as renewable energy parks and smart urban systems. Success stories in Vietnam's solar energy initiatives and India's Green Energy Corridor demonstrate how PPPs can drive sustainable development [7]. Replicating these models across the region can accelerate the implementation of large-scale projects.
6. **Inclusive Digital Transformation** Expanding internet infrastructure and digital platforms can reduce the digital divide, enabling rural and underserved communities to access opportunities in Industry 5.0. Programs like India's Digital India offer a scalable model for other countries [60]. These initiatives foster digital inclusion, ensuring broader economic participation and workforce readiness for Industry 5.0 technologies.
7. **Diversity and Inclusion Initiatives** Promoting workforce diversity by empowering women and differently-abled individuals can unlock untapped talent. Inclusive policies and assistive technologies can

drive innovation and create a truly human-centered industrial environment [14]. For instance, Japan's adoption of robotic exoskeletons by Panasonic empowers differently-abled workers, showcasing how inclusive technologies can enhance workforce participation.

17 Deep Dive into Challenges

The transition to Industry 5.0 in Asia presents immense opportunities for sustainable and human-centered development, but it also faces significant challenges. Two major obstacles are the lack of alignment in Environmental, Social, and Governance (ESG) standards across the region and the presence of cultural and societal barriers that hinder technological adoption. These challenges complicate the alignment of financial and technological objectives, delaying the widespread implementation of transformative innovations [5, 14].

17.1 Lack of Alignment in ESG Standards

While individual countries have made strides in sustainability initiatives, the absence of a unified ESG framework across Asia limits the region's ability to attract global investments and achieve cohesive progress. Variations in green taxonomies and reporting practices create barriers for cross-border investors and impede collaboration [4].

17.2 Cultural and Societal Barriers

Cultural resistance to new technologies and societal fears of job displacement further hinder the adoption of Industry 5.0 technologies. In rural and traditional sectors, skepticism toward automation and AI limits their integration into critical industries like agriculture and manufacturing [11].

18 Differing ESG Standards in Asia

18.1 Fragmented ESG Regulations Across Countries

Different Asian countries operate under varied regulatory frameworks, making it difficult to develop a unified sustainability strategy. For example, Japan and Singapore have advanced ESG policies, such as the Tokyo Stock Exchange's ESG disclosure mandates and Singapore's green finance incentives [56, 57]. In contrast, Bangladesh and Myanmar are still developing their ESG policies, leading to gaps in sustainable practices. This regulatory fragmentation creates inconsistencies that deter cross-border investments and reduce scalability for sustainability projects [4].

18.2 Inconsistent ESG Metrics and Reporting

Countries follow different reporting frameworks, complicating the comparison of ESG performance. For instance, India uses the SEBI Business Responsibility and Sustainability Reporting (BRSR) framework [58], while China adheres to the CSRC Green Bond Guidelines [59]. The lack of standardized ESG metrics results in mismatched data, making investment decisions more challenging for global investors.

18.3 Conflicting Priorities Between Development and Sustainability

Many developing Asian nations prioritize rapid industrialization over environmental sustainability. For example, Vietnam's ambitious industrial goals often clash with weak enforcement of ESG standards in its manufacturing sector [5]. Balancing economic growth and sustainability remains a significant challenge, as governments face pressure to meet economic targets while addressing global sustainability expectations.

18.4 Absence of Unified Green Taxonomy

Without a common definition of "sustainability," there is confusion regarding what qualifies as green finance. This lack of clarity limits investment scalability and reduces investor confidence, as additional due diligence costs are incurred [6]. A unified green taxonomy is essential to streamline green investments and foster greater trust among investors.

19 Cultural and Societal Barriers

1. 1. Resistance to Change in Traditional Industries

Many small and medium enterprises (SMEs) resist adopting advanced technologies due to cultural attachment to manual practices or fear of job losses. For instance, India's textile industry, known for its craftsmanship, often hesitates to integrate automation despite the potential benefits for worker well-being and productivity [60]. This resistance stems from fears that automation could erode traditional skills or lead to widespread unemployment, making it difficult to modernize legacy industries.

2. Limited ESG Awareness and Perception of Costs

In regions with low ESG literacy, businesses perceive sustainability as an added cost rather than an opportunity for long-term profitability. This mindset is prevalent in SMEs across Southeast Asia, where short-term financial gains often overshadow sustainable practices [4]. Many businesses lack awareness of the potential cost savings and market opportunities associated with sustainable practices, further hindering ESG adoption.

3. Socioeconomic Inequalities and Digital Divide

Marginalized communities in rural or underserved areas often lack the resources to participate in Industry 5.0 initiatives. In Central Asia, significant gaps exist between urban and rural regions in terms of internet access and technological infrastructure. These disparities limit access to financial tools, digital platforms, and skill-building opportunities, perpetuating economic inequalities and slowing technological adoption [6].

4. Gender and Workforce Inclusion Barriers

Deeply ingrained societal norms often limit workforce diversity, particularly in advanced industries. For example, in the Middle East, lower workforce participation rates among women result in the underutilization of skilled talent. Similarly, cultural biases hinder the inclusion of differently-abled individuals, reducing workforce diversity and innovation in human-centered industries [5]. Gender disparities not only impede equitable progress but also restrict industries from harnessing diverse perspectives critical to innovation.

20 Pathways to Overcome Challenges

Addressing the challenges in Asia's transition to Industry 5.0 requires coordinated efforts across regulatory, cultural, and technological fronts.

20.1 Harmonizing ESG Standards

Harmonizing ESG standards is a critical first step. Regional partnerships, such as the Asian Infrastructure Investment Bank (AIIB) and the ASEAN Taxonomy for Sustainable Finance, can develop unified frameworks to streamline ESG practices. For instance, the ASEAN Green Bond Standards offer a template for creating consistent sustainable finance regulations across member nations, ensuring a level playing field for investors and businesses [61].

20.2 Raising Awareness of ESG Benefits

Raising awareness of ESG benefits is equally important. Governments and organizations must conduct training programs and awareness campaigns to educate SMEs and local industries about the long-term advantages of sustainability. Japan's Ministry of Economy, Trade, and Industry (METI), for example, runs programs to help businesses integrate ESG principles into their operations, fostering a culture of sustainable innovation [62].

20.3 Bridging Societal Gaps

Bridging societal gaps is essential to ensure inclusivity. Governments can promote workforce diversity by offering incentives to companies that prioritize inclusive policies. The UAE's National Strategy for Advanced Innovation exemplifies this approach by focusing on empowering women in STEM fields to drive Industry 5.0 objectives [63]. Similarly, leveraging technology to bridge inequalities is critical. Initiatives like India's Digital India program aim to reduce the digital divide by expanding internet access in rural areas, enabling underserved communities to participate in Industry 5.0 advancements [64].

20.4 *Implications for Theory and Management*

These challenges and opportunities have direct theoretical and managerial implications. From a theoretical perspective, they redefine financial ecosystems to integrate sustainability, human well-being, and technology. Managerially, they emphasize the need for strategic investment in green technologies, harmonized regulations, and workforce readiness. By addressing these interconnected issues, Asia can unlock its potential to lead the global shift toward Industry 5.0, balancing innovation with sustainability and inclusivity. By addressing these challenges through harmonized standards, education, inclusivity, and equitable access to technology, Asia can unlock its full potential in transitioning to Industry 5.0. These measures will ensure that financial and technological objectives align with cultural and societal realities, fostering a sustainable and human-centered industrial future.

21 Theoretical Implications

This chapter provides meaningful contributions to the theoretical understanding of Industry 5.0 by advancing knowledge on the critical role of finance in creating human-centered and sustainable industrial systems. While Industry 4.0 largely revolved around technological automation and efficiency [1, 2], this study expands the discourse by integrating the role of financial ecosystems in facilitating the transition to a more inclusive and resilient Industry 5.0

The following theoretical implications emerge:

1. **Redefining Financial Ecosystems for Sustainability**

The chapter expands current theories on sustainable development [3] by demonstrating how financial ecosystems can act as enablers of environmental and social progress. It positions financial instruments like green bonds and sustainability-linked loans as foundational tools for integrating sustainability into industrial operations [4, 5]. This highlights the role of finance in moving beyond profitability to align with global sustainability goals.

2. **Bridging Human-Centered Development and Technological Innovation**

This study introduces a framework that connects financial systems with technological advancements like AI, IoT, and blockchain [6, 7], enabling industries to prioritize human well-being and resilience. It builds on innovation theory [8] to showcase how finance acts as a bridge, facilitating equitable adoption of emerging technologies in ways that address societal needs and environmental challenges.

3. **A Contextualized Approach to Sustainability in Emerging Economies**

The chapter contributes to regional development theories [9] by offering insights into how financial mechanisms operate differently in Asia. Case studies from Japan, India, Vietnam, and Singapore illustrate how financial strategies can be tailored to varying economic, cultural, and industrial contexts [10, 11], enriching the understanding of sustainable finance within emerging markets.

4. **4. Innovative Risk Mitigation Frameworks**

By incorporating advanced financial tools such as catastrophe bonds, climate risk insurance, and blockchain-enabled green financing [12, 13], this study builds on financial risk management theories. It provides a theoretical basis for understanding how financial innovation can reduce uncertainties and foster confidence among industries embracing Industry 5.0 technologies.

5. **Financial Inclusion as a Catalyst for Industrial Progress**

This research introduces financial inclusion as a key theoretical element in driving human-centric industrial development. By integrating fintech solutions and microfinance models [14, 15], the chapter highlights how financial accessibility fosters entrepreneurship, addresses societal inequalities, and accelerates the adoption of sustainable technologies in underserved communities.

In essence, this study broadens the theoretical scope of Industry 5.0 by presenting finance as a driving force that interlinks technology, sustainability, and human development. It provides a comprehensive framework that integrates financial systems with inclusive, resilient, and sustainable industrial transformation.

22 Managerial Implications

The findings of this chapter offer practical and actionable recommendations for policymakers, financial institutions, and business leaders who are tasked with driving Asia's transition to Industry 5.0. Managers can use these insights to design financial strategies that align technological innovation with human-centered and sustainable outcomes.

1. **Prioritizing Green and Sustainable Investments**: Financial institutions should proactively invest in projects that address environmental challenges while driving economic growth. Managers must allocate resources to renewable energy initiatives, smart grids, and circular economic models. Green bonds and sustainability-linked loans can incentivize businesses to adopt ESG (Environmental, Social, and Governance) goals and transition toward eco-friendly operations. For instance, institutions in Singapore and Vietnam have demonstrated how targeted funding can drive renewable energy adoption and innovation.
2. **Leveraging Fintech for Financial Inclusion**: Fintech platforms can revolutionize access to financial services by enabling microloans, AI-driven credit scoring, and blockchain-enabled transparency. Managers should leverage fintech to ensure financial inclusion for underserved populations, empowering SMEs and marginalized communities to participate in Industry 5.0. Platforms like Paytm in India and GCash in the Philippines have successfully demonstrated how digital ecosystems promote entrepreneurship, improve financial literacy, and enhance economic participation.
3. **Strengthening Public–Private Partnerships (PPPs)**: Policymakers and financial leaders must collaborate to develop large-scale infrastructure projects. Public–private partnerships (PPPs) combine governance with private-sector innovation, enabling the successful implementation of human-centered infrastructure. Managers can replicate models such as Vietnam's solar energy initiatives and

India's smart grid systems, which showcase how cross-sector collaborations can drive sustainable and scalable projects.

4. **Integrating Risk Mitigation Strategies**: Managers should adopt innovative financial tools like climate risk insurance, catastrophe bonds, and blockchain-enabled risk frameworks to reduce uncertainties associated with new technologies. By addressing financial risks, these tools can encourage businesses to invest confidently in advanced technologies and sustainable practices, fostering greater resilience within Industry 5.0 ecosystems.
5. **Workforce Development and Skill Building**: Financial investments in education and workforce upskilling are critical for ensuring that workers can adapt to Industry 5.0 technologies. Managers in both public and private sectors should sponsor vocational training, AI-integrated learning systems, and digital literacy programs. Examples from South Korea, where financial institutions collaborate with technical institutions to prepare workers for AI-driven industries, can serve as a blueprint for workforce resilience and inclusivity.
6. **Enhancing Transparency Through Financial Innovation**: Managers can utilize blockchain technology and AI-powered ESG tools to improve transparency, accountability, and investor confidence in sustainable projects. These tools ensure that funds are allocated appropriately, fostering trust among stakeholders and attracting global investment.
7. **Promoting Regional Collaboration**: Policymakers and business leaders must strengthen cross-border collaborations to harmonize sustainability standards and share best practices. Regional frameworks, such as the ASEAN Green Bond Standards, can provide a unified approach to implementing sustainable financial strategies across Asia, reducing fragmentation and accelerating Industry 5.0 adoption.

By implementing these managerial strategies, financial institutions, businesses, and governments can collaboratively foster a robust ecosystem that supports human-centered, sustainable, and technologically advanced industrial growth. These efforts will position Asia as a leader in Industry 5.0, setting an example for balancing economic aspirations with social and environmental responsibility.

23 Conclusion

The finance sector is at the heart of Asia's transformative journey toward Industry 5.0, where innovation, sustainability, and human-centric development intersect. This transition is not merely about adopting advanced technologies but about creating an inclusive ecosystem that ensures human well-being remains a central focus. Financial institutions are no longer passive enablers; they have become active agents of change by steering resources toward impactful projects that harmonize economic progress with environmental and social responsibility.

Through innovative instruments like green bonds, sustainability-linked loans, and climate risk insurance, the finance sector is driving investments in renewable energy, smart grids, and sustainable infrastructure. Fintech platforms, AI-driven credit scoring, and blockchain-based green financing are democratizing financial access, enabling small and medium enterprises (SMEs), rural populations, and marginalized communities to actively participate in Asia's industrial transformation.

Strategic public–private partnerships have emerged as a crucial tool in addressing large-scale infrastructure needs, combining governance, funding, and technological expertise to accelerate progress. Case studies from countries like Japan, Vietnam, Singapore, and India showcase how tailored financial solutions can foster clean energy adoption, digital transformation, and inclusive growth. These examples provide replicable models that highlight the effectiveness of regional collaboration and context-specific strategies.

As Asia solidifies its position as a global industrial hub, it carries the responsibility to balance economic aspirations with sustainability and inclusivity. By aligning financial strategies with Industry 5.0 principles, the region has an unparalleled opportunity to lead the global shift toward human-centered industrial development. The finance sector's role extends beyond facilitating economic growth; it lies in fostering a resilient, equitable, and future-ready society where technology serves humanity, not replaces it.

Ultimately, the chapter demonstrates that the finance sector's ability to innovate, collaborate, and prioritize sustainability will define Asia's success in achieving a harmonious blend of progress and purpose. By bridging the gap between ambition and implementation, financial systems are not just supporting Industry 5.0—they are shaping its very foundation. This journey is a testament to Asia's commitment to building a future where industry serves people, protects the planet, and leaves no one behind.

References

1. Schwab, K.: *The Fourth Industrial Revolution.* Crown Business, New York (2016)
2. European Commission: *Industry 5.0: Towards a sustainable, human-centric and resilient European industry* (2021)
3. United Nations: *Our Common Agenda – Report of the Secretary-General* (2023)
4. European Commission: *The European Green Deal.* https://commission.europa.eu (2020)
5. UNFCCC: *The Paris Agreement.* https://unfccc.int (2015)
6. Asian Development Bank (ADB): *Asian Development Outlook 2022 Update: Entrepreneurship in the Digital Age* (2022)
7. World Economic Forum: *The Future of Jobs Report* (2023)
8. OECD: *Financing for Sustainable Development Report* (2022)
9. UNEP: *Financing Circularity: Demystifying Finance for the Circular Economy* (2022)
10. Accenture: *Reinventing Sustainable Value Chains through Fintech* (2023)
11. OECD: *Green Finance and Investment* (2022)
12. UNDP: *Sustainable Infrastructure: Transforming Asia's Future* (2023)
13. MS&AD Insurance Group: *Integrated Report* (2023)
14. ILO: *World Employment and Social Outlook* (2023)
15. World Bank: *Fintech and Financial Inclusion in Asia* (2023)
16. Monetary Authority of Singapore (MAS): *Green Finance Action Plan* (2023)
17. Reserve Bank of India: *Report on Trend and Progress of Banking in India* (2023)
18. Government of India: *Digital India Programme.* https://digitalindia.gov.in (2023)
19. Ant Group: *Alipay Sustainability Report* (2023)
20. CredAvenue: *SME Lending Innovations in India.* https://credavenue.com (2023)
21. Grameen Bank: *Annual Report* (2023)
22. European Investment Bank: *Financing the Green Transition* (2023)
23. Climate Impact X (CIX): *Carbon Markets and Blockchain Solutions* (2023)
24. Korea Blockchain Association: *Annual Report* (2023)
25. Alibaba Group: *Smart Supply Chain Solutions* (2023)
26. Tanihub: *AgriTech and Financing Report* (2023)
27. Malaysian Palm Oil Council: *Sustainable Palm Oil Updates* (2023)
28. State Bank of Pakistan: *Raast - Pakistan's Instant Payment System* (2023)

29. TSMC: *Corporate Social Responsibility Report* (2023)
30. Toyota: *Manufacturing with Cobots for Ergonomics* (2023)
31. Foxconn: *Technology and Human-Centric Workspaces* (2023)
32. Siemens: *Smart Factory Human Engineering Report* (2023)
33. ST Engineering: *Augmented Reality in Aerospace Training* (2023)
34. NITI Aayog: *AR/VR in Indian Healthcare Sector* (2023)
35. Hyundai: *Ulsan Smart Green Plant Initiative* (2023)
36. Panasonic: *Assistive Robotics and Workforce Inclusion* (2023)
37. Infosys: *AI for Employee Mental Health Monitoring* (2023)
38. DBS Bank: *AI-Enabled Wellness Programs* (2023)
39. MUFG Bank: *Financing Innovation and Smart Manufacturing* (2023)
40. SBI: *India's Green Energy Corridor Report* (2023)
41. EBRD: *Renewable Projects in Kazakhstan* (2023)
42. AIIB: *Digital Infrastructure and Connectivity in Central Asia* (2023)
43. Public Investment Fund (Saudi Arabia): *NEOM Project Brief* (2023)
44. Saudi Vision 2030: *Official Vision Document*. www.vision2030.gov.sa
45. UAE Ministry of Energy: *Mohammed bin Rashid Solar Park Overview* (2023)
46. Nepal Electricity Authority: *Upper Tamakoshi Hydropower Project Report* (2023)
47. Indonesian Ministry of Finance: *Green Bond Framework* (2023)
48. Korean Ministry of Trade, Industry, and Energy: *Hydrogen Economy Strategy* (2023)
49. KB Financial Group: *Sustainability Report* (2023)
50. Taiwan Ministry of Economic Affairs: *AI and Semiconductor Policy* (2023)
51. Tokyo Stock Exchange: *ESG Disclosure Guidebook* (2023)
52. SEBI: *Business Responsibility and Sustainability Reporting (BRSR)* (2023)
53. China Securities Regulatory Commission (CSRC): *Green Bond Guidelines* (2023)
54. METI Japan: *ESG Training & Innovation Program* (2023)
55. UAE Ministry of Cabinet Affairs: *National Strategy for Advanced Innovation* (2023)
56. Foxconn: *Smart Manufacturing Report* (2023)
57. Asian Infrastructure Investment Bank (AIIB): *ASEAN Green Bond Standards* (2023)
58. Bangladesh Central Bank: *Sustainability Guidelines* (2023)
59. Myanmar Financial Commission: *ESG Implementation Strategy* (2023)
60. Accenture: *Automation & the Future of Skilled Crafts in Asia* (2023)
61. Vietnam Ministry of Industry and Trade: *Industrial Growth vs. ESG Enforcement* (2023)
62. TSMC: *ESG Facilities Modernization Report* (2023)
63. Panasonic Robotics: *Assistive Technology Case Study* (2023)

64. Infosys AI Lab: *Wellness Monitoring and AI Insights* (2023)
65. Paytm: *Financial Inclusion and Digital Payments* (2023)
66. GCash: *Rural Empowerment through Digital Finance* (2023)
67. Vietnam Renewable Energy Association: *Public-Private Solar Financing* (2023)
68. Singapore Urban Development Board: *Smart City Initiatives* (2023)
69. UAE Green Finance: *Sustainable Banking and Loans Framework* (2023)

Can Green Technologies, Renewable Energy Sources and Circular Economy for Sustainable Industry 5.0? An Explorative Study using Cross-Case Analysis

Jayanta Chakraborti, Sushil Kumar Maurya, and Sandeep Sharma

1 Introduction

The intersection of green technologies, renewable energy sources, and the circular economy is pivotal in the pursuit of Sustainable Industry 5.0 [7]. The evolution towards Industry 5.0 emphasizes not only technological advancement but also human-centric approaches that prioritize environmental sustainability and social equity [17].

J. Chakraborti (✉)
Global Institute of Business Studies, Bangalore, India
e-mail: jaychak072@gmail.com

S. K. Maurya
GNIOT MBA Institute Greater Noida, Greater Noida, India

S. Sharma
Swiss School of Applied Sciences for Economics and Management at Lausanne, Lausanne, Switzerland

© The Author(s), under exclusive license to Springer Nature Singapore Pte Ltd. 2025

P. Agarwal et al. (eds.), *Building a Human-Centred Infrastructure for Sustainable Industry 5.0 in Asia*,
https://doi.org/10.1007/978-981-95-0417-6_9

Green Technologies refer to "innovative processes, practices, and products that are environmentally sustainable [4]". These technologies aim to mitigate negative environmental impacts through efficient resource utilization, waste reduction, and pollution prevention. Examples include energy-efficient appliances, sustainable agricultural practices, and advanced waste management systems. Green technologies play a crucial role in mitigating climate change by reducing greenhouse gas emissions and promoting sustainable resource management [2].

Renewable Energy encompasses energy sources that are naturally replenished on a human timescale. This includes solar, wind, hydroelectric, geothermal, and biomass energy. In contrast to fossil fuels, which are finite and contribute significantly to environmental degradation, renewable energy sources provide clean alternatives that can substantially reduce carbon emissions. The transition to renewable energy is essential for achieving energy security and sustainability while addressing the critical challenges posed by climate change [10].

The Circular Economy is an economic model aimed at minimizing waste and optimizing resource utilization. It contrasts with the traditional linear economy, which follows a "take-make-dispose" pattern. In a circular economy, products are designed for longevity, reuse, refurbishment, and recycling. This approach not only conserves resources but also mitigates environmental impacts by closing the loop on product life cycles. By implementing a circular economy, industries can enhance resource efficiency and establish sustainable growth pathways [6].

Sustainable Industry 5.0 represents a paradigm shift in industrial practices that integrates advanced technologies with human-centric approaches to sustainability. This concept emphasizes the importance of balancing economic growth with ecological preservation and social equity. Industry 5.0 builds upon the foundations established by Industry 4.0—characterized by automation and data exchange in manufacturing technologies—by incorporating sustainability as a core principle [1].

The integration of green technologies and renewable energy into industrial processes is essential for achieving the objectives of Sustainable Industry 5.0. This approach not only enhances operational efficiency but also augments the resilience of industries against environmental fluctuations. Through the adoption of circular economy principles within this framework, industries can substantially reduce waste generation while optimizing resource utilization [14] .

As elucidated in recent studies, such as those conducted by Rajumesh [11], the implementation of human-centered infrastructure is crucial for realizing Sustainable Industry 5.0. This entails designing systems that prioritize the well-being of workers and communities while ensuring environmental sustainability. The research scholars posit that collaborative efforts among governments, industries, academia, and communities are indispensable for fostering innovation and establishing supportive policies that facilitate the transition to sustainable practices.

Several case studies demonstrate the successful application of green technologies and circular economy principles within various industries. Siemens AG has incorporated renewable energy sources into its manufacturing processes by utilizing wind turbines and solar panels at its facilities. This transition has not only reduced its carbon footprint but has also resulted in significant cost reductions in energy expenditures [18].

Unilever has implemented circular economy practices by designing products with sustainability as a primary consideration. Their initiatives encompass the utilization of recycled materials in packaging and the implementation of take-back programs to ensure that products are reused or recycled at the conclusion of their life cycle [8].

The outdoor apparel manufacturer Patagonia exemplifies a commitment to sustainability through its utilization of recycled materials and promotion of repairable products. Their business model emphasizes transparency and environmental stewardship while encouraging consumers to engage in sustainable practices [15]. These case studies provide valuable insights into how industries can effectively implement green technologies and circular economy principles to achieve Sustainable Industry 5.0.

In the Asian region, where industrial output drives nearly half of global manufacturing, the adoption of green technologies is accelerating. China, for instance, invests over $120 billion annually in clean energy solutions, leading the world in solar panel and electric vehicle production, which accounts for approximately 60% of global solar module supply.

India has also made significant strides through policies like the National Green Hydrogen Mission, targeting 5 million metric tonnes of green hydrogen production by 2030 to decarbonize heavy industries. These efforts highlight Asia's growing commitment to sustainable industrial practices, though barriers such as technological access and high implementation costs persist.

Renewable energy sources, including solar, wind, hydroelectric, geothermal, and biomass, offer viable alternatives to fossil fuels, which still dominate energy mixes in many Asian economies. With energy demand in Asia projected to rise by 50% by 2050, the shift to renewables is essential for energy security and carbon reduction. China boasts over 800 GW of renewable energy capacity as of 2024, driven by vast wind and solar installations, while India has achieved 45% of its power capacity from renewables, supported by initiatives like the PM Suryoday Yojana for rooftop solar adoption.

Notwithstanding the advancements made in comprehending the integration of green technologies, renewable energy sources, and circular economies within industrial frameworks, several research gaps persist. There exists a paucity of empirical studies examining the long-term impacts of implementing these strategies across diverse industrial contexts. While certain sectors have been extensively studied (e.g., manufacturing), others remain underexplored regarding their potential for adopting sustainable practices. Further research is necessitated on the systematic integration of human-centered design principles into infrastructure development for Sustainable Industry 5.0.

Conducting research on the integration of green technologies, renewable energy sources, and circular economies within sustainable Industry 5.0 is of paramount importance for several reasons. As climate change presents an existential threat to global ecosystems, elucidating how industries can mitigate their impacts is essential for fostering a sustainable future. Research can elucidate pathways for industries to achieve economic prosperity while concurrently reducing their environmental footprints. By prioritizing human-centered approaches within industrial development, research can contribute to social equity by ensuring that all stakeholders derive benefits from sustainable practices.

This research study aims to investigate how these elements can synergistically contribute to sustainable industrial practices, addressing the critical challenges posed by climate change and resource depletion. Advancing knowledge in this domain will provide valuable insights for policymakers, industry leaders, and researchers as they navigate the complexities of transitioning towards a more sustainable industrial landscape.

2 Literature Review

Contemporary literature underscores the pivotal role of green technologies in mitigating environmental impacts while augmenting operational efficiency. Renewable energy sources, including solar, wind, and bioenergy, are increasingly acknowledged for their potential to provide sustainable power alternatives, thereby reducing dependence on fossil fuels. The circular economy paradigm advocates resource efficiency and waste minimization through closed-loop systems, thus promoting sustainability in industrial processes.

Numerous studies highlight the obstacles to implementing these strategies, including substantial costs, insufficient awareness, policy inadequacies, and infrastructural limitations. Research suggests that addressing these challenges requires a comprehensive approach involving innovation, collaboration among stakeholders, and robust policy frameworks.

Initial research endeavors focused on defining green technologies and their potential impact on reducing environmental footprints. The seminal study by Yerram [19] investigated the factors driving the transition towards Sustainable Industry 5.0 through green manufacturing innovations. This research study emphasized the economic, environmental, and social impacts of sustainable industrial development. Utilizing a comprehensive analysis of existing literature on green manufacturing techniques and legislative frameworks, the study identified key drivers and obstacles influencing this transition. The research highlighted the substantial economic potential of Sustainable Industry 5.0 and underscored the necessity for robust regulatory frameworks, increased stakeholder engagement, and enhanced funding for research and development. It also noted limitations in data availability and generalizability.

Sulich [16] investigated the relationship between circular economy initiatives and Industry 5.0 within developed European nations. This study aimed to develop an econometric model to elucidate how circular economy activities influence advancements toward Industry 5.0. The research employed taxonomic methods and regression analysis. The data were collected from Eurostat indicators relevant to EU member states. The study reveals that circular economy principles are crucial for promoting green jobs and eco-innovation in conjunction with Industry 5.0 technologies.

Narula et al. [9] presented an interdisciplinary approach that integrated digital technologies with circular economy concepts in manufacturing industries under Industry 5.0. This research emphasized a human-centered design approach alongside technological advancements. The study utilized expert-based surveys of industry leaders combined with analytical hierarchical process techniques. The inference from the study was that digital technologies significantly enhance the implementation of circular economy practices in manufacturing, promoting sustainability through improved operational efficiencies.

Valette et al. [17] conducted a systematic literature review focusing on the human aspect within IoT-and CPS-based industrial systems as they transition from Industry 4.0 to Industry 5.0. The study identified a shift towards prioritizing human considerations in industrial research, emphasizing the importance of integrating societal aspects into technological advancements.

Dwivedi et al. [7] investigated interactions between Industry 5.0 and circular supply chains (CSC), advocating for a paradigm shift from linear to circular business models. A mixed-method approach was employed, utilizing modified Total Interpretive Structure Model (m-TISM) and Cross-Impact Matrix Multiplication Applied to Classification (MICMAC). The framework developed identified critical drivers for achieving synergy between I5.0 and CSC, highlighting management support and organizational readiness as key factors for successful implementation.

Rame et al. [12] examined the intersection of Industry 5.0 and sustainability within the context of global environmental challenges, emphasizing the collaboration between humans and machines. The research identified emerging trends that elucidate the potential of Industry 5.0 technologies to drive sustainability initiatives while balancing economic growth with environmental stewardship.

Atiku et al. [3] addressed socio-environmental challenges exacerbated by rapid industrialization, proposing eco-innovation as a pathway to sustainable development within Industry 5.0. The study advocated for a holistic approach that aligns economic growth with environmental sustainability, emphasizing the necessity for responsible business solutions.

Sharma and Gupta [14] investigated the integration of cleaner production practices with emerging technologies under Industry 5.0 in manufacturing firms within developing economies. Their research methodology employed Best Worst Method (BWM), Grey Decision-Making Trial and Evaluation Laboratory (Grey DEMATEL), and GRID Framework. The study identified key strategies, including the utilization of AI and IoT for optimization, which can potentially lead to sustainable competitive advantages while aligning with global sustainability objectives.

Shafique et al. [13] examined the impact of Industry 5.0 technological capabilities on circular economy practices within the Chinese manufacturing sector. Their research demonstrated that technological capabilities directly influence sustainable performance, with circular economy practices serving as mediators between these capabilities and sustainability outcomes.

Despite significant advancements in understanding the interplay between green technologies, renewable energy sources, and circular economy principles within Sustainable Industry 5.0, several research gaps persist. While existing studies highlight the role of green technologies and circular economy principles in promoting sustainability, there is a lack of comprehensive frameworks that integrate these elements effectively across diverse industrial contexts. Furthermore, the interplay between digital technologies and human-centered design in facilitating sustainable practices remains underexplored, necessitating further investigation into stakeholder engagement and regulatory frameworks to enhance implementation strategies. Addressing the research gaps will be essential for advancing knowledge and practice in this critical area. The research questions that have arisen from the identification of gaps are:

RQ1: How can green technologies and renewable energy sources be effectively integrated into industrial practices to promote sustainability?
RQ2: What role does the circular economy play in enhancing resource efficiency within Sustainable Industry 5.0?
RQ3: How can human-centered design principles be incorporated into infrastructure development to ensure environmental sustainability and social equity?

This research study will endeavor to answer the research questions through the following research objectives:

RO1: To analyze the impact of green technologies and renewable energy on sustainable industrial practices.
RO2: To evaluate the effectiveness of circular economy principles in resource management.

RO3: To explore the integration of human-centered design in developing sustainable infrastructures.

3 Research Methodology

This study adopts a cross-case analysis methodology to explore the integration of green technologies, renewable energy sources, and circular economy principles within Sustainable Industry 5.0, with a focus on diverse global and Asian industrial contexts [5]. The research focused on organizations demonstrating advanced implementation of Industry 5.0 principles and sustainability practices. The scope of the research was limited to global and Asian corporations across various industrial sectors.

The case studies of the following companies were selected for the research study: **Siemens Digital Industries Factory**, Amberg, Germany; **Interface Inc.**, Atlanta, Georgia; **Kalundborg Symbiosis**, Denmark; **Tesla Gigafactory**, Nevada, **Phillips Lighting (Signify),** Netherlands, **Tata Steel** in India, and **BYD** in China. The selection criteria matrix comprised of primary and secondary criteria. The primary criteria for the selection of the companies were Industry 5.0 implementation, adoption of green technologies, circular economy practices and sustainability integration. The secondary criteria used for the selection of the companies were geographic diversity and industry sector variety. Siemens, Signify and Kalundborg were chosen for their European representation while Tesla and Interface gave the North American representation. Siemens represented the manufacturing sector, Tesla represented automotive/energy, Kalundborg represented the industrial symbiosis of energy, processing, pharmaceutical, medical, and cleantech sectors, Interface represented the Consumer Goods and Signify represented the Lighting/Electronics Industry. Tata Steel and BYD were included to capture Asian advancements, with Tata Steel representing India's steel sector, which recycles 90% of its waste, and BYD showcasing China's electric vehicle industry, powered by 70% renewable energy. The companies selected for the research study demonstrated advanced automation and digitalization, human-centric manufacturing approaches, smart factory implementation, digital twin technology usage, AI and IoT integration. They also demonstrated circular economy practices, renewable energy adoption, waste reduction initiatives, green technology implementation and environmental impact reduction.

The selection process started by reviewing Fortune 500 companies and analyzing sustainability rankings. The companies who won industry awards were given preference. The academic literature on the companies were studied and expert opinion was taken to create the final list. The final list of companies and the selection criteria are given in Table 1.

The data was collected from company sustainability reports, academic publications, industry white papers, expert interviews and environmental impact assessments. The analysis was done by assessing environmental impact metrics, economic performance indicators, social impact measures, technology adoption levels, implementation challenges and measuring the

Table 1 Companies selected for conducting research and selection criteria

Sl No	*Company*	*Selected for*	*Represents*	*Strengths*	*Data availability*	*Innovation level*
1	Siemens digital industries	Advanced digital manufacturing implementation	European manufacturing sector	Digital transformation, automation	High	Leading
2	Tesla gigafactory	Sustainable manufacturing practices	North American energy sector	Vertical integration, renewable energy	Moderate	High
3	Kalundborg symbiosis	Industrial ecosystem approach	Collaborative industrial model	Resource sharing, circular economy	High	Pioneering
4	Interface Inc.	Circular economy leadership	Manufacturing/ consumer goods	Sustainability integration	High	Leading
5	Philips lighting (Signify)	Business model innovation	Electronics/ Lighting sector	Service-based sustainability	High	Advanced
6	Tata steel	Green steel production	Steel sector in India	Waste recycling and renewable energy	High	Advanced
7	BYD	Sustainable mobility solution	Automotive and energy sector in China	Battery recycling and renewable energy	High	Leading

success factors. The cross-case analysis was done by comparing implementation strategies across different industries, identifying common success factors and challenges, analyzing the role of technology in enabling sustainability and evaluating economic viability of different approaches.

4 Significant Findings

The cross-case analysis of sustainable practices across various industries reveals both commonalities and unique strategies in their approaches to implementing sustainability. Preliminary findings suggest that industries implementing green technologies report substantial reductions in carbon emissions and operational costs. Additionally, companies embracing circular economy principles demonstrate improved resource utilization and waste reduction. The significant findings are shown in the Word Cloud generated with MAXQDA software (Fig. 1).

A common thread across Siemens, Tesla, Interface, Kalundborg, Signify, Tata Steel, and BYD is the significant reduction in carbon emissions and operational costs achieved through green technologies, with firms reporting up to 30% energy savings. Each case also exhibited a phased implementation of digital technologies, ensuring that changes

Fig. 1 Word cloud generated with MAXQDA software

are manageable and effective. The integration of circular economy principles and a focus on human-centric manufacturing further underscores a long-term vision for sustainability.

However, key differences emerged in the specific strategies employed by each organization. For instance, Kalundborg adopted an ecosystem approach through industrial symbiosis, while Tesla emphasized vertical integration to enhance its supply chain. Signify transitioned to a service-based model, contrasting with Siemens, which focused on leveraging digital twin technology. Lastly, Interface prioritized biomimicry and nature-inspired design in its operations.

In terms of technology integration, all cases utilized advanced technologies such as IoT sensor networks, Artificial Intelligence and Machine Learning (AIML), and automated systems to enhance operational efficiency. The organizations implemented digital twin technology and real-time monitoring capabilities to optimize processes. Distinctive features highlight their individual technological advancements: Siemens integrated advanced PLC systems, Tesla innovated in battery technology, Signify developed connected lighting systems, Kalundborg focused on resource exchange networks, and Interface advanced material recycling technologies.

The analysis of sustainability metrics reveals shared achievements across the cases, including the use of 100% renewable energy and significant waste reduction exceeding 80%. All organizations also made strides in reducing their carbon footprints and conserving water while implementing circular economy practices. However, their focuses varied: Tesla concentrated on battery recycling and energy storage metrics; Kalundborg developed metrics around industrial symbiosis; Interface emphasized raw material sourcing; Signify utilized product-as-service metrics; and Siemens focused on production efficiency metrics.

The companies shared several human-centric approaches, such as workforce development programs and enhanced safety systems. They also prioritized ergonomic workplace designs and collaborative robotics to improve employee engagement. Different emphases were noted: Siemens implemented operator assistance systems, Tesla invested in advanced automation training, Signify fostered a service-oriented workforce, Interface engaged employees in sustainability initiatives, and Kalundborg promoted cross-company collaboration. Human-centric approaches, such as workforce training, are prevalent, with India's Tata Steel skilling

10,000 workers annually for sustainable operations and China's BYD implementing ergonomic designs in smart factories.

Common strategies for implementing the circular economy included waste reduction programs, material recycling initiatives, resource optimization efforts, product lifecycle management, and supply chain sustainability practices. Unique approaches distinguished each organization: Signify introduced a "Light as a Service" model; Interface launched the Net-Works program; Tesla established a battery recycling ecosystem; Kalundborg continued its industrial symbiosis efforts; and Siemens focused on digital waste tracking.

However, strategies diverge by context: Kalundborg's industrial symbiosis contrasts with Tesla's vertical integration, while Interface's biomimicry differs from Signify's service model. In Asia, Tata Steel's slag recycling recovers 1.5 million tonnes yearly, and BYD's battery recycling ecosystem achieves 95% material recovery, showcasing region-specific circular economy innovation. Technology integration varies, with Siemens leveraging PLC systems, BYD advancing battery technology, and Tata Steel using AI for predictive maintenance. Sustainability metrics show universal gains, like 100% renewable energy use, but focus areas differ: BYD emphasizes energy storage, Tata Steel prioritizes material efficiency, and Interface targets raw material sourcing. Challenges include high investment costs and supply chain complexities, with Asian firms like BYD addressing these through government subsidies and Tata Steel via public–private partnerships. Performance impacts include enhanced productivity and environmental benefits, with BYD leading China's electric vehicle market and Tata Steel reducing India's industrial emissions by 10%. Emerging trends point to increased AI integration and advanced recycling, with Asia's rapid adoption of smart manufacturing positioning it as a sustainability leader. These findings underscore the importance of tailoring Industry 5.0 strategies to regional contexts while balancing technology, sustainability, and human factors for transformative outcomes.

Despite their successes, these organizations faced common challenges such as initial investment costs, technology integration hurdles, workforce adaptation issues, supply chain transformations, and system complexities. Their solutions varied significantly: Kalundborg fostered collaborative partnerships; Tesla pursued vertical integration; Signify innovated its business model; Interface opted for incremental transformations, while Siemens concentrated on digital solutions.

The performance impacts of these strategies yielded shared benefits like reduced environmental impacts and enhanced productivity alongside cost savings. Distinct outcomes emerged from each case: Kalundborg realized ecosystem benefits; Tesla achieved market leadership in electric vehicles; Signify experienced growth in service revenue; Interface excelled in material innovation; and Siemens attained digital excellence.

Looking ahead, common trends indicate a push towards enhanced AI integration, expanded automation capabilities, improved sustainability metrics, advanced recycling technologies, and ongoing digital transformation efforts. Specific priorities include Tesla's focus on battery technology innovation, Signify's development of smart lighting solutions, Interface's exploration of biomaterials, Kalundborg's network expansion initiatives, and Siemens' advancements in digital twin technology.

This analysis highlights critical success factors, including the necessity of leadership commitment and strategic technology integration while emphasizing that employee engagement is vital for achieving measurable sustainability goals. It also points to emerging innovation patterns where technology facilitates sustainability efforts while circular economy principles drive innovation across sectors. As industries move towards Industry 5.0, the integration of human-centric approaches will expand alongside accelerated technology adoption and the normalization of circular economy practices.

This cross-case analysis illustrated that while diverse strategies exist for implementing sustainable practices within Industry 5.0 frameworks, common patterns emerge that underscore the importance of balancing technological advancements with sustainability objectives and human factors in achieving transformative outcomes across industries.

5 Discussion

Sustainable Industry 5.0 implementation strategies are crucial for organizations aiming to balance technological advancement with environmental stewardship. This approach emphasizes a comprehensive understanding of industry-specific challenges while fostering economic viability and long-term sustainability goals.

In manufacturing, global leaders like Siemens and Tesla demonstrate automation and renewable energy integration, mirrored in Asia by China's BYD and India's Tata Steel. BYD powers its electric vehicle production with 70% renewable energy, achieving a 25% reduction in lifecycle emissions, aligning with China's 2060 carbon neutrality goal. Tata Steel, leveraging green technologies like hydrogen-based smelting, has cut energy intensity by 20%, supporting India's 2070 net-zero target. These Asian examples highlight heavy investment in research and development, though high capital costs and technological scaling remain challenges.

In contrast, the chemical and industrial sectors, as demonstrated by the Kalundborg Symbiosis, adopted a network-based approach that emphasizes resource sharing and waste reduction. This collaborative ecosystem fosters long-term partnerships that enhance resource efficiency and minimize environmental impact. The focus on creating a symbiotic relationship among industries exemplifies how sustainability can be achieved through shared resources and collective innovation.

The consumer goods sector, represented by companies like Interface and Signify, highlights the importance of service-based business models and customer-centric approaches. These organizations prioritize product lifecycle management and material innovation, with a strong emphasis on the circular economy. By rethinking product design and end-of-life processes, they not only meet consumer demands but also contribute to sustainable practices.

Common success factors across these industries include a clear leadership vision, commitment to long-term sustainability goals, and measurable performance metrics. Engaging stakeholders is essential to foster an innovation-driven culture that supports sustainability initiatives. Operationally, a phased implementation approach combined with comprehensive employee training ensures that organizations can adapt to new technologies while maintaining efficiency.

However, implementing these strategies is not without challenges. Technical issues such as integrating legacy systems and managing data complexity must be addressed. Additionally, organizational resistance to change, skill gaps, and resource allocation pose significant hurdles. Financially, high initial investments and uncertainty regarding return on investment (ROI) can deter organizations from pursuing sustainable practices.

Technology plays a pivotal role in enabling sustainability within Industry 5.0. Digital technologies like the Internet of Things (IoT), artificial intelligence (AI), digital twins, blockchain, and cloud computing enhance operational efficiency while supporting environmental goals. These technologies facilitate real-time monitoring, optimize resource usage, improve waste management, and enable better maintenance scheduling.

Economic viability is another critical aspect of sustainable implementation strategies. The manufacturing sector often requires the highest capital investment but promises long-term ROI through efficiency gains. In contrast, the chemical industry may see medium-term returns via resource-sharing initiatives, while consumer goods companies can achieve shorter ROI cycles through innovative service models.

To ensure successful implementation of sustainable Industry 5.0 strategies, organizations should develop tailored approaches that consider their specific industry contexts. Key recommendations include establishing a clear sustainability roadmap with measurable targets, engaging stakeholders throughout the process, and focusing on pilot projects that can scale effectively. Resource management should prioritize circular approaches and efficient allocation to maximize sustainability efforts.

Looking ahead, emerging trends such as increased automation, enhanced connectivity, advanced materials, smart manufacturing, and sustainable design will shape the future of industry practices. As market demands for sustainability grow alongside stricter regulations and evolving consumer preferences, organizations must remain agile in their strategies to adapt to these changes effectively.

The successful implementation of Sustainable Industry 5.0 requires a balanced approach that integrates technology with sustainability objectives while addressing industry-specific challenges. By fostering an innovation-driven culture focused on long-term economic viability, organizations can thrive in an increasingly eco-conscious marketplace. The findings affirm that integrating green technologies with renewable energy sources fosters sustainability within industrial frameworks. Furthermore, adopting circular economy practices not only enhances efficiency but also promotes economic resilience amidst global challenges. The incorporation of human-centered design principles is essential for ensuring that infrastructure developments align with societal needs while maintaining ecological integrity.

6 Research Implications

This research underscores the necessity for policymakers to create supportive environments that facilitate the adoption of sustainable practices across industries. It also highlights the importance of collaborative efforts among governments, businesses, and communities to realize the full potential of Sustainable Industry 5.0.

The research study emphasizes the critical integration of these elements to foster a sustainable industrial framework. This approach is essential in addressing the pressing challenges posed by climate change, resource depletion, and the need for economic resilience.

Green technologies are pivotal in minimizing environmental impacts while enhancing operational efficiency. They encompass innovative processes and products designed to reduce negative environmental effects through efficient resource use and waste reduction. The adoption of such technologies can significantly mitigate climate change by lowering greenhouse gas emissions and promoting sustainable resource management. For instance, energy-efficient appliances, sustainable agricultural practices, and advanced waste management systems exemplify how green technologies can contribute to a more sustainable industrial landscape.

Renewable energy sources—such as solar, wind, hydroelectric, geothermal, and biomass—are crucial for transitioning away from fossil fuels. They provide clean alternatives that can substantially reduce carbon footprints and enhance energy security. The shift towards renewable energy is not merely an environmental necessity but also an economic opportunity, as it encourages job creation in emerging sectors and reduces dependency on finite resources. The integration of renewable energy into industrial processes can lead to significant cost savings and operational efficiencies.

The circular economy presents a transformative model that contrasts sharply with the traditional linear economy characterized by a "take-make-dispose" mentality. By focusing on minimizing waste and maximizing resource efficiency through closed-loop systems, the circular economy fosters sustainable growth pathways. This model encourages industries to design products for longevity, reuse, refurbishment, and recycling, thereby conserving resources and reducing environmental impacts. Implementing circular economy principles not only enhances resource efficiency but also drives innovation in product design and manufacturing processes.

Despite the clear benefits of integrating green technologies, renewable energy sources, and circular economy principles into Industry 5.0, several barriers hinder widespread adoption. These include high implementation costs, lack of awareness among stakeholders, insufficient policy frameworks, infrastructural limitations, technological constraints, and resistance from established industries. Addressing these challenges requires a comprehensive approach that encompasses financial incentives, robust policies, infrastructure investment, innovation promotion, and collaboration among various stakeholders.

A significant aspect of Sustainable Industry 5.0 is the emphasis on human-centered infrastructure that prioritizes worker well-being and community engagement. This approach integrates human-centric design principles—such as accessibility, inclusivity, and safety—into infrastructure development. By ensuring that industrial advancements consider the social implications alongside environmental sustainability, industries can foster a more equitable future.

Successful implementation of these concepts necessitates collaboration among governments, industries, academia, and communities. Case studies from various sectors illustrate how collaborative efforts can lead to innovative solutions that drive sustainability. For example, companies like Siemens AG have successfully integrated renewable energy sources into their manufacturing processes, resulting in reduced carbon footprints and cost savings.

The implications of this research extend beyond theoretical understanding; they provide actionable insights for policymakers and industry leaders. By identifying pathways for sustainable practices that align economic growth with ecological preservation and social equity, this research contributes to a broader understanding of how industries can thrive in an environmentally conscious manner.

The integration of green technologies, renewable energy sources, and circular economy principles is not just beneficial but essential for achieving Sustainable Industry 5.0. Continued research in this area will be vital for developing strategies that effectively address the challenges posed by climate change while promoting economic resilience and social equity across diverse industrial contexts.

7 Conclusion, Limitations and Directions for Future Studies

The research emphasizes the pivotal role of green technologies, renewable energy, and circular economy principles in achieving a sustainable industrial future. These elements form the cornerstone of Sustainable Industry 5.0, addressing critical challenges such as climate change, resource depletion, and economic resilience. Green technologies mitigate environmental impacts while improving operational efficiency and cost management, offering industries a competitive edge in eco-conscious markets. Renewable energy sources like solar and wind reduce carbon footprints, foster innovation, and create green jobs. The circular economy complements these efforts by minimizing waste and promoting resource efficiency through closed-loop systems. Human-centered infrastructure, prioritizing worker well-being and community engagement, is equally crucial in creating inclusive and equitable industrial development. Despite evident benefits, challenges such as high initial costs, inadequate awareness, policy gaps, and infrastructural limitations hinder implementation. The research concludes that a holistic, collaborative, and innovation-driven approach is necessary for industries to transition towards sustainability while balancing ecological preservation, economic growth, and social equity.

This study acknowledges several limitations. First, its focus on specific case studies limits generalizability across industries and regions with diverse economic, cultural, and regulatory contexts. Second, the absence of longitudinal studies constrains understanding of the long-term impacts of sustainable practices. Third, there is a lack of empirical evidence to substantiate the effectiveness of these strategies in diverse settings, which could help convince stakeholders to adopt them. Fourth, while human-centered infrastructure is emphasized, the research lacks detailed exploration of methodologies to integrate these principles into existing industrial frameworks systematically. Lastly, the barriers to adopting sustainable practices, such as high costs and insufficient policies, are identified but not deeply analyzed to propose actionable solutions.

Future research should address these limitations by adopting several approaches. Longitudinal studies are necessary to track the long-term impacts of sustainability practices on environmental and economic outcomes. Comparative research across regions and industries can reveal tailored strategies suited to specific local contexts, considering regulatory, cultural, and economic differences. Additionally, exploring emerging technologies such as artificial intelligence, blockchain, and advanced manufacturing can provide innovative tools for implementing sustainable practices. Developing comprehensive policy frameworks is crucial to incentivize investment in sustainable infrastructure and eco-friendly practices. Future studies should also focus on designing effective stakeholder engagement models that foster collaboration among governments, businesses, communities, and academia to drive innovation and resource sharing. Lastly, human-centric approaches need further exploration to create inclusive systems prioritizing social equity alongside environmental sustainability. By addressing these directions, researchers can provide actionable insights for industries and policymakers to navigate the complexities of sustainability transitions.

Annexure—i: Detailed Case Studies of Five Companies

Siemens Digital Industries Factory, Amberg, Germany

The Siemens Electronic Works facility in Amberg, established in 1989, has become a leading example of digital manufacturing and sustainability, primarily focusing on the production of Simatic programmable logic controllers (PLCs). Spanning 104,000 square meters, the facility manufactures over 1,200 product variants and assembles approximately 17 million components daily. A significant portion of the production process is automated, with 75% of the value chain relying on the integration of more than 1,000 PLCs. This smart manufacturing approach utilizes digital twin technology and virtual modeling to optimize operations. Siemens AG, recognized as a global technology leader, integrates advanced technologies into industrial processes to enhance operational efficiency across various sectors.

Siemens employs cutting-edge technologies such as artificial intelligence (AI), machine learning, and quality control automation to create sustainable solutions tailored to modern industrial demands. One key area of focus is predictive maintenance systems that leverage real-time data analytics to anticipate equipment failures, allowing organizations to optimize maintenance schedules and resource allocation. This proactive maintenance strategy reduces downtime and costs while extending the lifespan of critical assets. Furthermore, Siemens emphasizes quality control automation through intelligent monitoring systems that ensure products meet high standards while optimizing production scheduling.

Sustainability is a cornerstone of Siemens' strategy, with a goal of achieving 100% renewable energy usage through initiatives like on-site solar installations and wind energy contracts. The company is also pioneering smart grid integration and energy storage systems to enhance energy distribution efficiency. By implementing AI-driven energy optimization techniques, Siemens has successfully reduced energy consumption by up to 30%. Additionally, smart building management systems utilizing Internet of Things (IoT) technology help optimize energy usage within buildings.

In line with its sustainability objectives, Siemens promotes resource efficiency through innovative practices such as closed-loop water systems and material recycling programs. The company's commitment to waste reduction is reflected in its precise manufacturing techniques that minimize excess material usage. Digital tracking of material consumption provides actionable insights that support efficient resource allocation throughout the production cycle.

Siemens Technology Works exemplifies how advanced technologies can transform industries by enhancing operational efficiency and promoting sustainability. As part of the Industry 5.0 revolution, Siemens emphasizes a human-centric approach that integrates advanced technology while prioritizing worker well-being and productivity. Collaborative robots (cobots) are employed alongside human workers to enhance productivity and reduce physical strain. Advanced operator assistance systems and ergonomic workstation designs further support this initiative.

Siemens has achieved significant milestones in sustainability integration, reaching carbon–neutral operations by 2020 and adhering to circular economy principles that emphasize zero-waste initiatives and biodiversity programs. These efforts have led to a remarkable reduction in CO_2 emissions by 70% since 2015 and an 80% reduction in waste.

Despite its successes, Siemens faces challenges typical of technological advancement, including high initial investment costs and workforce resistance to new technologies. These challenges are addressed through phased implementation strategies with clear return on investment metrics and comprehensive training programs for employees.

Looking ahead, Siemens plans to expand its initiatives by further integrating AI into quality control processes and enhancing circular economy programs. Areas for future research include quantum computing applications, advanced materials recycling, bio-based manufacturing materials, and improved energy storage solutions. Overall, Siemens Technology Works serves as a blueprint for sustainable Industry 5.0 implementation, showcasing how digital transformation can be achieved while maintaining a strong focus on human factors and environmental sustainability.

Interface Inc. (Carpet Manufacturing)

Interface Inc., a global leader in modular carpet manufacturing, has established itself as a pioneer in implementing circular economy principles through innovative practices and a strong commitment to sustainability. Founded in 1973 by Ray Anderson, the company has transformed its operations over the decades, focusing on minimizing environmental impact and promoting resource efficiency. In 1994, Interface launched its Mission Zero program, which aimed for zero environmental impact by 2020. This initiative has been instrumental in achieving a remarkable 96% reduction in carbon emissions, underscoring the company's dedication to sustainability goals. A key component of this program is the ReEntry® recycling initiative, which facilitates the collection and reuse of old carpet materials, effectively reducing landfill waste and conserving resources. By 2023, Interface had collected over 31,750 tonnes of post-consumer carpet tiles, significantly advancing its circular economy efforts.

To enhance its manufacturing processes, Interface has embraced Industry 5.0 technologies. These advancements include the use of advanced robotics for efficient carpet tile production, AI-powered material sorting systems that optimize resource use, blockchain tracking to ensure material provenance, and smart factory systems designed with a human-centric approach. Such technological integration not only streamlines production but also contributes to a more sustainable operational model.

Interface's commitment to circular economy principles is further evidenced through various initiatives. The Net-Works program collects discarded fishing nets for recycling into ECONYL yarn, which is then used in carpet production. Additionally, the Random Design process has successfully reduced waste by 80%. The company has also implemented biomimicry-inspired product designs that draw inspiration from nature to enhance sustainability and operates a closed-loop manufacturing system that ensures continuous reuse and recycling of materials. As of 2023, Interface reports that 48% of raw materials used are from recycled or bio-based sources, and it operates on 99% renewable energy, showcasing significant strides toward sustainability.

The measurable impacts of Interface's sustainability efforts are substantial, including a 93% reduction in water consumption and a 56% reduction in waste sent to landfills. These achievements underscore the effectiveness of Interface's strategies in promoting environmental stewardship while maintaining operational efficiency.

Recognizing the importance of the human element in its operations, Interface emphasizes worker empowerment through technology, enabling employees to leverage advanced tools for enhanced productivity. The company also invests in comprehensive skill development programs that prepare workers for evolving industry demands and implements collaborative robotics to enhance workplace safety and efficiency. This focus on human–machine collaboration reflects a holistic approach to sustainability that aligns with Industry 5.0 principles prioritizing human welfare alongside technological advancement.

Overall, Interface Inc.'s transformation represents a comprehensive implementation of circular economy principles integrated with cutting-edge technologies. Through its Mission Zero program and various sustainability initiatives, Interface not only reduces its environmental impact but also sets a benchmark for other companies aiming for similar goals. With clear metrics on waste reduction and carbon footprint, Interface exemplifies how businesses can thrive while prioritizing ecological responsibility. Its journey over the past 25 years serves as an excellent documentation of successful sustainability practices that others can emulate in their quest for a more sustainable future.

Kalundborg Symbiosis, Denmark

The Kalundborg Symbiosis in Denmark is recognized as the world's first industrial symbiosis network, exemplifying the principles of a circular economy through the integration of smart technologies for resource optimization. This innovative collaboration, established in 1972, involves multiple industries—including a power plant, pharmaceutical companies, and a plasterboard manufacturer—working together to optimize resource use and reduce waste. The extensive data available on resource savings and environmental impact illustrates how this model can enhance existing sustainable practices, particularly as it transitions from Industry 4.0 to Industry 5.0.

Kalundborg Symbiosis operates as a pioneering model where private and public companies collaborate to maximize resource efficiency and sustainability. The network consists of eight core companies, including major players such as Novo Nordisk, Novozymes, and Ørsted's Asnæs Power Station. This partnership embodies a circular economy approach by transforming the by-products of one entity into resources for another, yielding significant environmental benefits and economic efficiencies.

The structural backbone of Kalundborg Symbiosis comprises interconnected facilities that facilitate effective resource exchanges. For instance, steam and hot water are circulated between facilities, biological sludge from wastewater treatment is converted into fertilizer, fly ash from the power station is repurposed in cement production, and surplus yeast from insulin production is utilized as animal feed. These exchanges not only minimize waste but also enhance resource efficiency across the network.

The diverse resource exchanges at Kalundborg include the circulation of steam and hot water for energy efficiency, conversion of biological sludge into fertilizer, utilization of fly ash in cement production to reduce landfill waste, and repurposing surplus yeast as animal feed. Collectively, these initiatives contribute to an impressive resource recovery rate of 98%, showcasing the effectiveness of the circular economy model in practice.

Moreover, Kalundborg Symbiosis integrates modern technology to further enhance its operations. Key elements include smart grid systems that monitor energy flows for optimal distribution, AI-powered optimization for streamlining resource exchanges, real-time monitoring with IoT sensors to facilitate quick adjustments, and digital twin technology for process optimization through digital simulations. These innovations highlight a commitment to incorporating digital solutions within the framework of Industry 5.0.The environmental impact of Kalundborg Symbiosis is substantial. Recent data indicates an annual reduction of approximately 635,000 tons of CO2 emissions, conservation of about 3.6 million cubic meters of water, and a decrease of around 87,000 tons of waste each year. These achievements underscore the effectiveness of industrial symbiosis in mitigating environmental impacts while promoting sustainable business practices. In summary, Kalundborg Symbiosis serves as a powerful example of how collaboration between public and private sectors can achieve sustainability goals. By transforming waste into resources and integrating advanced technologies, this model not only enhances economic resilience but also significantly reduces environmental footprints. As industries globally seek sustainable solutions, Kalundborg provides a blueprint for successful industrial symbiosis that can inspire similar initiatives worldwide.

Tesla Gigafactory, Nevada

Tesla's Gigafactory Nevada, also known as Gigafactory 1, is a landmark facility in sustainable manufacturing and renewable energy. Established in 2014 and operational since 2016, it is located in Sparks, Nevada, and aims to revolutionize battery production while adhering to sustainability principles.

Gigafactory Nevada spans approximately 5.3 million square feet, with plans to expand to 10 million square feet. The factory represents a substantial investment of over $6.2 billion and employs more than 7,000 individuals. It has the capacity to produce batteries for around 500,000 electric vehicles annually, making it one of the largest manufacturing facilities globally.

A key feature of the Gigafactory is its dedication to renewable energy. The facility operates entirely on renewable sources, including a 70 MW solar array and on-site energy storage systems that enhance reliability. It incorporates a zero net energy concept and smart microgrid technology to optimize energy use. Additionally, a closed-loop water recycling system ensures minimal waste, with rainwater harvesting techniques contributing to water efficiency.

The Gigafactory exemplifies vertical integration by managing all stages of battery production—from raw material processing to cell production and assembly. This approach streamlines operations and improves quality control. Advanced technologies such as automated guided vehicles (AGVs) optimize logistics, while AI and machine learning enhance process efficiency through real-time monitoring systems.

Tesla prioritizes worker safety and ergonomics at the Gigafactory. Collaborative robotics assist human workers, while advanced safety protocols ensure a safe working environment. Real-time feedback systems empower workers to adjust processes dynamically, boosting productivity.

Sustainable operations are central to the Gigafactory's resource management strategies. A comprehensive battery recycling program aligns with circular economy principles by recovering valuable materials from used batteries. Material recovery systems minimize waste throughout production cycles, complemented by supply chain optimization strategies.

The Gigafactory has achieved impressive performance metrics, including an annual battery production capacity of 20 GWh, a 30% reduction in battery costs, and a 50% improvement in production speed. It operates with zero direct emissions and an 80% water recycling rate, committing fully to renewable energy usage.

Significant innovations have emerged from the Gigafactory, particularly in battery technology. New cell chemistries have improved energy density and extended battery life while reducing production costs. Automated assembly techniques and enhanced quality control measures have streamlined operations further.

Despite its successes, the Gigafactory has faced challenges such as scaling up operations, supply chain issues related to raw material sourcing, and skilled labor shortages. Tesla has addressed these through phased expansion strategies, vertical integration practices, local sourcing initiatives, and training programs in collaboration with educational institutions.

Looking ahead, Tesla plans to expand the Gigafactory's capabilities by adding new production lines and recycling facilities to meet increasing demand for electric vehicle batteries. Research and development will continue focusing on new battery chemistries and advanced manufacturing processes aimed at enhancing efficiency and sustainability.

Tesla's Gigafactory Nevada stands as a pioneering model for sustainable manufacturing within the electric vehicle sector. By integrating renewable energy with advanced manufacturing techniques and adhering to circular economy principles, it not only supports Tesla's mission but also sets a precedent for future manufacturing endeavors globally. The facility highlights that strong vision combined with sustainability practices is crucial for long-term success in the industry.

Phillips Lighting (Signify)

Signify, previously known as Philips Lighting, has undergone a transformative shift from traditional manufacturing to a sustainable, service-oriented business model since its rebranding in 2018. This transformation is characterized by innovative concepts such as "Light as a Service" (LaaS), the adoption of circular economy principles, integration of smart manufacturing technologies, and a commitment to renewable energy.

At the heart of Signify's transformation is the Light as a Service (LaaS) model, which aligns with circular economy principles. Instead of selling lighting products outright, Signify offers customers the option to pay for lighting services based on usage. This pay-per-lux model not only reduces upfront costs for clients but also allows Signify to maintain ownership of the lighting systems, facilitating responsible end-of-life management through recycling and refurbishment. The service package includes maintenance and upgrades, ensuring continuous improvement without additional costs for customers. Sustainable product design is emphasized through modular designs that extend product lifespans and utilize recyclable materials, contributing to reduced energy consumption and environmental impact.

Signify has embraced smart manufacturing by incorporating Internet of Things (IoT) technologies and real-time monitoring systems. These advancements enable predictive maintenance and more efficient resource management. The introduction of 3D printing and advanced automation has streamlined production processes while minimizing waste. A robust digital infrastructure supports these innovations, enhancing collaboration and operational efficiency across various functions. AI-powered quality control systems ensure high standards throughout production.

The company's commitment to sustainability has led to significant achievements, including achieving carbon neutrality in its operations by 2020 and utilizing 100% renewable electricity. Additionally, Signify has diverted 85% of its waste from landfills, reinforcing its dedication to circular economy initiatives.

Signify's approach aligns with Industry 5.0 principles by focusing on human-centric innovation. The integration of collaborative robotics and enhanced safety measures improves workplace conditions and productivity. Skill development programs and ergonomic designs promote employee engagement and well-being, fostering an inclusive work environment.

Several projects highlight Signify's innovative spirit and sustainability commitment. The Brainport Industries Campus in Eindhoven features smart lighting systems that optimize energy use through advanced technologies like occupancy sensing. The Dubai Lamp Initiative aims to develop energy-efficient LED solutions tailored for local manufacturing needs, reducing overall energy consumption while extending product lifetimes.

The impact of Signify's transformation is reflected in its performance metrics; in 2022, the company reported revenues of 6.7 billion EUR, with a significant portion from connected lighting solutions. Notably, 84% of its revenues stemmed from sustainable products, demonstrating the effectiveness of its innovative business model.

Despite its successes, Signify encountered challenges during its transition from a product-centric to a service-oriented model. Customer education was essential for acceptance of the new approach, while integrating legacy systems with new technologies required a phased digital transformation strategy to avoid disruptions.

Looking ahead, Signify plans to enhance its offerings by expanding circular economy programs and advancing connected lighting solutions. Research into smart city integration and biodegradable components will keep the company at the forefront of sustainable innovation in the lighting industry.

Signify's transformation exemplifies how traditional industries can innovate their business models through sustainability and technology integration. By adopting circular economy principles and embracing Industry 5.0 concepts, Signify enhances operational efficiency while setting a benchmark for other companies aiming for sustainability. Its journey illustrates how strategic vision, strong leadership commitment, and stakeholder engagement can drive significant change within an industry striving for sustainability.

Tata Steel, India

Tata Steel, one of India's largest steel manufacturers, has emerged as a leader in sustainable industrial practices, aligning with Industry 5.0 principles through its integration of green technologies, renewable energy, and circular economy strategies. Established in 1907, the company operates major facilities in Jamshedpur and Kalinganagar, producing over 20 million tonnes of steel annually. Employing approximately 75,000 workers, Tata Steel has invested heavily in sustainability, with a $1 billion commitment to green initiatives by 2030.

The company leverages advanced technologies like AI-driven predictive maintenance and digital twins to optimize production, reducing energy intensity by 20% over the past decade. Its adoption of green technologies includes hydrogen-based steelmaking pilots, which have cut CO2 emissions by 15% in trial phases, and waste heat recovery systems that generate 10% of its energy needs. Renewable energy plays a growing role, with 200 MW of solar and wind capacity installed across its plants, contributing to 25% of its energy mix by 2024.

Tata Steel's circular economy efforts are exemplified by its slag recycling program, recovering 1.5 million tonnes annually for use in cement and road construction, achieving a 90% waste recycling rate. The company prioritizes human-centric design through ergonomic workstations and extensive skill development, training 10,000 workers yearly to operate sustainable technologies. Sustainability metrics include a 30% reduction in water consumption and a 10% decrease in overall emissions since 2015, aligning with India's net-zero goal by 2070.

Challenges include high capital costs for green transitions and regulatory complexities, addressed through public–private partnerships and government subsidies. Tata Steel's innovations, such as carbon capture utilization and storage trials, position it as a pioneer in decarbonizing heavy industry. Looking ahead, the company plans to scale hydrogen production and expand renewable energy to 50% of its mix by 2035, with research focused on biocomposites and low-carbon alloys. Tata Steel's journey illustrates how traditional industries can embrace Sustainable Industry 5.0, balancing economic growth with environmental and social imperatives in a high-growth market like India.

BYD, China

BYD (Build Your Dreams), a leading Chinese electric vehicle and battery manufacturer, exemplifies Sustainable Industry 5.0 through its integration of renewable energy, green technologies, and circular economy principles. Founded in 1995, BYD operates major facilities in Shenzhen and Xi'an, producing over 1.5 million vehicles annually and employing 400,000 workers. With a $10 billion investment in sustainability by 2025, BYD powers 70% of its production with renewable energy, primarily solar and wind, supported by a 500 MW on-site solar array.

Advanced technologies, including AI for battery optimization and IoT for real-time monitoring, enhance efficiency, reducing production energy use by 25%. BYD's green technology innovations include high-density battery chemistries that extend vehicle range by 20% and modular designs for easy repair, aligning with circular economy goals. Its battery recycling ecosystem recovers 95% of materials from used batteries, diverting 100,000 tonnes from landfills yearly.

Human-centric approaches include collaborative robotics and ergonomic factory designs, with 50,000 workers trained annually for smart manufacturing roles, supporting China's 2060 carbon neutrality target. Sustainability achievements include zero direct emissions in key plants and an 80% water recycling rate.

Challenges like raw material supply chain volatility are mitigated through vertical integration and local sourcing, while government green subsidies ease financial burdens. BYD's innovations, such as blade battery technology, have lowered costs by 15%, strengthening its global market leadership. Future plans involve expanding recycling facilities and integrating smart grid systems, with research into solid-state batteries and vehicle-to-grid solutions. BYD's model demonstrates how Asia's industrial giants can lead in Sustainable Industry 5.0, leveraging technology and policy support to drive environmental and economic resilience.

References

1. Aheleroff, S., Huang, H., Xu, X., & Zhong, R. Y. (2022). Toward sustainability and resilience with Industry 4.0 and Industry 5.0. *Frontiers in Manufacturing Technology*, *2*, 951643.
2. Alestra, C., Cette, G., Chouard, V., & Lecat, R. (2024). How can technology significantly contribute to climate change mitigation? *Applied Economics*, *56*(41), 4925-4937.
3. Atiku, S. O., Jeremiah, A., Semente, E., & Boateng, F. (Eds.). (2024). Eco-Innovation and Sustainable Development in Industry 5.0. *IGI Global*.
4. Barbieri, N., Marzucchi, A., & Rizzo, U. (2023). Green technologies, interdependencies, and policy. *Journal of Environmental Economics and Management*, 118, 102791.
5. Borman, K. M., Clarke, C., Cotner, B., & Lee, R. (2012). Cross-case analysis. In Handbook of complementary methods in education research (pp. 123–139). Routledge.
6. Castro, C. G., Trevisan, A. H., Pigosso, D. C., & Mascarenhas, J. (2022). The rebound effect of circular economy: Definitions, mechanisms and a research agenda. *Journal of Cleaner Production*, *345*, 131136.
7. Dwivedi, A., Agrawal, D., Jha, A., & Mathiyazhagan, K. (2023). Studying the interactions among Industry 5.0 and circular supply chain: Towards attaining sustainable development. *Computers & Industrial Engineering*, 176, 108927.
8. Iglesias, O., Mingione, M., Ind, N., & Markovic, S. (2023). How to build a conscientious corporate brand together with business partners: A case study of Unilever. *Industrial Marketing Management*, *109*, 1-13.
9. Narula, S., Tamvada, J. P., Kumar, A., Puppala, H., & Gupta, N. (2023). Putting digital technologies at the forefront of Industry 5.0 for the implementation of a circular economy in manufacturing industries. *IEEE Transactions on Engineering Management*.
10. Østergaard, P. A., Duic, N., Noorollahi, Y., & Kalogirou, S. (2022). Renewable energy for sustainable development. *Renewable Energy*, *199*, 1145-1152.

11. Rajumesh, S. (2024). Promoting sustainable and human-centric industry 5.0: a thematic analysis of emerging research topics and opportunities. *Journal of Business and Socio-economic Development*, *4*(2), 111–126.
12. Rame, R., Purwanto, P., & Sudarno, S. (2024). Industry 5.0 and sustainability: An overview of emerging trends and challenges for a green future. *Innovation and Green Development*, 3(4), 100173.
13. Shafique, M. N., Adeel, U., & Rashid, A. (2024). The Synergy Between Industry 5.0 and Circular Economy for Sustainable Performance in the Chinese Manufacturing Industry. *Sustainability*, 16(22), 9952.
14. Sharma, R., & Gupta, H. (2024). Harmonizing sustainability in industry 5.0 era: Transformative strategies for cleaner production and sustainable competitive advantage. *Journal of Cleaner Production*, *445*, 141118.
15. Shourkaei, M. M., Taylor, K.M. & Dyck, B. (2023). Examining sustainable supply chain management via a social-symbolic work lens: Lessons from Patagonia. *Business Strategy and the Environment*. Volume 33, Issue 2. https://doi.org/10.1002/bse.3552
16. Sulich, A. (2023). Model of Relationship Between Circular Economy and Industry 5.0. In IFIP International Workshop on Artificial Intelligence for Knowledge Management (pp. 220–236). Cham: *Springer Nature Switzerland.*
17. Valette, E., El-Haouzi, H. B., & Demesure, G. (2023). Industry 5.0 and its technologies: A systematic literature review upon the human place into IoT-and CPS-based industrial systems. *Computers & Industrial Engineering*, 184, 109426.
18. Yang, Y., Brosch, G., Yang, B., & Cadden, T. (2020). Dissemination and communication of lessons learned for a project-based business with the application of information technology: a case study with Siemens. *Production Planning & Control*, *31*(4), 273-286.
19. Yerram, S. R. (2021). Driving the Shift to Sustainable Industry 5.0 with Green Manufacturing Innovations. *Asia Pacific Journal of Energy and Environment*, *8*(2), 55–66.

Green Accounting and its Role in Industry 5.0 Sustainability Framework

Garima Agarwal

1 Introduction to Green Accounting

In the coeval landscape of economic development, environmental debasement has emerged as a pressure refer that demands a paradigm transfer in accounting practices. Traditional accounting, which predominantly focuses on commercial enterprise and economic dimensions, often neglects the intricate interplay between worldly activities and their environmental consequences. In response, the concept of "Green Accounting" has gained prominence as a vital tool for aligning economic increase with sustainable development goals [11].

1.1 Definition and Scope

Green Accounting, also known as situation accounting or sustainable accounting, is an innovative model that seeks to bridge the gap between worldly activities and their environmental impacts. The traditional notion of Gross Domestic Product (GDP) as a sole measure of worldly progress

G. Agarwal (✉)
ACED, Amity University Uttar Pradesh, Noida, India
e-mail: enterpreneurdr@gmail.com

© The Author(s), under exclusive license to Springer Nature Singapore Pte Ltd. 2025

P. Agarwal et al. (eds.), *Building a Human-Centred Infrastructure for Sustainable Industry 5.0 in Asia*,
https://doi.org/10.1007/978-981-95-0417-6_10

falls short in addressing the environmental costs incurred during production and consumption. [15] Green Accounting recognizes the need to incorporate environmental considerations into the method of accounting systems, providing a comprehensive understanding of the true undefined benefits of economic activities [27].

The earmark of Green Accounting lies in its desegregation of environmental factors alongside traditional financial metrics. It aims to quantify and attribute environmental impacts such as resource depletion, pollution, and carbon paper emissions to economic activities [8].

I. **Valuation of Natural Resources**: Putting Green Accounting acknowledges the finite nature of natural resources and endeavours to assign economic values to them. This valuation aids in comprehending the trade-offs between resource exploitation and conservation [2].

II. **Lifecycle Perspective**: Unlike the conventional method of accounting that preponderantly focuses on production and consumption stages, Green Accounting adopts a lifecycle perspective. It evaluates the environmental impacts across the entire lifecycle of products or services, encompassing extraction, production, distribution, use, and disposal phases [1].

III. **Monetary and Physical Units**: The method of green accounting employs both monetary and natural science units for measurement. While monetary units help worldly comparisons, physical unit's volunteer insights into the quantitative undefined of environmental degradation.

IV. **Policy Informing Tool**: It serves as a powerful tool for policy formulation and decision-making by offering a comprehensive understanding of the environmental consequences of various choices. Green Accounting aids policymakers in designing operational strategies for property development [28].

The scope of Green Accounting is undefined and multifaceted, spanning various dimensions of worldly and situational interactions:

I. **Corporate Level:** Within the corporate sector, Green Accounting enables companies to assess the state of affairs and performance of their operations. It assists in identifying areas for improvement, optimizing imagination utilization, and integrating sustainability into business strategies [6].

II. **National Level:** On a national scale, Green Accounting contributes to assessing a nation's progress in a holistic manner. By incorporating environmental indicators, countries can evaluate their worldly undefined vis-à-vis environmental preservation [27].

III. **Policy Development**: Green Accounting provides worthy insights for the preparation of policies that promote sustainable development. Governments can design regulations and incentives that advance industries to internalize environmental costs [9].

IV. **International Comparisons**: Through standardized frameworks and indicators, Green Accounting facilitates international comparisons of environmental performance. This supports global efforts to turn to Trans-boundary environmental challenges [12].

V. **Education and Awareness**: Green Accounting enhances public awareness by elucidating the environmental implications of everyday choices. It empowers individuals to make educated decisions that contribute to a more sustainable future [10].

1.2 Importance in Sustainability

Sustainability is important in green accounting because it bridges the gap between economic growth, environmental protection, and social equality. Green accounting, often known as environmental accounting, incorporates environmental considerations into regular financial accounting and decision-making procedures. Several significant aspects illustrate the significance of sustainability in green accounting, including:

i. **Reflects True Economic Cost:** Traditional accounting frequently fails to account for environmental costs (such as pollution, resource depletion, and biodiversity loss). Green accounting accounts for these externalities, resulting in a more accurate portrayal of a company's or nation's genuine economic performance [11].

ii. **Promotes Long-term Value Creation:** Companies that use green accounting procedures acknowledge the value of natural resources and the advantages of preserving environmental capital for future generations [2].

iii. **Encourages Responsible Resource Management:** Companies are encouraged to track and control their energy, water, and raw material use in order to decrease waste and minimize environmental impact. Sustainable practices are incorporated into a company's financial reports [18].

iv. **Enhances Regulatory Compliance and Risk Management:** Companies that embrace sustainable practices early might avoid regulatory penalties and lessen the risk of noncompliance (ISO 14001:2015).

v. **Supports Stakeholder Transparency:** Companies that publicly disclose their environmental footprint and sustainability activities may attract more customers, investors, and workers that value corporate social responsibility (CSR) [1].

vi. **Encourages Innovation:** Businesses are driven to invest in technology that reduce resource use, enhance efficiency, or reduce emissions by recognizing environmental costs and opportunities, resulting in new avenues for competitive advantage and growth [19].

vii. **Attracts Green Investments:** Green accounting positions businesses to attract such investments by demonstrating a commitment to environmental stewardship and long-term viability [21].

1.3 Environmental Costing and Benefits

Environmental Costing and its benefits, helps in integrating environmental factors into consideration at the time of financial decision making. Environmental costing meant to Identifying, Measuring and accounting of environmental costs.

Environmental cost generally represents the cost associated with the company's environmental impact, which largely includes Direct cost in the nature of Waste Management, Raw material resources, Energy Consumption cost, Pollution Control related cost, Emissions and Carbon Taxes associated cost [7].

Besides the above direct cost, it includes Indirect costs in the nature of Environmental Damage costs (deforestation, long term pollution impacts), reputation cost, Health and Hygiene cost, Regulatory compliance costs, and foregone opportunity Costs [15].

Environmental benefits are the positive effects of sustainable activities that can improve financial performance and societal well-being. Green accounting quantifies and integrates these advantages into decision-making to emphasize the worth of environmentally friendly measures.

Types of Environmental Benefits:

i. **Cost Savings**: Companies that implement green technologies and practices can typically generate long-term cost advantages, such as energy savings, reduced waste disposal expenses, and lower water usage [22].
ii. **Improved Market Competitiveness**: Sustainable enterprises frequently get a competitive advantage by differentiating themselves in the market. Benefits may include recruiting customers who choose eco-friendly products, building brand loyalty, and having access to green funds or incentives [2].
iii. **Regulatory and Legal Benefits**: Adherence to environmental standards can lower the danger of legal penalties while also increasing compliance. Companies that invest in sustainability might prevent future costs associated with environmental infractions, including fines and punishments, as well as insurance premiums [14].
iv. **Intangible Benefits**: Green accounting also helps to recognize intangible benefits, such as improved public relations, increased staff morale and retention owing to a dedication to sustainability, better stakeholder connections, and health benefits [19].
v. **Long-Term Value Creation:** Companies that invest in sustainable practices might create a more resilient company model. The long-term benefits may include sustainable resource use, safeguarding the company's future growth through diverse revenue streams and enhanced brand value [11].

2 The Role of Industry 5.0 in Sustainability

The integration of innovative technologies within the Industry 5.0 framework is closely matched with sustainability objectives, resulting in a positive feedback loop. These technologies, such as artificial intelligence (AI), robotics, and the Internet of Things (IoT), help companies meet environmental goals by enhancing efficiency and resource optimization [24] e.g.:

i. **Energy Efficiency**: Smart manufacturing systems, enabled by AI and IoT, save energy by optimizing production schedules and avoiding waste.
ii. **Circular Economy**: Advanced technologies promote the circular economy by enabling product recycling, remanufacturing, and reuse, reducing raw material extraction and landfill waste.
iii. **Carbon Neutrality**: Companies can achieve carbon neutrality and lower their environmental footprint by utilizing renewable energy sources, AI-driven energy management systems, and emissions tracking.

2.1 Human-Centric Innovation and Environmental Goals

Industry 5.0 represents the intersection of human-centric innovation with environmental sustainability, with the goal of creating a future in which technology benefits both people and the environment. Industry 5.0 enables industries to accomplish sustainability targets while also developing a more inclusive and resilient society by putting human well-being first and supporting green technologies. As the industrial landscape shifts, this paradigm promises a harmonic mix of technical advancement, environmental care, and human empowerment [3].

2.2 Synergy of Advanced Technologies and Sustainability

The confluence of cutting-edge technologies and sustainability in Industry 5.0 focuses on creating a harmonic balance between economic progress, human wellbeing, and environmental responsibility.

i. **Collaborative Robotics (Cobots)**: Cobots serve a critical role in improving industrial process efficiency and safety. These robots are designed to work alongside human operators, helping to limit human exposure to hazardous tasks and enhance worker capabilities [20].
ii. **Artificial Intelligence (AI) and Machine Learning**: AI improves operational efficiency by improving resource allocation, forecasting maintenance requirements, and lowering energy consumption [1].
iii. **Internet of Things (IoT)**: Companies that deploy IoT-enabled sensors throughout their factories and supply chains may measure

resource consumption in real time and find areas for improvement. These sensors also contribute to predictive maintenance, decreasing machine downtime and preventing wasteful waste [29].

iv. **Additive Manufacturing (3D Printing)**: Additive manufacturing, also known as 3D printing, is transforming how goods are created and manufactured. This technology reduces material waste by manufacturing goods layer by layer, utilizing just the materials needed. It also enables the creation of personalized items, which reduces the need for mass production and surplus inventories [21].

v. **Blockchain Technology**: In supply chains, it may trace the origin of raw materials, ensuring that they are farmed sustainably and produced ethically. Blockchain also enables businesses to manage carbon credits and emissions data more efficiently, maintaining environmental compliance and contributing to sustainability goals [26].

2.3 *Sustainable Business Practices in Smart Manufacturing*

In the shifting landscape of Industry 5.0, smart manufacturing is critical to rethinking corporate processes with a strong emphasis on sustainability. Resource efficiency is a core sustainability factor in smart manufacturing. Industry 5.0 allows for the use of modern technology to optimize material and energy usage, decreasing waste and minimizing environmental effect. AI-powered predictive analytics and IoT sensors continuously monitor energy use, raw material consumption, and waste creation in real time, allowing businesses to spot inefficiencies and make adjustments. AI systems, for example, may optimize production schedules to save energy during peak hours and adapt workflows to prevent material waste [16].

2.4 *Circular Economy and Green Accounting Frameworks*

A circular economy differs from the usual linear "take-make-dispose" model. Instead, it focuses on the continual reuse, refurbishing, and recycling of materials to reduce waste and reliance on virgin resources. Smart manufacturing in Industry 5.0 promotes the application of circular economy ideas, which extend the lifecycle of products through repair, reuse, and recycling. IoT-enabled systems can monitor product health and performance, enabling predictive maintenance and extending equipment lifespan [9]. Similarly, data-driven manufacturing allows organizations to design products that are easier to deconstruct and recycle at the end of their life cycle, allowing for the reuse of materials in future production processes. The most important sustainable practices in smart manufacturing are energy efficiency and renewable integration and the optimization of energy Consumption. Industry 5.0 technology, such as AI and smart grids, offer real-time energy management, allowing firms to shift energy use to off-peak hours or change production to take advantage of renewable energy availability [19]. Furthermore, energy-efficient systems and machinery powered by smart sensors and automation can significantly lower manufacturing's carbon impact, helping to reach carbon neutrality targets [29].

3 Financial Implications of Green Accounting

In the context of Industry 5.0, green accounting assists businesses in determining how sustainable practices affect their financial performance and long-term viability, ensuring that they make decisions that balance profit, people, and the environment. Key features of green accounting frameworks in Industry 5.0 include:

I. **Environmental Costing**: Green accounting entails determining and measuring environmental expenses, including direct costs like as energy, water, materials, and waste management, as well as indirect costs such as regulatory compliance, environmental fines, and reputational harm. The data-driven approach enables businesses to discover areas for improvement and lower their total environmental impact [7].

ii. **Environmental Profit and Loss (EP&L)**: The EP&L paradigm provides monetary value to environmental impacts like carbon emissions, water usage, and biodiversity loss. It enables businesses to realize the true cost of their environmental effect and encourages them to take proactive measures to reduce it. In Industry 5.0, AI and machine learning algorithms can be used to quantify the environmental costs of various business activities and incorporate this data into financial decisions [2].

III. **Natural Capital Accounting**: Natural capital accounting measures the value of the natural resources and ecosystems on which a firm depends. This paradigm includes evaluating the depletion of natural resources such as forests, water, and minerals and factoring them into financial statements. By incorporating natural capital into their business models, companies in Industry 5.0 can better match their growth objectives with environmental sustainability, ensuring that their activities do not deplete the resources on which they depend [11].

IV. **Sustainability Reporting and Transparency**: Green accounting models prioritize transparency in sustainability reporting. Companies can use digital platforms and blockchain technology to give transparent and verifiable data about their environmental effect, supply chains, and sustainability policies [26].

3.1 Profitability and Sustainability Trade-Offs

One of the main trade-offs in green accounting is the initial cost of establishing sustainable practices vs the long-term financial rewards. In the long run, these improvements can result in cost savings through lower energy bills, reduced waste management expenses, and increased efficiency [11].

i. **Operational Efficiency versus Environmental Impact** derives from balancing operational efficiency with environmental stewardship. Although these strategies increase profitability, they frequently incur environmental costs that are not recognized in traditional accounting. Green accounting attempts to account for these external expenses, but businesses may discover that pursuing more environmentally friendly alternatives, such as utilizing less toxic materials or using cleaner technology, can lower operational efficiency and raise production costs. As a result, businesses must strike a balance between preserving profitability and minimizing their negative environmental impact [15].

ii. **Short-Term Gains versus Long-Term Reputation** Green accounting highlights the necessity of accounting for environmental risks such as regulatory compliance, environmental deterioration, and resource scarcity, which can have a substantial impact on a company's long-term profitability. While the initial costs of sustainable practices may lower revenues in the short term, they can improve a company's long-term image and brand value [19].

iii. **Regulatory Compliance versus Operational Flexibility** Green accounting requires firms to account for the expenses of complying with environmental rules and standards, such as emissions reductions, waste management, and reporting obligations. This may affect profits in the short term, but compliance also protects the organization against potential environmental and financial fines in the future (ISO 14001:2015).

3.2 Long-term Financial Planning with Green Metrics

As environmental issues become more essential to corporate strategy, organizations are increasingly implementing green accounting to guarantee that sustainability is represented in their financial decisions. Green metrics enable businesses to make more informed decisions that lead to long-term profitability and sustainable growth. Green metrics are methods and indicators for assessing the environmental impact of corporate activity. These measures include carbon emissions, energy use, water consumption, garbage output, and other environmental footprints. Green accounting incorporates these measures into regular financial accounts, allowing organizations to understand their environmental costs and discover areas for efficiency improvement.

In the context of long-term financial planning, green metrics can serve several key purposes:

Identifying Environmental Risks and Opportunities Green metrics assist businesses in determining the environmental risks they face, such as resource scarcity, legislative changes, and climate change consequences [12].

Evaluating the Cost of Environmental Impact Green accounting ensures that these expenditures are included in financial planning. For example, the cost of carbon emissions can be calculated and incorporated into a company's cost structure, thereby reflecting the genuine environmental cost [2].

Enhancing Decision-Making through Sustainable Investment Green accounting may help lead investments in technology and projects that not only generate financial benefits but also contribute to environmental sustainability. For example, investing in energy-efficient technology, water recycling systems, or green supply chains can result in lower operational costs and better environmental performance [1].

Long-Term Profitability through Circular Economy Green accounting can measure the success of circular business models such product recycling, refurbishing, and material reuse [9].

3.3 Investment in Green Technologies and Innovation

Green accounting enables businesses to analyze, evaluate, and incorporate the environmental costs and benefits of their operations into their financial management systems. One of the most important components of green accounting is investing in green technologies and innovation, which can promote sustainability while also contributing to financial success. Green technologies are developments that help to reduce environmental impact, increase resource efficiency, and promote sustainability.

Green technologies include renewable energy sources (solar, wind, and hydropower), energy-efficient systems, waste-to-energy solutions, carbon capture technology, electric vehicles, and environmentally friendly manufacturing methods [21]. These technologies are critical for accomplishing company sustainability objectives and are strongly related to green accounting concepts.

For example, installing solar panels to save money on electricity or switching to LED lights to save energy can have a long-term financial benefit. Green accounting aids in the calculation of payback period and lifetime savings, taking into account not only direct monetary savings but also environmental advantages such as lower carbon emissions [23]. Investing in green technologies and innovation not only promotes environmental stewardship, but it also makes financial sense over time. Furthermore, sustainability-driven innovation can lead to new revenue streams. As customer demand for sustainable products and services rises, businesses who innovate in eco-friendly solutions can capitalize on a profitable market [2].

4 Regulatory Framework and Compliance

The combination of green accounting, industry rules, and Industry 5.0 technology offers firms a comprehensive strategy to aligning their operations with sustainability objectives.

4.1 *Environmental Regulations and Industry Standards*

As global environmental concerns develop, governments and regulatory agencies have implemented a variety of environmental legislation to address challenges such as climate change, resource depletion, and pollution. These requirements mandate businesses to monitor and reduce carbon emissions, manage waste, optimize energy use, and limit their environmental impact. Industry standards such as ISO 14001 (environmental management system), ISO 50001 (energy management), and Global Reporting Initiative (GRI) guidelines are also important in ensuring that organizations meet environmental requirements. These standards give frameworks for organizations to assess their environmental impact, define sustainability targets, and monitor progress.

i. **Environmental Costing and Compliance**: Green accounting enables firms to quantify environmental costs such as carbon taxes, emissions trading, and penalties for noncompliance with environmental regulations. It assists in tracking these costs, ensuring that enterprises stay within legal boundaries and avoid financial penalties. For example, firms can use green accounting to track and report their carbon emissions in compliance with carbon tax policies or emission cap rules, ensuring that they meet regulatory obligations while minimizing expenses [23].
ii. **Real-Time Monitoring and Reporting**: Companies that integrate IoT sensors, AI, and big data analytics into Industry 5.0 may continually monitor environmental metrics such as energy use, trash generation, and emissions. Green accounting solutions may combine these real-time data flows, allowing organizations to rapidly compare their performance to regulatory criteria. This dynamic method enables organizations to make swift adjustments, maintaining continued compliance while avoiding costly fines or penalties [29].
iii. **Lifecycle Assessment**: Industry 5.0 technologies enable more extensive lifetime evaluations (LCAs) of products, which analyze environmental effect at every stage of manufacturing, use, and disposal. Green accounting frameworks can use LCA data to create a comprehensive view of a product's environmental footprint, assisting businesses in complying with rules requiring environmental effect disclosure. This is especially important in industries with

strict product stewardship rules, such as electronics and manufacturing, where the environmental impact of raw material extraction, manufacture, and disposal is carefully monitored [9].

4.2 Green Accounting's Role in Compliance

It entails calculating environmental costs and benefits and including them in the company's financial reporting system. For organizations working in Industry 5.0, which requires high accuracy and creativity, this system provides a framework for properly measuring and reporting on environmental compliance.

i. **Tracking Environmental Impact and Compliance:** Businesses must remain comply with increasingly stringent environmental rules, such as carbon levies, emission reduction objectives, and waste management legislation, in order to avoid penalties and protect their reputations. Green accounting helps by collecting environmental data in real time, ensuring that organizations satisfy compliance standards [23].
ii. **Automated Reporting for Regulatory Bodies:** Industry 5.0 technologies, such as artificial intelligence and blockchain, offer automated compliance reporting by incorporating real-time environmental performance data directly into regulatory frameworks. Green accounting systems can produce transparent, verifiable reports that adhere to standards such as ISO 14001 (Environmental Management Systems), ISO 50001 (Energy Management Systems), and regional regulatory requirements [14].
iii. **Cost Management and Carbon Accounting:** Carbon accounting—the tracking and reduction of carbon emissions—is a vital part of environmental compliance. Industry 5.0 technology make it easier to track carbon footprints in real time. Green accounting integrates carbon prices into total financial assessments, ensuring that businesses meet emission reduction objectives or carbon pricing plans [26].

4.3 *Anticipating and Adapting to Future Regulations*

As the global economy emphasizes sustainability, the regulatory framework for environmental challenges is fast evolving. Future environmental laws are anticipated to be more stringent, with more pressure on corporations to reduce their environmental footprints, enhance resource efficiency, and adopt cleaner technology. In this context, green accounting is crucial for firms to foresee and react to future requirements, particularly within the framework of Industry 5.0. Industry 5.0 combines new technologies and sustainability, allowing firms to not only comply with existing standards but also proactively plan for future issues 13.

Anticipating Future Regulations

i. **Regulatory Forecasting through Real-Time Data Analysis** Companies can predict the direction of future rules by evaluating historical data and tracking regulatory patterns, whether they are concerned with carbon emissions, resource utilization, or waste management [29].
ii. **Scenario Planning and Risk Assessment:** Businesses that incorporate green metrics such as carbon emissions, water use, and energy use can estimate the risks associated with noncompliance and devise solutions to avoid those risks. For example, if a company predicts that harsher waste disposal restrictions will be implemented, it might begin investing in waste reduction technologies or embracing circular economy principles before the regulations are enacted [9].

Adapting to Future Regulations

i. **Real-Time Monitoring and Continuous Compliance:** Real-time monitoring is an important part of Industry 5.0's adaptation to future laws. Businesses can use IoT sensors, AI analytics, and smart factories to continuously track environmental data such as energy use, emissions, water usage, and trash generation. Green accounting solutions may automatically include this information into environmental reporting, ensuring that organizations remain in compliance with changing rules at all times [1].
ii. **Adaptation through Sustainability Innovation:** Industry 5.0 emphasizes human-centered innovation. By investing in green technology such as renewable energy sources, energy-efficient

machinery, and circular supply chains, firms may reduce their environmental impact and future-proof their operations [21].

iii. **Carbon and Resource Management:** As climate change policies tighten, industry will likely face higher restrictions for carbon emissions and resource management. Green accounting provides the tools needed to track and report on these aspects, allowing businesses to take proactive efforts to lessen their environmental effect. Businesses that integrate carbon accounting and resource usage indicators may assess their emissions, identify reduction opportunities, and plan investments in low-carbon solutions [23].

With a growing global emphasis on environmental, social, and governance (ESG) standards, firms must comply with obligatory disclosure frameworks such as the EU Green Deal or the Task Force on Climate-related Financial Disclosures (TCFD). Green accounting allows firms to analyze and report on environmental parameters, making it easier to comply with legislation.

5 Emerging Trends in Green Accounting

In the framework of Industry 5.0, sustainability is no longer a prerequisite, but rather an essential component of company strategy. As businesses embrace the combination of human-centric innovations and modern technologies such as Artificial Intelligence (AI), sustainability reporting becomes increasingly comprehensive, precise, and integrated into overall business performance 4.

5.1 Artificial Intelligence in Sustainability Reporting

AI-powered IoT sensors embedded in manufacturing lines, supply chains, and facilities can monitor environmental data in real time. These sensors generate a continuous stream of data on energy consumption, emissions, waste levels, and other environmental parameters, which AI systems immediately assess. AI can recognize patterns, identify inefficiencies, and estimate future environmental consequences, giving organizations actionable insights for improving operations and lowering environmental expenses [17, 29].

Artificial intelligence can be used to track carbon footprints, allowing firms to determine how diverse activities or operations contribute to overall emissions. By automating the data collecting and analysis process, AI enables businesses to produce more accurate and timely sustainability reports, minimizing human error and assuring compliance with demanding regulatory requirements [1].

5.2 *Blockchain for Transparent Environmental Data*

AI, when integrated with blockchain technology, can improve the credibility of sustainability reports by making the data verifiable and tamper-proof. Blockchain creates a safe, immutable ledger for capturing environmental data, which AI analyzes and interprets. This combination ensures that sustainability reports contain accurate and transparent information, instilling confidence in investors, regulators, and consumers. Blockchain's decentralized, immutable, and transparent nature provides distinct advantages for tracking and validating environmental data, ensuring authenticity and trust in sustainability claims [5, 26].

For example, firms can use blockchain to monitor the carbon footprint of their whole supply chain, from raw material extraction to product disposal. AI may then evaluate this data to create thorough sustainability reports that flag areas for concern or development [2].

This transparent, AI-enabled reporting solution ensures that businesses can demonstrate their commitment to sustainability through verifiable, accurate data. This open, AI-enabled reporting solution ensures that businesses can demonstrate their commitment to sustainability through verifiable and accurate data.

5.3 *Real-time Environmental Data Analytics*

Real-time data gathering and processing are critical in the context of Industry 5.0, where organizations must be responsive to regulatory and market changes. AI-driven sustainability reporting enables businesses to continuously monitor and report on their environmental performance, making it easier to comply with changing legislation and requirements [29].

AI can automate the creation of sustainability reports, ensuring that they are constantly current, accurate, and compliant with the most recent legal requirements, such as the EU Green Deal, ISO 14001, and Global Reporting Initiative (GRI) standards [10, 14].

This real-time reporting capabilities allows firms to keep ahead of potential concerns and take proactive steps to reduce environmental risks. AI can also assist businesses track ESG (Environmental, Social, and Governance) parameters, which are growing more relevant to investors and stakeholders. Automated AI systems can constantly update ESG reports, allowing firms to give accurate, transparent, and timely information to investors, regulators, and the general public.

Predictive Analysis for Sustainability Decisions can be made with AI. AI systems can scan massive datasets from numerous sources, find trends, and anticipate future environmental impacts using present practices. By combining historical data and real-time inputs, AI can forecast how future business decisions or operational changes would effect sustainability measures.

Key Benefits of Real-time Environmental Data Analytics

Timely Decision-Making and Corrective Actions The most major benefit of real-time environmental data analytics in green accounting is the capacity to make quick choices and take corrective action [26].

Enhanced Accuracy and Accountability Real-time data analytics solves this problem by automating the gathering and reporting of environmental variables. With IoT sensors and AI-powered systems, data is continuously collected from numerous processes, eliminating human error and inconsistency. This data automation improves the dependability and quality of reports, which are critical for audits, regulatory compliance, and stakeholder visibility [29].

Predictive Capabilities and Future Planning Real-time data analytics not only helps businesses evaluate current environmental performance, but it also delivers predictive insights that enable proactive planning. Based on present habits, AI-powered systems can anticipate future environmental consequences, such as energy consumption or emissions, by evaluating previous data and patterns [23].

Optimization of Resources and Costs Businesses can make modifications by monitoring energy consumption and material use in real time [9].

Sustainability Reporting and Compliance Real-time data collection and analysis enable accurate and timely sustainability reporting, which is becoming increasingly crucial to stakeholders, regulators, and investors. Real-time data analytics enables businesses to provide up-to-date reports that reflect their current environmental impact, providing stakeholders with transparency and confidence [1].

6 Challenges in Implementing Green Accounting

As the world moves toward Industry 5.0, which emphasizes human-centered innovation and the incorporation of modern technologies into industrial operations, green accounting becomes increasingly important. However, new paradigms in technology and industrial processes, as well as standardization and worldwide consensus in green accounting, provide considerable hurdles.

i. **Divergence in Environmental Reporting Standards:** One of the most significant issues in green accounting for Industry 5.0 is a lack of consistency in environmental reporting across countries, industries, and organizations. Currently, numerous frameworks and principles are utilized around the world to monitor and report environmental sustainability. For example, the Global Reporting Initiative (GRI), ISO 14001, and the Sustainability Accounting Standards Board (SASB) all use different methodologies to report on environmental impacts, while carbon accounting protocols like the Greenhouse Gas (GHG) Protocol and the Carbon Disclosure Project (CDP) focus on emissions reporting.
ii. **Complexity of Supply Chain Integration:** With **Industry 5.0**, Businesses are becoming increasingly reliant on extremely complex, interdependent supply chains that use automation, smart manufacturing, and sustainable sourcing practices. These complex supply networks make it difficult to standardize green accounting indicators throughout the whole manufacturing process, from raw material procurement to end product disposal.
iii. **Data Privacy and Security Concerns** As AI, IoT, and big data analytics become more integrated into green accounting in Industry 5.0, the massive volume of data generated raises worries about data privacy and security. Real-time environmental data may contain sensitive information about a company's operations, energy usage, waste management methods, and resource utilization. This data can be utilized to improve operations and reduce environmental impact, but it also includes sensitive company information.
iv. **Integration of Technology and Human-Centric Approaches** The integration of human labor with modern technologies such as robots, AI systems, and augmented reality is central to Industry 5.0. As a result, green accounting must evolve to accommodate both

human capital and technology-driven efficiencies. The problem is finding how to compare the environmental benefits of human-centered innovation to those of technological advancements. For example, using AI to forecast energy usage, optimize manufacturing processes, or reduce waste can greatly improve a company's environmental performance.

v. **Regulatory Compliance and Evolution of Laws** The regulatory landscape for environmental reporting is always changing, and each country has its own set of laws and sustainability criteria. As new technologies develop and industries expand with Industry 5.0, regulatory organizations must update and unify environmental regulations to keep up with these advancements.

6.1 Standardization and Global Consensus

Standardizing how sensitive environmental data is collected, exchanged, and reported on a worldwide scale becomes difficult as businesses must strike a balance between transparency and the preservation of proprietary information. Concerns surrounding data sovereignty, or the ownership and jurisdiction of data, hamper the standardization process because certain countries may have stronger constraints on data storage and transmission than others.

Industry 5.0 technology must solve these security and privacy concerns while maintaining the accuracy and transparency of environmental data. Standardization of data protection and privacy rules, as well as environmental reporting, will be critical to achieving worldwide green accounting consensus. Achieving standardization and worldwide consensus in green accounting for Industry 5.0 poses substantial obstacles. The quickly changing world of new technologies, the requirement for consistent environmental reporting, and the complexities of global supply networks all make generally accepted accounting rules challenging to apply. Concerns regarding data security, privacy, and regulatory compliance exacerbate the dilemma. [10, 14].

To successfully integrate green accounting with Industry 5.0, stakeholders—governments, industries, and technology providers—must work together to develop consistent standards that are adaptable to emerging technologies and capable of meeting the diverse and evolving environmental needs of a global economy [23].

6.2 Data Accuracy and Reporting Challenges

The integration of technology with new accounting patterns, such as Industry 5.0 technologies, creates substantial data accuracy and reporting difficulties in green accounting, which must be solved to provide credible sustainability reporting, regulatory compliance, and relevant decision-making.

i. **Complexity of Environmental Data Collection:** One of the most difficult difficulties in green accounting is gathering correct environmental data. Industry 5.0 is largely reliant on interconnected systems enabled by IoT sensors, AI, and real-time data analytics. The difficulty is to ensure that all data collected from diverse sources—from factories and warehouses to transportation systems and product life cycles—is accurate, consistent, and aligned throughout the business [29].
ii. **Lack of Standardized Metrics and Reporting Frameworks:** The absence of globally acknowledged standards for environmental data reporting creates a substantial barrier to accurate green accounting. Although frameworks like as the Global Reporting Initiative (GRI) and the Sustainability Accounting Standards Board (SASB) help, there is no universally accepted standard for measuring, tracking, and reporting on environmental data. This lack of uniformity causes reporting disparities between areas, industries, and organizations, making it difficult to compare statistics and analyze enterprises' genuine environmental performance [10].
iii. **Real-time Data Overload and Interpretation:** The sheer volume of data collected by continuous monitoring might cause data overload. Companies may struggle to adequately evaluate and analyze data when it is created at a greater rate than ever before. The AI-driven analytics required to evaluate this data may fail to provide actionable insights if the data is not effectively integrated or if its source is inconsistent. Furthermore, predictive models intended to forecast environmental impact might be faulty if the real-time data fed into them is incorrect or missing [26].
iv. **Transparency and Auditing of Environmental Data** In Industry 5.0, the incorporation of modern technologies such as AI, robotics, and blockchain might result in a black box effect, in which the

underlying algorithms or automated processes that drive environmental decisions are not completely visible or understood. This opacity raises questions regarding the traceability and auditability of environmental data. Integration of data from many technologies and processes. Without a unifying platform to aggregate this disparate data, businesses would struggle to produce a clear and accurate picture of their environmental effect. Furthermore, variations in data collected by various devices, especially those driven by human's vs machines, might bring inconsistencies and inaccuracies that jeopardize the integrity of green accounting [2].

6.3 *Data Privacy and Security*

While green accounting data is not generally considered extremely sensitive, its combination with other business data may expose a corporation to data protection and compliance problems, such as the General Data Protection Regulation (GDPR). Ensuring that environmental data is safely kept and sent while still being accessible for auditing purposes is a hard balance to strike.

6.4 *Overcoming Resistance to Change*

Despite the potential benefits, many firms encounter resistance to change when implementing green accounting processes and new technology in accordance with Industry 5.0 principles. Overcoming this reluctance is critical to realize the full potential of green accounting and accomplishing sustainability objectives [21].

7 Conclusion

At the heart of Industry 5.0 is the merging of human-centric innovation with modern technologies, with the goal of creating a more sustainable, inclusive, and efficient industrial landscape. Green accounting provides a critical framework for firms to analyze, report, and improve their environmental effect while remaining consistent with overall sustainability goals. Green accounting allows businesses in Industry 5.0 to take a more holistic approach to sustainability. The incorporation of Industry 5.0 technologies, such as blockchain and real-time data analytics, has improved organizations' ability to offer accurate, transparent, and verified environmental data. As organizations increasingly operate in a global market, integrating with international standards and frameworks—such as the Global Reporting Initiative (GRI), ISO 14001, and the Sustainability Accounting Standards Board (SASB)—is crucial to unify reporting indicators and ensure that environmental impacts are consistently tracked and communicated.

The circular economy strives to decrease waste, improve resource efficiency, and extend product lifecycles through recycling, reuse, and remanufacturing. Green accounting frameworks can be used to evaluate the financial implications of implementing circular economy concepts, allowing firms to make educated decisions that balance economic and environmental objectives.

Looking ahead, the future of green accounting in Industry 5.0 relies on continued innovation and integration. As new technologies develop, such as quantum computing, AI breakthroughs, and next-generation robotics, green accounting systems must evolve to accommodate the intricacies of these innovations. The capacity to combine human experience with new technologies will be a distinguishing element of Industry 5.0's sustainable business practices.

References

1. **Accenture.** (2020). *The Green Economy: How AI and Data Analytics Are Shaping the Future of Sustainability*. Accenture Insights.
2. **Bebbington, J., & Larrinaga, C.** (2014). *Accounting for sustainability: an exploration. Accounting, Auditing & Accountability Journal*, 27(6), 1141-1160.
3. **Benghozi, P., & André, A.** (2019). *From Industry 4.0 to Industry 5.0: The Transition Toward the Human-Centric Future of Work. Technological Forecasting and Social Change*, 146, 23-33.
4. **Binns, A., & Cavanagh, G.** (2021). *Using AI to Enhance Sustainability Reporting and Green Accounting: A Case Study Approach. Business Strategy and the Environment*, 30(5), 2134-2145.
5. **Cheng, J., & Li, Y.** (2019). *Leveraging Blockchain for Environmental Sustainability: The Role of Green Accounting in Industry 5.0. Journal of Business Ethics*, 159(4), 1109–1123.
6. **Deloitte.** (2021). *The Human Side of Industry 5.0: The Future of Work in the Fourth Industrial Revolution*. Deloitte Insights.

7. **Ditz, D., Ranganathan, J., & Banks, R.** (1995). *Measuring the Environmental Performance of Companies: The Role of Green Accounting. World Resources Institute.*
8. **Eccles, R. G., & Krzus, M. P.** (2018). *The Role of Integrated Reporting in the Corporate Sustainability Framework. Journal of Applied Corporate Finance*, 30(1), 32-40.
9. **European Commission.** (2020). *European Green Deal: Pathways for Decarbonization and Green Finance*. European Commission.
10. **Global Reporting Initiative (GRI).** (2016). *Sustainability Reporting Standards*. GRI.
11. **Gray, R., & Bebbington, J.** (2000). *Environmental Accounting, Managerialism, and Sustainability: Is the Planet Safe in the Hands of Business and Accounting? Accounting, Organizations and Society*, 25(1-2), 47-72.
12. **International Federation of Accountants (IFAC).** (2018). *Sustainability and Integrated Reporting: Enhancing Value Creation*. IFAC.
13. **International Monetary Fund (IMF).** (2019). *The Role of Green Accounting in the Transition to a Sustainable Green Economy*. IMF.
14. **ISO 14001:2015.** *Environmental Management Systems: Requirements with Guidance for Use*. International Organization for Standardization.
15. **Jones, M. J.** (2010). *Sustainability and the Role of Green Accounting: Moving Forward in the Green Economy. Business Strategy and the Environment*, 19(5), 315-327.
16. **Kagermann, H., Wahlster, W., & Helbig, J.** (2013). *Industry 4.0: The Digital Transformation of Manufacturing*. Springer Vieweg.
17. **Kiron, D., Kruschwitz, N., & Vos, M.** (2018). *Artificial Intelligence and Its Role in Sustainability Reporting and Green Accounting. MIT Sloan Management Review*, 59(1), 22-31.
18. **KPMG.** (2020). *KPMG Survey of Corporate Responsibility Reporting: Global Trends and Insights*. KPMG International.
19. **McKinsey & Company.** (2019). *The Green Transformation: How Business is Driving Sustainability Through Digital Innovation*. McKinsey.
20. **Pereira, A., & Romero, F.** (2021). *Industry 5.0: The Next Industrial Revolution and its Role in Sustainable Development. Computers & Industrial Engineering*, 151, 106890.
21. **PwC.** (2020). *Future-Fit Business Benchmark: Aligning Profit with Purpose in Industry 5.0*. PwC.
22. **PwC.** (2021). *The Future of Sustainability Reporting: A New Era in Corporate Transparency*. PwC.
23. **Schaltegger, S., & Burritt, R.** (2018). *Corporate Sustainability and Environmental Accounting*. Springer.

24. **Sung, T. K.** (2020). *Industry 5.0: A New Paradigm for Human-Centric Manufacturing. Journal of Manufacturing Science and Engineering*, 142(10), 1–10.
25. **Sustainability Accounting Standards Board (SASB).** (2021). *SASB Standards for Reporting Environmental, Social, and Governance Metrics*. SASB.
26. **Tan, K., & Lee, S.** (2019). *Blockchain as a Tool for Enhancing Transparency in Environmental Data Reporting. Environmental Science & Technology*, 53(15), 8902-8911.
27. **United Nations Environment Programme (UNEP).** (2017). *Green Accounting and Policy Making: Concepts and Applications*. UNEP.
28. **World Economic Forum (WEF).** (2021). *Sustainability in Industry 5.0: Challenges and Opportunities*. WEF.
29. **Xu, J., & Wang, W.** (2021). *AI-Powered Real-Time Environmental Data Analytics for Green Accounting in Industry 5.0. Computers in Industry*, 125, 103319.

Enhancing Employee Wellbeing in Industry 5.0: A Comprehensive Literature Review

Pooja Singh and Rashi Chaudhary

1 Introduction

1.1 Overview of Industry 5.0

While the concept of Industry 4.0 is still ongoing and dominates the market, Research development is transferring the focus towards the next Industrial Revolution, which is established as Industry 5.0, [1]. European Commission was the very first organization to start a discussion on Industry 5.0 agenda in 2021 and recognizes the early stage of elevation of Industry 4.0 and still on demand. The current literatures are focused on increasing consciousness of Industry 5.0 among Policy makers, Industrial units, high level scientists, etc. In regard to the many literatures on Industry 4.0, it is imperative to have a comprehensive and profound understanding of the concepts, origin, evolution, principles and progress of Industry 4.0 [2]. Several academic contributions vouch for

P. Singh (✉) · R. Chaudhary
G L Bajaj Institute of Management and Research, Greater Noida, India
e-mail: drpoojasingh3112@gmail.com; Pooja.singh@glbimr.org

R. Chaudhary
e-mail: rashi.1@glbimr.org

© The Author(s), under exclusive license to Springer Nature Singapore Pte Ltd. 2025

P. Agarwal et al. (eds.), *Building a Human-Centred Infrastructure for Sustainable Industry 5.0 in Asia*,
https://doi.org/10.1007/978-981-95-0417-6_11

this discipline and the potential of this discipline which is quite unique. It theorised Industry 4.0 as implementation of the underlying technologies within the factory walls [3].

Source Author constructed

The phenomenon of paradigm shifts in value creation and involving the value partners in digital mode is a new conventional mode of elaboration. The tangible transformation driven by Industry 4.0 has not only reached to the production sections but are starting to arise with primary sector ideas like Agriculture 4.0 [4]. Numerous literatures exist on the frameworks being formed and the models and designs being developed that explain the growing awareness and comprehension of Industry 4.0 capabilities [5]. On the contrary side of Industry 4.0 researchers are remain studying Industry 5.0 compared to its predecessor. The mechanisms and identify constituents of Industry 5.0 are less elaborated and understudied [6]. Now, shifting the gear towards the era of development in Industries, industry 5.0 slowly and in ignorance, co-existing with Industry 4.0 as a parallel phenomenon posing confusion and scepticism towards the pathway of Industrial revolution [7].

In the initial context, there are two different insights leading along with interpreting the principle of Industry 5.0, that is the paradigm of Industry 4.0 indicating the advancement in technologies like artificial intelligence, 6G, augmenting marketing, etc. are transforming the future concern regarding the workplace, combination with the machines, technologies with the humans [8]. Another outlook desires the growing concentration towards the drawback of originating the profit from technology (profit centric approach). On the latter perspective, the agenda of European Commission (EC) on Industry 5.0 is strongly concentrating the resilient industry, human centric and eco-friendlier industries [9]. Industry 5.0 growth and its controversies are closely connected with the growth of Industry 5.0 and researchers are still drilling down towards its exploration.

1.2 *Overview of Employee Wellbeing*

At workplace, non-monetary benefits which are given to an employee to ensure a better and a healthy work-life like Insurance plans, yoga classes, meditation centres, flexibility in work hours etc. are termed as Employee wellbeing [10]. Such benefits and perks usually boost up the employee's morale and provide them work-life balance. Employee wellbeing is a broad concept in itself and it encompasses many scopes like mental wellbeing, physical wellbeing and career wellbeing, etc. [11]. According to Gallup Report (2022) 76% employees are suffering with symptoms of burnout due to over-excessive workload, unfair treatment at workplace and poor management conditions where employees are not appreciated. Approximately 37% Employees are facing absenteeism due to stressful conditions and almost 89% employees are facing presenteeism (present physically but mentally absent) due to stressful working conditions or other condition due to stressful workplace conditions, [12–14].

According to Conway (2009), Employee wellbeing consists of few core constructs like- clarity of role and sense of participation, support from peer colleagues and sub-employees, control over workload, workplace relationships, and manageable workload, etc. Wellbeing can also be shaped in terms of strain. Strain is basically the response associated with the behavioural, physical or psychological stressor [15]. The term Stressor defines the environmental factors which requires the adaptive responses from the workers and staff members of a certain organisation [16]. That stressor which leads to change negatively impact the employee's wellbeing whereas conditions which impact in either neutral or positive way does not lead to be them in stressor condition (refers to performance, efficiency effectiveness and satisfaction) in given environment. The most extreme considerations of strain are depression, stress and anxiety, expanded heart rate, expanded pulses, heartbeat, absenteeism, negative presenteeism, terrible execution, disengagements and so forth.

Hence to conclude wellbeing can be binding force towards individual commitment and it is an antecedent of commitment. From the perspective of the organisation, commitment is a multidimensional construct in which the normative and affective commitment are measured. There are two types of commitments normative and affective [17]. It is assumed that an employee with a well-sound wellbeing, for evaluating the potential gain or loss and being emotionally attached with the organisation and therefore, normative or affective commitment belongs to a positive mental state of the individuals. Let us elaborate with the help of an example; An employee who is dedicated towards his/her organisation along with the emotional associations may have a different feeling on the profit or Loss transactions [18].

1.3 Significance of Employee Wellbeing in Industry 5.0

There are many international events held recently such as Coronavirus pandemic and Russia-Ukraine war, have emphasised the predisposition of economies and organisation; anticipating a quick adjustment to the circumstances over the new normal [19]. After facing the war of COVID-19, it has been proved that wellbeing is the utmost priority of Individual life. Unlike to the operations, one of the toughest challenges in management techniques are based on sustainability, resilience and human centrism, all are the vitals of Industry 5.0. Embracing the concept of Digitalisation is another recognised important factor paved from Industry 4.0 towards Industry 5.0. In order to achieve, the exceptional socio-economic framework of respective organisation, the adaptation towards utilisation and acquisition of soft skills are mandatory. Smart Manufacturing for the future is the next best agenda of industry 5.0, which will increase the innovativeness and productivity in the industry. Integrating augmented and virtual reality, ambient intelligence, smart factories, big data, Artificial Intelligence and cloud computing are the major objectives of accomplishing smart manufacturing [20].

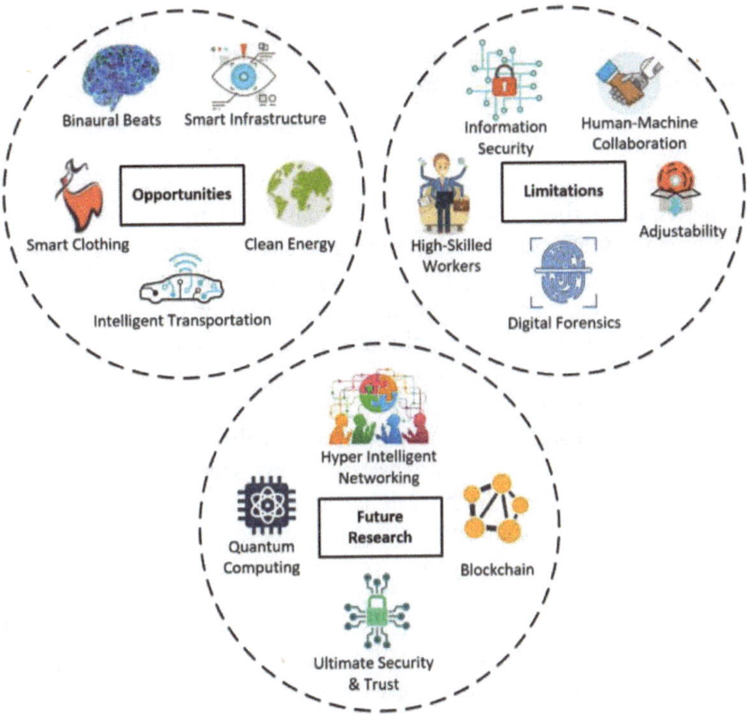

Source Author constructed

The principle, outlined in Industry 4.0 consists of integrating the advanced technologies such as Big data, Artificial Intelligence, smart factories, cloud computing etc. In spite of several advancements of Industry 4.0, it is also facing a lot of challenges that includes the human costs occurring due to insufficient environmental consciousness and process optimisation [21]. Among the all over challenges, one of the prominent questions arising to how to effectively manage the human resources in the digital era. Adaptation of new technology could increase labour shortages, decrease human involvement, and compel the organisations to allocate value added capacities for human resources [22].

This era signifies a departure from the purely mechanized and digitized processes of Industry 4.0 towards a model that places human welfare at its nucleus.

The regular engagement of human resources in industry 4.0, has a great significance such as nurturing the holistic health of employees transcends mere corporate responsibility and subsequently, it becomes an indispensable strategic imperative for humans [23]. On the advancement note Industry 5.0 only nurtures the development and technology where employees are valued, aided, and empowered. From the technostress permeating the overwhelming digitalization to the reorganization of traditional work setups and the requisite of consistent upskilling, numerous obstacles impede this clear blueprint [24]. In a fast-moving change and uncertainty, creating an environment of psychological safety, inclusion and trust remains an uphill task. But within these challenges are opportunities for innovation and growth [25].

They can adopt comprehensive wellbeing programs that address not only physical but also mental and emotional health to individuals who are resilient and adaptable. Flexible work can align work responsibilities with personal growth, offering independence and work-life balance that is at its best and work-life integration [26] It enables employees with the knowledge required to adeptly navigate the changing landscape of Industry 5.0, encouraging confidence and a culture of continuous Learning. Further, creating an organizational culture that encourages support and collaboration helps organizations leverage innate organizational potential that drives innovation and sustainable growth [27]. Using technology not just to improve operational efficiency but also to drive employee wellbeing is a core strategy here, providing them digital tools to facilitate remote collaboration, mental health support, and wellness tracking. Also, these various approaches allow Industry 5.0 to not just be an economic driving force, but a paradigm that encourages human flourishing and fulfilling the promise of a genuinely human centric evolution of industry [28].

Source Author constructed

1.4 Historical Perspectives on Industrial Revolutions and Their Impact on Employee Wellbeing

From gathering the pieces from our history, the industrial revolutions have been pivotal ages that reshaped the fabric of societies and economies, fundamentally altering the nature of work and the lives of individuals [29]. The first industrial revolution, characterized by mechanization and the beginning of steam power, marked a profound shift from agrarian to industrial economies. While it brought unparalleled economic growth and technological advancement, it also introduced harsh working conditions in factories, often at the disbursement of employee wellbeing [30]. The second industrial revolution driven by electricity, mass production and the assembly line, further enhanced industrialization leading to increased productivity but also harming issues such as labour mistreatment and urban congestion [31].

The third industrial revolution based on automation, computers, and digital skills was brought on by an age of globalization and interdependence that created new possibilities for efficiency and growth [32]. At the same time, it raised concerns regarding employment displacement and the erosion of the traditional model of engagement thus threatening employee wellbeing by inducing uncertainty and insecurity [33]. Now, at the face of Industry 5.0 that focuses on human set and holistic productivity, employee wellbeing is again being recognized as instrumental. Learning from the past, Industry 5.0 focuses on improving technology while prioritising the working population, creating a future that is more equitable and sustainable for every person.

Factors Influencing Employee Wellbeing in Industry 5.0

Numerous interconnected elements shape an employee's wellbeing in the industry 5.0 era, but three main features are organizational culture, individual experiences in the workplace and work environment. In Industry 5.0 is the integration of cutting-edge technologies with human-centric philosophies including an awareness of the interdependence between technological progress and an employee-friendly workplace. The nature of work itself is a significant determinant of employee well-being in Industry 5.0. As routine tasks become automated and human capabilities are extended by means of artificial intelligence and robotics, job tasks are evolving, demanding new skills and abilities from workers [34]. Workers face uncertainty and anxiety in response to such progress, especially those who risk being expatriates among technology and those who cannot acquire the necessary skills to accommodate changes in the work requirements. Hence, continuous learning, upskilling, and reskilling are essential for nurturing employee self-confidence and wellbeing in Industry 5.0 [35].

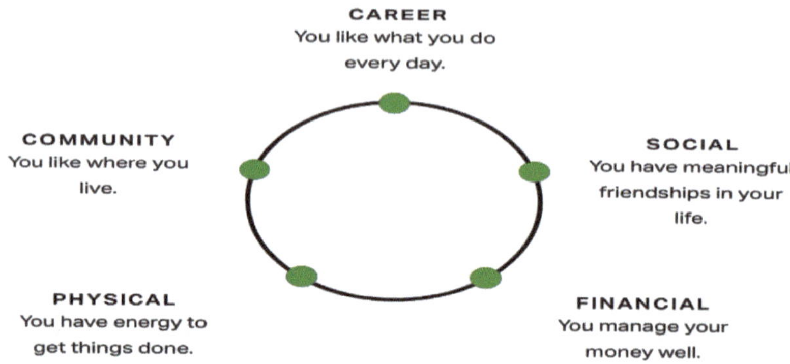

Source Author constructed

The impact of the organizational culture and guidance practices within companies operating in Industry 5.0 plays a crucial role in determining employee wellbeing. Joining Good corporate culture and employee wellbeing, a culture of psychological safety, open communication as well as trust nurtures a sense of security and empowerment in employees [36]. Conversely, toxic work environments marked by micromanagement, lack of transparency and a dismissal of employee input can impact mental health and job satisfaction. Good leadership that empowers all aspects of the environment —uniqueness, compassion for others, collaboration is essential to a healthy workplace culture and an environment where everyone feels valued, appreciated, recognized and ready to contribute their best efforts [37].

Any new technology brings challenges and opportunities regarding work-life balance and digital wellbeing as well. According to this, the lack of work life balance between work and personal lives as a result of remote work arrangements and global inter-connectivity could also result in employee burnout, stress and separation [38]. So, organizations need to incorporate policies and work-life balance, support flexible work arrangements. In addition, making use of technology to promote employee health, like wellness applications, mindfulness tools and virtual support networks can increase resilience and coping skills in response to digital overwork and technostress [39].

Another critical component in Industry 5.0 in persuading employee wellbeing is also the work environment which they have to work in [40]. Well-being facilities access to natural light and an ergonomic design all lead to satisfied and productive employees. however, creativities that encourage diversity, equity and inclusion in the landscape encourage a workplace environment where all employees feel valued, respected and supported to be their best selves [41]. The wellbeing of employees in Industry 5.0 is more multifaceted and affected by interplay of work characteristics, organisational culture, technology development and physical work environment along with work-life balance [42]. Indeed, organizations can nurture an empowered, resilient and engaged workforce fit to thrive in the industry 5.0 age through continuous learning, supportive leadership and organizational culture, work-life integration, use of technology for digital wellbeing and holistic work environments [43].

1.5 Technological Advancements and Their Impact on Work Environments

From automation through the industrial revolution to the 21st-century digital revolution, technology is seen as both a path to progress as well as a wrecking ball in a traditional job structure. In this chapter, we examine the broad range of impacts that technological advancements have on work environments from productivity, collaboration, job design and skills development to the future of work. One of the most significant effects of technology on work environment is the rapid increase in productivity and efficiency. Production processes are also revolutionized with Artificial Intelligence, Robotics and Automation [3]. They are more accurate and processes can now be completed faster and cheaper. Activities that used to require much manual effort and time are now streamlined or automated, allowing humans to refocus on more complex and creative tasks [44].

Moreover, technological breakthroughs have changed how people work and interact with each other in corporate settings. The rise of digital communication tools including email, instant messengers, video calls and collaborative platforms has made it possible to work in real-time and through remote work setups [45]. Such geographically widespread teams can easily work together on projects, exchange information and plan work around, transcending geographical boundaries and facilitating global connectivity. Virtual collaboration tools have emerged as an essential resource in the current global climate, especially since the outbreak of COVID-19 [46]. Yet these tools, while providing never-before-seen levels of accessibility and interconnectedness come with their own set of challenges: information overload, digital distraction and opportunities for misunderstanding. So organizations need to balance technology for collaboration against the right skills and support for employees to operate effectively in digital work spaces [47].

2 Employee Autonomy and Empowerment

Key values that shape contemporary organizational management involve employee autonomy and empowerment. These storying devices point towards a transition from vertical hierarchies to horizontal networks as governance [48]. Furthermore, authors have also connected what and how the autonomy and empowerment is, its benefits to people and organizations, and ways to promote a culture of autonomy and empowerment. What is employee autonomy? It refers to the amount of freedom a person has when making decisions in their job function. It involves allowing employees to create ownership of their work, set their own goals and discover the most effective way to get the job done [49]. Unlike consulting, coaching is a process that supports individuals in creating the confidence and skillset they require to create action that adds value to the organization. When combined, autonomy and empowerment can nurture a work environment where managers experience engaged employees who are motivated to perform at their best [50].

Job satisfaction and enhanced engagement are the biggest advantages of employee autonomy and empowerment. When people can decide on their own articulate their unique ideas and skills, they find meaning and significance in their work. This improves motivation, productivity and commitment towards organizational goals [22]. Moreover, when employees possess autonomy and empowerment, they are much more likely to be motivated and to contribute with ideas that enhance processes and therefore creating a culture of innovation and creativity [51]. Employee autonomy and empowerment have also been linked to increased organizational performance and competitive advantage. Having access to all that data allows companies to decentralise decision-making and empower teams throughout the organisation, tapping into the expertise of employees and empowering them- this drives ownership and accountability [5]. That enables more speed of decision-making, greater agility to respond to change and a closer alignment of individual and organizational goals. Moreover, empowered employees also tend to take ownership of their work hold themselves accountable for the results of their actions and become more competent at their role ultimately leading to greater client satisfaction and loyalty [52].

Another factor contributing to autonomy and empowerment within an organization is the distribution of decision-making power as well as opportunities for decision-making involvement. That could range from decentralizing authority more than it is now, allowing people to define their own working and collaborating paths and asking for input and recommendations from employees at all levels of the organization [3]. Indeed, organizational culture is also incredibly strong for making the leap toward the future as well, creating an environment for exploration and learning where employees are pushed to experiment take risks, fail with dignity and, ultimately, continue tracking opportunities for growth and enhancement [53].

3 Challenges to Employee Wellbeing in Industry 5.0

Industry 5.0 introduces a new ecosystem, where advanced technologies are integrated based on human principles to promote a new human-centric agenda of employee well-being. As we transition to this paradigm that will encourage great new opportunities for innovation and growth, it is a conundrum of multiple layers of complexity of issues yet to be solved to promote integrated wellbeing of the workforce. Technostress a poor outcome caused by the overwhelming speed of digitalization and technological evolution is the main obstacle on the way to employee wellbeing in Industry 5.0. Digital workplaces also render disconnecting virtually impossible which is giving rise to overwhelm anxiety and burnout (on the rise). Add to this the dissolution of the boundaries of work and home enabled by mobile devices and at-home working, making it even harder for people to unplug and recharge. Moreover, the rapid pace of technological evolution can create anxiety and insecurity in employees who can no longer meet the new requirement of workplace standard and competence.

A major challenge to employee wellbeing in Industry 5.0 is the changing paradigm of work set up and the rise in non-traditional forms of employment. Gig economy workers are people who engage in short term contracts or freelance which give them rise of independence but can appear unstable and with less protection and or benefits than say a 9 to 5. This can lead to diminished financial security and the added costs of unaffordable access to medical care and other benefits as well as isolation and disengagement from the larger workforce. Developing a sense of belonging or identity that owners obtain from their work will also be eroded as the traditional employment relationship which could lead to reduced job satisfaction as well as get health outcomes.

Additionally, the new adoption of technology like automation, artificial intelligence and robots also compromises employee well-being due to job losses and skills obsolescence (Anthony, 2018). While these technologies do provide an opportunity for productivity and efficiency gains, along with their ability to eliminate some jobs and tasks particularly those that are repetitive or fixed in nature. This has given rise to the worker being replaceable, the worker losing their livelihood on the job and to worker disempowerment and disillusionment and the fast pace of technological change requires continuous upskilling and reskilling to keep up with the new labor market, which adds another layer of pressure for people to adjust and gain new abilities throughout their career.

Additionally, Industry 5.0 employee wellbeing extends into the out-of-work scope into the four walls of society with issues related to socioeconomic inequality, discrimination and systemic barriers to access and opportunity all affecting employee wellbeing. Discrimination, bias and lack of representation in leadership roles can affect employees feeling excluded from the workplace as well as their ability to thrive within the workforce. Also, socioeconomic conditions for example, income distribution; access to health and education services; and place of residence can impact people's access to prospects for work, career advancement and wellbeing.

4 Isolation and Disconnection in Virtual Work Environments

Digital transformation is increasing isolation and disconnection in virtual workplaces. As companies adapt to remote work setups and further adopt digital technologies for collaboration, these physical gaps between workers can create feelings of loneliness, isolation, and disconnection. Author have explored some of the reasons and effects of isolation and disconnection in virtual work environments as well as strategies you can implement to help bring connection, collaboration and wellbeing into remote workspaces.

The trend is also shaped by such technological tools ranging from video conferencing to instant messaging to collaborative software that enable employees to communicate and collaborate no matter where they are physically located. These types of technologies provide unparalleled flexibility and convenience but are a killer combination for remote teams hoping to maintain social connections and healthy relationships. And as the number of virtual meetings increase at a much higher rate than in-person ones, the absence of those chance encounters and discussions that happen as a result of shared office space can leave employees with a sense of disconnection from their colleagues and the company as a whole specifically employees who depend on social interaction. The lack of physical presence can further deteriorate communication, contribute to miscommunication, misunderstanding, and a feeling of disconnection of team members in virtual work setups. Face-to-Face communication has a lot of non-verbal cues such as body language, facial expressions which are difficult to consider when we work on online platforms.

Source Author constructed

Furthermore, the blurring of boundaries between work and personal life in virtual work environments can aggravate feelings of isolation and disconnection. Without the delineation of a physical workspace, employees may find it challenging to disconnect from work and maintain work-life balance, leading to feelings of burnout, stress, and fatigue. The lack of social interaction and informal interactions that occur in traditional office settings can also contribute to a sense of disengagement from the broader organizational culture, values, and community, further intensifying feelings of isolation and disconnection among remote employees.

The consequences of isolation and disconnection in virtual work environments extend beyond individual wellbeing to impact team dynamics, organizational culture, and performance. When employees feel disconnected from their colleagues and the broader organization, they may become disengaged, demotivated, and less committed to team goals. This can delay collaboration, innovation, and creativity, as individuals are less likely to share ideas, seek feedback, and collaborate on projects. Furthermore, the lack of social support and companionship in virtual work environments can erode trust and cohesion among team members, leading to increased conflict, turnover, and absenteeism. To address isolation and disconnection in virtual work environments, organizations must prioritize initiatives that foster connection, collaboration, and wellbeing among remote teams. One strategy is to leverage technology to create opportunities for virtual socialization and informal interaction. This may include virtual coffee breaks, team-building activities, and social events that allow employees to connect on a personal level and build relationships outside of work-related tasks. Additionally, organizations can establish clear communication norms and expectations for virtual meetings and interactions, ensuring that all team members have the opportunity to participate and contribute effectively.

Moreover, organizations can promote a culture of inclusion and belonging by recognizing and celebrating the unique contributions and perspectives of remote employees. This may involve providing opportunities for remote employees to represent their work, participate in decision-making processes and receive recognition and feedback from colleagues and leaders. By developing a sense of connection and belonging among remote teams, organizations can increase morale, engagement, and performance, ultimately driving success in virtual work environments.

Source Author constructed

Designing human-centric work systems and implementing ergonomic practices are very crucial aspects of creating work environments that focus on health, safety and well-being of employees. Human-centric design places the needs, abilities, and preferences of workers at the forefront of workplace design, while ergonomic practices aim to optimize the physical and cognitive demands of work tasks to prevent injury and enhance performance. In this essay, we explore the principles of human-centric design and ergonomic practices, their importance in creating sustainable and productive work environments, and strategies for implementing them effectively.

Human-centric design revolves around understanding the needs, capabilities and preferences of individuals to create products, systems and environments that are intuitive, usable, and satisfying. In the context of work systems, human-centered design involves considering factors such as physical ergonomics, cognitive ergonomics, and socio-technical systems to ensure that work environments support the health, safety and well-being of employees. This approach acknowledges that humans are diverse beings with unique strengths, limitations and preferences and seeks to accommodate these differences through thoughtful design and consideration of user feedback.

Physical ergonomics focuses on prioritizing the physical aspects of work tasks to minimize the risk of musculoskeletal injuries and discomfort. This may involve designing workstations, tools and equipment to accommodate the range of body sizes and shapes, ensuring proper posture, alignment, and movement patterns. For example, adjustable desks and chairs allow employees to customize their workstation to their individual needs, while ergonomic keyboards and mouse reduce strain on the wrists and hands during typing and pointing tasks. Moreover, proper lighting, ventilation, and temperature control contribute to a comfortable and productive work environment, enhancing employee well-being and performance.

Cognitive ergonomics, on the other hand, addresses the mental demands of work tasks and seeks to optimize cognitive processes such as attention, memory, decision-making, and problem-solving. This may involve simplifying complex tasks, providing clear instructions and feedback, and reducing cognitive load by eliminating unnecessary distractions and information overload. For example, well-designed interfaces and software applications prioritize usability and intuitiveness, allowing employees to navigate tasks efficiently and effectively. Moreover, ergonomic practices such as regular breaks, task rotation, and stress management techniques help mitigate mental fatigue and prevent burnout, promoting cognitive well-being and performance. Socio-technical systems theory emphasizes the interaction between people, technology and organizational structures in shaping work systems and environments. It recognizes that work is inherently social and that the design of work systems must consider the social dynamics, communication patterns, and collaborative processes that influence employee well-being and performance. For example, fostering a culture of trust, respect, and collaboration promotes psychological safety and teamwork, enhancing employee engagement and satisfaction. Moreover, providing opportunities for social interaction, feedback and recognition strengthens social bonds and develop a sense of belonging and community among employees.

Implementing human-centric work systems and ergonomic practices requires a holistic approach that integrates design principles, organizational policies and employee feedback. Organizations can start by conducting ergonomic assessments and risk assessments to identify potential hazards and areas for improvement in the work environment. This may involve consulting with ergonomics experts, occupational health professionals and employee representatives to gather insights and recommendations for enhancing workplace design and practices.

Moreover, organizations can involve employees in the design process through participatory design workshops, surveys, and focus groups to gather feedback on their needs, preferences, and experiences in the workplace. This collaborative approach ensures that the design of work systems reflects the diverse perspectives and requirements of the workforce, enhancing usability, satisfaction, and performance. Additionally, organizations can provide training and education on ergonomic principles and practices to raise awareness and empower employees to take proactive measures to protect their health and well-being.

5 Emerging Trends and Innovations in Promoting Employee Wellbeing

Emerging trends and innovations in promoting employee wellbeing represent a dynamic response to the evolving needs and expectations of the modern workforce. As organizations recognize the intrinsic link between employee wellbeing and organizational success, they are increasingly investing in initiatives that prioritize physical, mental, and emotional health in the workplace. In this essay, we explore some of the latest trends and innovations in promoting employee wellbeing, including technology-driven solutions, holistic wellness programs, and organizational culture initiatives.

One of the most notable trends in promoting employee wellbeing is the adoption of technology-driven solutions that leverage digital tools and platforms to support employee health and wellness. From wearable devices that track physical activity and monitor vital signs to mobile apps that provide access to mental health resources and mindfulness exercises, technology offers unprecedented opportunities for individuals to monitor and manage their health in real-time. Moreover, artificial intelligence (AI) and data analytics enable organizations to personalize wellness interventions, identify trends and patterns in employee health data, and proactively address emerging issues before they escalate. For example, AI-powered chatbots and virtual assistants provide on-demand support and guidance for employees seeking information or assistance with health-related concerns, while predictive analytics algorithms can identify individuals at risk of burnout or other mental health challenges and intervene with targeted interventions.

6 Conclusion

Overall, this study reviews and studies the existing literature on how to improve employee wellbeing in the current and emerging industry 5.0. This essay examines various perspectives to highlight that employee wellbeing is both a moral and business imperative, such as organizations seek to thrive during Industry 5.0. There are numerous ways to facilitate employee wellbeing, from the integration of technology with human-centric philosophies to push towards holistic wellness programs and enabling organizational environments.

In fact, further collaboration is needed, because every step in Industry 5.0 requires a whole lot of interplay between technology, organization and society, so what you learn now is embedded into what we can't unlearn. Organizations need to proactively design work environments that balance the benefits of digital transformation with the essential human needs for engagement, purpose and well-being. This includes the merging of ethical AI, automation and smart technologies with empathetic leadership and mental health initiatives to ensure that employees do not feel alienated or overwhelmed by rapid technological shifts.

Furthermore, Industry 5.0 ushers in the potential for organizations to reimagine work arrangements, putting flexibility, inclusiveness, and employee agency front and center. Building trust at scale underlines a culture of psychological safety, constant upskilling and open communication. Organizations can shape a motivated and high-performing workforce by implementing employee-oriented policies such as remote working, well-being programs and employee-involved decision-making processes.

A focus on employee wellbeing improves organizational performance, but it also leads to collective economic and social progress. Workers empowered and esteemed can more robustly lend to innovation, sustainability and ethical business practices. Promoting initiatives focused on well-being allow organizations to not only boost productivity but also be part of a successful and humane 'Future at Work'.

Indeed, the core of the sustainable business success of Industry 5.0 is formed through the employee wellbeing as the other takeaways from the literature review of this paper. As companies learn and grow, the balance between advancement and people-centricity will ultimately set the stage for their sustainability and competitive edge. Organizations that support their employees will capitalize on the full potential of their human resources, ensuring that they not only transition successfully into the future of work, but flourish within it.

Theme	*Key Aspects*
Human centric approach 5.0	Transitional shift from automation to human machine compilation Customisation in work environments Artificial intelligence support for employee empowerment
Technological integration and employee wellbeing	Online digital tools for mental wellbeing Digital integration for employee wellbeing Job displacement of technology's ethical concerns
Psychosocial wellbeing in the smart workplace	Hyperconnectivity and digital burnout Strategies of prevent burnout Status of social interaction and workplace culture
Work flexibility and hybrid work models	Harmonizing automation with remote/hybrid work Employee self-government and job satisfaction Challenges in controlling remote employee performance
Sustainability and employee wellbeing	Green HRM and sustainable work practices Eco-friendly factories' impact on mental health CSR and happiness initiatives
Skill development and lifelong learning	Reskilling and upskilling for human-AI collaboration Constant learning as a job satisfaction driver Psychological impression of adapting to new technologies
Ethical considerations and workplace inclusion	AI-driven decision-making and equality Addressing workplace disparities in automation

(continued)

(continued)

Theme	*Key Aspects*
Future research and policy implications	Inclusion of disabled employees Gaps in research on happiness in Industry 5.0 Need for ethical AI policy frameworks Future trends in workplace wellbeing

References

1. Adekanmbi, F. P., & Ukpere, W. I. (2022). Sustaining organizational performance and employee wellbeing in the 4IR: the impact of leadership 4.0, PSYCAP, and high-performance HR practices. *EUREKA: Social and Humanities*, (3), 24–39.
2. Adel, A. (2022). Future of industry 5.0 in society: human-centric solutions, challenges and prospective research areas. *Journal of Cloud Computing*, *11*(1), 40.
3. Antonaci, F. G., Olivetti, E. C., Marcolin, F., Castiblanco Jimenez, I. A., Eynard, B., Vezzetti, E., & Moos, S. (2024). Workplace Well-Being in Industry 5.0: A Worker-Centered Systematic Review. *Sensors*, *24*(17), 5473.
4. Bai, C., Dallasega, P., Orzes, G., & Sarkis, J. (2020). Industry 4.0 technologies assessment: A sustainability perspective. *International journal of production economics*, *229*, 107776.
5. Chauhan, M. (2023). Industry 4.0 and Employee Wellbeing: The Mediating Role of Creative Climate. *Issue 3 Int'l JL Mgmt. & Human.*, *6*, 2747.
6. CIPD report, 2020 https://www.cipd.org/globalassets/media/knowledge/knowledge-hub/reports/resourcing-and-talent-planning-2020_tcm18-85530.pdf
7. Coetzee, D. (2024). *The readiness of HR practitioners to address the influence of the Fourth Industrial Revolution on employee wellbeing: An exploratory study* (Doctoral dissertation, Stellenbosch University).
8. Dalenogare, L. S., Benitez, G. B., Ayala, N. F., & Frank, A. G. (2018). The expected contribution of Industry 4.0 technologies for industrial performance. *International Journal of production economics*, *204*, 383-394.
9. Dewi, R. P. (2020) Empower Employees: Understanding Wellbeing in the Era of Industry 4.0 Through Flexibility working arrangement. *Psisula: Prosiding Berkala Psikologi*, *6*, 273–291.

10. Dewi, R. P., & Prahara, S. A. (2025). How does job insecurity among employees affect employee well-being in the era of the Fourth Industrial Revolution?. In *Economic Sustainability and Social Equality in the Technological Era* (pp. 247–255). Routledge.
11. du Plessis, M. (2021). Enhancing psychological wellbeing in industry 4.0: The relationship between emotional intelligence, social connectedness, work-life balance and positive coping behaviour. In *Agile coping in the digital workplace: Emerging issues for research and practice* (pp. 99–118). Cham: Springer International Publishing.
12. Fedorova, A., Dvorakova, Z., & Atas, H. (2022, February). Workplace Well-Being in Employee Estimates. In *Proceedings of the International Scientific Conference "Smart Nations: Global Trends In The Digital Economy" Volume 1* (pp. 529–540). Cham: Springer International Publishing.
13. Frank, A. G., Dalenogare, L. S., & Ayala, N. F. (2019). Industry 4.0 technologies: Implementation patterns in manufacturing companies. *International journal of production economics*, *210*, 15-26.
14. Frutos-Bencze, D., Sokolova, M., Zubr, V., & Mohelska, H. (2022). Job satisfaction during COVID-19: industry 5.0 as a driver of sustainable development and gender equality. *Technological and Economic Development of Economy*, *28*(5), 1527–1544.
15. Galjak, M., Nikolić, V., Miladinović, T., & Jovanović, (2024) B. EMPLOYEE WELLBEING IN THE DIGITIZATION AGE. *The authors are responsible for the professional and linguistic accuracy of their papers.*, 58.
16. Gallup report, 2022 https://www.gallup.com/workplace/467699/gallup-top-workplace-stories-2022.aspx
17. Guest, D., & Conway, N. (2009). Health and well-being: The role of the psychological contract. *International handbook of work and health psychology*, 7–23.
18. Gupta, A., & John, S. (2023). Strengthening Industry 5.0 through Emotional Intelligence. *Disruptive Business Environment*, 387.
19. Iqbal, M. N. (2025). Leveraging Technology for Employee Well Being and Organizational Resilience. In *Human-Centric, Sustainable, and Resilient Organizations in the Digital Age* (pp. 147–172). IGI Global Scientific Publishing.
20. Javaid, M., Haleem, A., Vaishya, R., Bahl, S., Suman, R., & Vaish, A. (2020). Industry 4.0 technologies and their applications in fighting COVID-19 pandemic. *Diabetes & Metabolic Syndrome: Clinical Research & Reviews*, *14*(4), 419–422.
21. Kaasinen, E., Anttila, A. H., & Heikkilä, P. (2022). New industrial work: Personalised job roles, smooth human-machine teamwork and support for well-being at work. In *Human-technology interaction: Shaping the future*

of industrial user interfaces (pp. 271-301). Cham: Springer International Publishing.

22. Kadir, B. A., & Broberg, O. (2020). Human well-being and system performance in the transition to industry 4.0. *International Journal of Industrial Ergonomics*, *76*, 102936.
23. Koropets, O., Fedorova, A., & Shkurin, D. (2022). INVESTIGATION OF THE EMPLOYEES'WELL-BEING UNDER INDUSTRY 4.0 DEVELOPMENT. *Журнал «Human Progress»* http://progress-human.com, *8*(4).
24. Le Fevre, M., Kolt, G. S., & Matheny, J. (2006). Eustress, distress and their interpretation in primary and secondary occupational stress management interventions: which way first?. *Journal of Managerial Psychology*, *21*(6), 547-565.
25. Leng, J., Sha, W., Wang, B., Zheng, P., Zhuang, C., Liu, Q., ... & Wang, L. (2022). Industry 5.0: Prospect and retrospect. *Journal of Manufacturing Systems*, *65*, 279-295.
26. Lu, Y., Zheng, H., Chand, S., Xia, W., Liu, Z., Xu, X., ... & Bao, J. (2022). Outlook on human-centric manufacturing towards Industry 5.0. *Journal of Manufacturing Systems*, *62*, 612–627.
27. Madero-Gómez, S. M., Rubio Leal, Y. L., Olivas-Luján, M., & Yusliza, M. Y. (2023). Companies could benefit when they focus on employee wellbeing and the environment: a systematic review of Sustainable Human Resource Management. *Sustainability*, *15*(6), 5435.
28. McKinsey report, (2022) https://www.mckinsey.com/featured-insights/insights-store, accessed on 12 February 2025
29. Nurrohmat, S. M., Khuzaini, K., & Shaddiq, S. (2024). The Influence of Industry 4.0 on Work Behavior and Employee Productivity in Technology Companies. *Proceeding: Islamic University of Kalimantan.*
30. Panday, P., & Kaur, G. (2023). Talent management and employee outlook on industry 5.0. In *Handbook of Research on Education Institutions, Skills, and Jobs in the Digital Era* (pp. 299–306). IGI Global.
31. Papetti, A., Gregori, F., Pandolfi, M., Peruzzini, M., & Germani, M. (2020). A method to improve workers' well-being toward human-centered connected factories. *Journal of Computational Design and Engineering*, *7*(5), 630-643.
32. Poláková, M., Suleimanová, J. H., Madzík, P., Copuš, L., Molnárová, I., & Polednová, J. (2023). Soft skills and their importance in the labour market under the conditions of Industry 5.0. *Heliyon*, *9*(8).
33. Raj, A., Dwivedi, G., Sharma, A., de Sousa Jabbour, A. B. L., & Rajak, S. (2020). Barriers to the adoption of industry 4.0 technologies in the manufacturing sector: An inter-country comparative perspective. *International Journal of Production Economics*, *224*, 107546.

34. Rosca, C. M., & Stancu, A. (2024). Fusing Machine Learning and AI to Create a Framework for Employee Well-Being in the Era of Industry 5.0. *Applied Sciences (2076–3417)*, *14*(23).
35. Rosin, F., Forget, P., Lamouri, S., & Pellerin, R. (2020). Impacts of Industry 4.0 technologies on Lean principles. *International Journal of Production Research*, *58*(6), 1644–1661.
36. Sagar, S., Garg, V., & Rastogi, R. (2022). Employee Wellness Without Stress and Strain: Application of Yoga and Meditation in Management With an Industry 5.0 Perspective. In *Handbook of Research on Innovative Management Using AI in Industry 5.0* (pp. 204–221). IGI Global.
37. Saharan, T., & Sharma, H. (2022). Intellectual Impact of Spiritual Wellbeing, Self-Determination, and Employee Outlook on Industry 5.0. In *Handbook of Research on Innovative Management Using AI in Industry 5.0* (pp. 118–135). IGI Global.
38. Salvadorinho, J., & Teixeira, L. (2023). Happy and engaged workforce in industry 4.0: a new concept of digital tool for HR based on theoretical and practical trends. *Sustainability*, *15*(3), 2781.
39. Tripathi, M. A., Sawant, P. D., Kaur, H., Almahairah, M. S., Chandel, P. S., & Balakumar, A. (2024, March). Human-Robot Collaboration in the Workplace: Assessing the Impact on Employee Well-Being and Productivity. In *2024 Third International Conference on Intelligent Techniques in Control, Optimization and Signal Processing (INCOS)* (pp. 1–7). IEEE.
40. Xu, X., Lu, Y., Vogel-Heuser, B., & Wang, L. (2021). Industry 4.0 and Industry 5.0—Inception, conception and perception. *Journal of manufacturing systems*, *61*, 530-535.
41. Zheng, T., Ardolino, M., Bacchetti, A., & Perona, M. (2021). The applications of Industry 4.0 technologies in manufacturing context: a systematic literature review. *International Journal of Production Research*, *59*(6), 1922–1954.
42. Rosca, C. M., & Stancu, A. (2024). Fusing Machine Learning and AI to Create a Framework for Employee Well-Being in the Era of Industry 5.0. *Applied Sciences (2076-3417)*, *14*(23).
43. Kuru, H. (2023). Understanding employee wellness in industry 5.0: A systematic review. *Journal of Ekonomi*, *5*(1), 32–35.
44. Khaled, G., & Alena, F. (2022). The evolution of well-being approach within the industry 5.0 concept. *Human Progress*, *8*(3), 12.
45. Davila-Gonzalez, S., & Martin, S. (2024). Human digital twin in industry 5.0: A holistic approach to worker safety and well-being through advanced AI and emotional analytics. *Sensors*, *24*(2), 655.
46. Chulakit, S., Sadun, A. S., Jalaludin, N. A., Hashim, H., Hassan, H., Mahmood, S., ... & Fauzi, M. A. (2024). A Review of HRV and

EEG Technology Applications in Industry 5.0: Emphasising Manufacturing Efficiency and Worker Well-Being. *International Journal of Integrated Engineering*, *16*(5), 324–340.
47. Passalacqua, M., Pellerin, R., Magnani, F., Doyon-Poulin, P., Del-Aguila, L., Boasen, J., & Léger, P. M. (2025). Human-centred AI in industry 5.0: a systematic review. *International Journal of Production Research*, *63*(7), 2638–2669.
48. Grybauskas, A., & Cárdenas-Rubio, J. (2024). Unlocking employer insights: Using large language models to explore human-centric aspects in the context of industry 5.0. *Technological Forecasting and Social Change*, *208*, 123719.
49. Sharma, R. (2024). Analysis of Industry 5.0 contributions to sustainable development: from welfare to wellbeing. In *Modern Technologies and Tools Supporting the Development of Industry 5.0* (pp. 259–300). CRC Press.
50. Trstenjak, M., Benešova, A., Opetuk, T., & Cajner, H. (2025). Human Factors and Ergonomics in Industry 5.0—A Systematic Literature Review. *Applied Sciences*, *15*(4), 2123.
51. Abe, I. I. (2021). The dynamics of workplace relationships, employee well-being, and the fourth industrial revolution: Perspectives of workplace relationships and Industry 4.0. In *Future of Work, Work-Family Satisfaction, and Employee Well-Being in the Fourth Industrial Revolution* (pp. 99–112). IGI Global Scientific Publishing.
52. du Plessis, M. (2021). Enhancing psychological wellbeing in industry 4.0: The relationship between emotional intelligence, social connectedness, work-life balance and positive coping behaviour. In *Agile coping in the digital workplace: Emerging issues for research and practice* (pp. 99-118). Cham: Springer International Publishing.
53. Olga, K., Alena, F., & Denis, S. (2022). INVESTIGATION OF THE EMPLOYEES'WELL-BEING UNDER INDUSTRY 4.0 DEVELOPMENT. *Human Progress*, *8*(4), 18.

Women-Led Social Enterprises in Industry 5.0: Pioneering Sustainable and Inclusive Growth in South Asia

Ritesh Dwivedi and Mouripa Deb

1 Introduction

1.1 Background and Context

In recent years, there has been a growing recognition of women's role in promoting social and economic development. It has turned into a positive and significant change-making agent in South Asia and the global scenario, especially in women-led social entrepreneurship. The women's entrepreneurial approach and the ability to overcome all the difficulties have been significant in combating urgent social issues and making positive changes toward effective development in South Asia [1]. The advancement of women to the working force and their participation in business ventures have helped boost the economic needs of the country and have shifted gender roles and inequalities in today's society.

R. Dwivedi (✉) · M. Deb
Symbiosis Institute of Business Management, Noida, Symbiosis International (Deemed University), Pune, India
e-mail: ritesh.dwivedi@sibmnoida.siu.edu.in

M. Deb
e-mail: mouripa.deb2026@sibmnoida.siu.edu.in

© The Author(s), under exclusive license to Springer Nature Singapore Pte Ltd. 2025

P. Agarwal et al. (eds.), *Building a Human-Centred Infrastructure for Sustainable Industry 5.0 in Asia*,
https://doi.org/10.1007/978-981-95-0417-6_12

1.2 Importance of Women-Led Social Enterprises

The reason that women-led social enterprises are vital is due to their ability to create social value and economic value. Several such businesses support both the financial goals alongside the sustainable and social goals, which in turn supports the inclusion of sustainable development. Women can notice social issues that most regular companies will not care about due to the difference in skills and perspectives. In addition, SDG entrepreneurship and women's rights are critical for realizing the SDGs and people's welfare because of the powerful effect of women's entrepreneurship, the advocacy for social justice and equity, and the promotion of sustainability. In as much as we look at the development likely to unlock the political, social, and even economic dimensions of society, there is no doubt that women are crucial. The literature also suggests that as half of the population is women, any change or improvement is only possible with their participation [2]. Education of women is essential to the overall well-being and development of any nation since it empowers women economically [3]. Women's entrepreneurship also has a high level of effectiveness in pursuing the overall national development objectives to empower women folk in their economic status and enhance their social status.

1.3 Objectives and Scope of the Study

It intends to examine how women-headed development organizations engage themselves in establishing social businesses in the South Asian Region, particularly in India, to address socio-economic problems. Although the focus of this study is social responsiveness, including supporting entrepreneurship to fight for social justice and equality to foster social change, community upliftment, and sustainable development, the study aims to identify and understand the nature of these businesses. In order to understand the challenges, opportunities, and impact of women-led social firms in the area, the scope of this study embraces a review of case studies, quantitative/qualitative data, and published papers. Furthermore, the research also tries to find policy recommendations and support structures that would help enhance the capability and capacity of women entrepreneurs in South Asia.

1.4 *Industry 5.0*

The Next Evolution of the Industrial Path is Industry 5.0, which is focused on human-centric innovation, sustainability, and technological integration. While Industry 4.0 mainly worked on automation and smart technologies, Industry 5.0 puts humans and smart systems in a harmonious collaboration with one another. Key characteristics of Industry 5.0 include focusing on human abilities instead of automating them, ensuring egocentric production processes, and minimizing the eco prints. Resilience and Inclusivity—Creating adaptive and inclusive business ecosystems. Sustainable Development Through Women's Social Enterprises: Generators for Economic and Social Transformation The women's social enterprises' models of sustainable development are innovative business models that address social challenges. The enterprises that these schools produce are intended to contribute to the economy and job creation and to provide means for community empowerment, specifically in South Asia, for which gender inequalities continue to be an impediment to economic participation.

1.5 *The Importance of Gender Inclusion in Industry 5.0*

The concept of Industry 5.0 understands the pivotal contribution of gender diversity to the innovation and sustainable growth of the industry. The women integrated into leadership and entrepreneurship within Industry 5.0 ensure Women Entrepreneurs, meaning that they took part in greater economic participation. It will enhance diverse perspectives on systemic gender disparities by focusing on addressing systemic gender disparities through targeted policies and support systems.

2 Literature Review

2.1 *The Role of Women in Economic and Social Development*

The role of women in any society plays a critical role in enhancing social and economic development. women's representation in labour and entrepreneurship brings out good societal values like healthcare and education for women and families as well as economic improvement [3]. South Asian Women have been involved in various sectors of the economy, as entrepreneurs in small and medium enterprises or as producers of small scale production in manufacturing including handicrafts and agriculture. However, most often the efforts that single mothers put in their work are not acknowledged and, in some cases, even unappreciated. A few development projects targeting to better support and diversify female businesses and economic management and leadership in the area have been launched in recent years due to the increasing concern on women's economic and social role.

2.2 Current Landscape of Women-Led Social Enterprises in India and South Asia

Today, the opportunities for women-led social entrepreneurs, based in South Asia and India in particular, are growing dramatically as more women make the decision to create startups that solve social and environmental issues. Many sectors benefit from the services of these enterprises and their application of business strategies that seek to have sustainable financial returns and address the welfare of society that they are well known for. The women social entrepreneurs in the area are very actively contributing to improved social and gender equality, social participation, and sustainable development, albeit the prevailing challenges are social rejections and scarce funding. A shift marks continuous growth in social enterprise in South Asia and India as more women opt for entrepreneurship to solve social and environmental challenges. The majority of Indian women entrepreneurs are involved in the manufacture of products such as apparel and cosmetics, and services which include interiors and consultancy, among others. Most will start a business or a service in the commerce industry and prefer less high-tech, low-capital ventures. Some of them, as they gain experience, transition into the manufacturing end of the business. Incumbents in this industry are educationally more endowed, and a lower proportion inherited their businesses compared with traders and manufacturers. Specialisation is rife for most women-owned SMEs in that they mainly deal with a single product or service; hence, diversification, which is an exception, is occasioned by necessity. As highlighted by Rajalakshmi [3], the present picture has a favourable picture; women enter almost all sectors and show good skills in the strategic management of businesses and their growth and profitability. Of course, the acknowledgement of women's economic efforts through self-employment and industrial undertakings has started gaining tempo, and the various agencies and non-governmental organizations are thoroughly assisting these women in their endeavours. From welfare-oriented to development and empowerment-oriented, women have become more involved in entrepreneurial activities. Even if it is so, women of India and other SAARC countries have shown that they are abler and are already important active members in the social and economic stratum of society. As per the analysis of Rajalakshmi [3], it is becoming better day by day that women entrepreneurs are involved in most of the industries of the economy, and they are also showing their ability to manage their businesses and grow them successfully. Greater awareness of the involvement of women in the economy through their participation in self-employment and industrial production continued, and there are agencies both in the government and non-government bodies that assist these women in their endeavours. South Asian women's entrepreneurship, including the Indian, has been even more supported since the change of the strategy from welfarism to development and empowering approaches. Indeed, working women of India and the South Asian region are transforming the scenario and are coming forward to play their roles in both social and economic sectors despite some hindrances. These have been noted to go beyond the generation of economic value and encompass social justice, the environment, and the poor. But even if the latter is still in charge, the reality of the narrative unveils the possible huge capacity and capabilities of women social entrepreneurs in shaping a better future for the region that is more sustainable and equal.

3 The Nexus Between Social Enterprises and Social Problem Solving

3.1 Understanding Social Enterprises as a Vehicle for Social Change

Social businesses are different categories of companies that do not aim only at making high revenue an profit but consider the impact on the environment and the change they bring to society as well. One of the chief objectives of these groups is to have an answer to social concerns and to engage in change for the benefit of the societies. It is, therefore, different from firms that are profit-making organisations that only focus on profits. Enterprises sourced by women focus on the mission to solve social problems in ways through their unique perspectives, innovative ideas and forces of thought patterns and positive features that will introduce novelty into the strategies. Also, their concern is simply to identify and magnify some chosen problem issues when it comes to issues and policies relating to education, health, and employment, which will undoubtedly be more acute for women and other vulnerable people. This may be a lack of concern for society or the future of their initiatives, but social enterprises, on the other hand, plough back their profits to enable society to find sustainable solutions for the problems affecting societies. It has also established that most women-centered social businesses exhibit strong concern for social justice, democracies, and community well-being, boosting the chances of bringing about positive change in South Asia and other countries.

3.2 *How Women-Led Enterprises Address Social Issues*

Through providing necessities, creating employment and as well as advocating for economic freedom, WMEs play a crucial role in advocating for integration and the improvement of the poor in society. It also makes their work more sustainable, thus making their work effective, enduring, and, in the process, does not affect the environment. South Asian women entrepreneurs use diverse strategies in presenting solutions to social issues in enterprises for employment because, considering the social inclusion drive a lens, they introduce distinct approaches to addressing the challenges (Kampoowale and Khalid 2024). The literature says that such enterprises are likely to respond to the needs of the women and the disadvantages such as education, health and employment [4].

It is worth appreciating the efforts that women-led enterprises are making towards social inclusion, poverty eradication, and improved livelihood since they meet some of the most basic needs, create job opportunities, and empower the people (Kampoowale and Khalid 2024). The emphasis on sustainability, in turn, leads to the stability/sustainability of the ventures as well as the effect on the physical terrain. The literature suggests that WMEs also emphasize social justice, equality, and community empowerment, making them effective agents of social change in the region.

3.3 *Case Studies of Successful Women-Led Social Enterprises*

Various successful cases observed in South Asia have made a good example on how entrepreneurship can be tapped into social issues and cause change. For example, "RangSutra Crafts India" has helped aspiring rural women artisans to be economically independent through creative skill development and selling handmade crafts they produce market very well [5]. Likewise, ideas such as "Moeda Seeds" approach e-commerce stores and utilize cryptocurrency platforms to provide economic services and enhance female's status within the developing countries' societies [6]. Below mentioned case discussion focuses on the positive impact of women as they embark on the social entrepreneurship initiatives toward the formation of the sustainable society. There are numerous examples in South Asian region indicating successful women led social enterprises. Firms that have demonstrated outstanding accomplishments in their endeavors to solve social problems and support the Sustainable Development Goals. For instance, SEWA, the Self-Employed Women's Association in India has assisted numerous women through its cooperative bank and micro financing, that grants women an opportunity to access loans and finance to start and grow their businesses as noted by ESCAP [4]. Disbursement of loans among the women entrepreneurs, particularly has been supported and assisted largely by BWCCI. Women's entrepreneurship development in Bangladesh: Capacity Building Programs, Advocacy and Access to Finance [4]. Some of the case studies indicate that, among others, impact of improving the lives of women and communities in South Asia through different women lead social enterprise.

- Rifa Musthapha is the attorney of the law as well as business lady from Sri Lanka. She also sits as a president to Women's Chamber of Commerce and Industry within her country. That is why she address the gender inequity in the realm of business and supports the laws that empower women owning small and mid- sized businesses.
- Shamama Arbab of Pakistan, is not only a vice president 'Women Chamber of Commerce and Industry- Pakistan' but also having own food processing industry in Peshawar. She also sees the women empowerment as an important part of the development process of the country and also the importance of the women being incorporated into the mainstream economies.
- Nepali Rita Bhandary inspires women to do this while running their businesses. Besides being a successful businesswoman, she is also the President, Federation of Women's Entrepreneurs Associations of Nepal. She has played a tremendous role in the setting down of finances for government funding and market for women ventures.

- Dr. Manju Kalra Prakash is an Indian executive at the Federation of Indian Chambers of Commerce and Industry. She offers women entrepreneurship training and development solution which are customized for their needs to enable them grow their businesses.
- Selima Ahmad, a woman for instance, who has been the founder of Bangladesh Women's Chamber of Commerce and Industries believes that more funding and education should be made available for women entrepreneurs. She explains how women's economic empowered is prosperous to their communities and families.

3.4 *Linking Women Entrepreneurship with Industry 5.0 Principles*

Women entrepreneurs are pioneering new business models that align with Industry 5.0's objectives. Some key models include the following: Women entrepreneurs are creating new business models in line with the objectives of Industry 5.0. Women entrepreneurs use cooperative networks as a powerful model where women zone together and share resources and market access. An instance of this is the Self-Employed Women's Association (SEWA) of India, which has been able to create a framework for female entrepreneurs rooted in a community-based model. Microfinancing initiatives are another impactful model that offers small-scale funding platforms to empower women-led businesses to grow. Empowering women financially and helping them to start or grow their businesses, the Grameen Bank in Bangladesh has been one of the driving forces in lending microloans. Businesses also look towards sustainable supply chains, such as putting progressive work into the sourcing of their products to ensure that it is ethical and fair trade. The approach is shown by Malavika Sharma's Avika in India, which creates both a positive economic and environmental impact through eco-friendly and ethical fashion.

3.5 *Digital Transformation and Smart Infrastructure:*

AI and Automation—Optimizing production and customer service. Blockchain—Ensuring transparent transactions and ethical sourcing. E-commerce and Digital Marketing—Expanding market access through platforms like Shopify and Etsy. Social Implications of Industry 5.0 Women-led enterprises play a huge role in addressing social justice, economic disparity, and environmental sustainability. Their businesses: Provide employment opportunities for marginalized women. Dedicated to environmental sustainability through eco-friendly production techniques. Help develop the community by reinvesting profits in social causes. Gender Barriers and How Industry 5.0 Can Help Remove Them Women entrepreneurs must contend with several challenges, though: lack of access to capital, lack of digital literacy, socio-cultural restrictions, and so forth. Industry 5.0 can help overcome these barriers through digital banking and fintech solutions that help to improve financial inclusion in the Southeast Asia region. Expanding educational and skill-building programs. Encouraging gender-sensitive policies and investment incentives.

4 Challenges and Opportunities for Female Entrepreneurs

Gender-Specific Barriers in Entrepreneurship Despite the growing awareness of the importance of WOMEN ENTREPRENEURS in South Asia, women entrepreneurs still face a number of gender-related barriers that hinder progress. The societies make it quite challenging for women to commence and manage profitable ventures [4]. Also, the literature highlights how pervasive sexism in the workplace is, how women are paid less, and how there are few opportunities for the advancement of women, which all contribute to the challenges women face when trying to become entrepreneurs.

Some of the societies in the region are also polygamous, and this has led to restrictions on women's mobility and decision-making. This makes it difficult for women to start and run businesses that can be profitable, a factor that has contributed to a high rate of loan default. Therefore, developing a complex approach is essential to explain institutional and societal constraints and remove these challenges. However, many barriers continue to hamper the progress of the women in the region in achieving their business drive in the country. The last challenge is role strain due to the efforts made to try to balance between home and business responsibilities. Women company owners are usually expected to run businesses and perform the conventional womanly responsibilities of a wife, mother, and daughter-in-law. This place a lot of pressure on their time as well as other resources that can be utilized more efficiently elsewhere. In most cases, a woman is exposed to a dual role whereby she is expected to work and at the same time fend for the family, especially in a joint family arrangement, and the additional load is even more apparent in the case of rural women [7].

The other important challenge is the immobility. Studies have indicated that whenever women are employed and have to travel in search of work, they always have to take along with them male relations, especially if they are from rural areas. Because of their dependence on men, they are often incapable of making timely decisions or closing profitable transactions, which also affects their opportunities for expansion. In addition, there are so many opportunities for women business owners in the new corporate world. The new generation of women can thus overcome barriers to market entry and movement owing to the emergent e-commerce and digital platforms. Through the use of these tools, women can penetrate new markets and hence be able to sell their products. Still, financial help and training aspects are identified to be funded by government schemes, including the Prime Minister Rojgar Yojana and Swarna Jayanti Swarozgar Yojana to support women aspiring to develop their businesses or looking to expand on their endeavors [7]. These interventions are billed as measures to promote women's entrepreneurship. markets and potentiality, and is detrimental to the company's operations [7]. Furthermore, in consideration of women entrepreneurs, especially those with rural backgrounds, poor professional and technical competence is another challenge they encounter. It also shows that many women lack confidence and are insecure in employing themselves since they are barred from pursuing technical education or any form of learning. However, the education levels and skills possessed by the women entrepreneurs remained low incompetitive markets. [7].

However, several barriers remain and south Asian woman entrepreneurs have many opportunities to chart their path to success. Lately, awareness of women's entrepreneurship has gained attention, resulting in the establishment of women-friendly programs to support women-owned businesses. Some of these activities include funding opportunities, educational prospects, networking opportunities, and mentoring opportunities, amongst others. The opportunities that allow empowering women's social companies are quite limited, and it is becoming possible for women's social companies to create positive societal impacts because of the increasing popularity of social and sustainable needs among consumers. Despite these hurdles, the women entrepreneurs of India have a rich opportunity profile to grow and evolve. Another important reason that has made women undertake entrepreneurship has been the increased support from families, particularly from spouses. [7].

The women entrepreneurs of South Asia have availability of a number of opportunities available for to cater to the needs of women-led firms and help them in financing, training, and markets, government policies and initiatives are important as described by Rajalakshmi [3]. Non-governmental organizations and social impact investors are major attractions for opportunities in networking, training, and other relevant support in building capacity. Moreover, with the enhancement and popularity of the use of digital technology and particularly e-commerce platforms, it became possible for women entrepreneurs to diversify their businesses and become recognized beyond the borders. Female entrepreneurs cannot survive without support systems in place or want to build.

Many Government and non-government organizations in India provide financial support, guidance, and training to women involved in business. For instance, The Trade Related Entrepreneurial Assistance and Development (TREAD) project offers capital support and entrepreneurial skill support among women living in rural, urban, and semi-urban regions. Like this, low-income women now have restricted access to financial hindrances for the commencement and growth of their businesses due to Rashtriya Mahila Kosh microcredit [7]. Thus, for female entrepreneurs to be successful, the support of their families has not lost its significance. Several authors have pointed out that being blessed with good family support, especially from a husband, increases women's chances of excelling at entrepreneurship. With this support, women can concentrate on their businesses; the situation also reduces some role stress [7]. Hence, access to mentors and networking opportunities are critical focal points for the advancement of the growth of female entrepreneurship, in addition to financial and familial resources. Provided women have access to professional networks and experienced mentors, then they ought to be able to access those fortified needs in order to manage the challenges encountered in entrepreneurship. In addition, these networks imply cooperation, exchange of information, and market access, which are crucial to the evolution and viability of companies [7]. In South Asia, many organizations have played an important role in supporting female entrepreneurs in a number of programs.

For women entrepreneurs in India who are running businesses at various levels of development, FLO exists, which offers training, business consultancy, and courses. FLO also launched communication rights for

African women, and it established a forum for young female professionals. Another Pakistan based microfinance institution namely First Women's Bank Limited (FWBL) provides only credit facility and assistance but only to female entrepreneurs. Almost all its business center owners are women, it has high recovery rate. BWCCI supports female business people by incubating them, providing market opportunities, and providing capital support. Policy lobbying is also on its behalf. Women Entrepreneurs Association of Nepal WEAN provides funding projects, networking, advocacy, and training to the women in Nepal. Eventually, by using the programs and the networks that have been developed for some time and learning more about the techniques that can help overcome some of the challenges, female entrepreneurs in India can further develop their companies and make them grow. Thus, it is important for the government and other organizations to continue enhancing women's empowerment through prototypes of friendly strength mentorship, funding, and education so as to support and create reactive environments for women within all countries.

5 The Impact of Women-Led Social Enterprises on Society

The Indian Government characterizes a woman-owned business as an organization that is owned by a woman, or multiple women, and 51% of the stake in the organization is held by women. Women contribute to nearly 48% of the population of India, yet they are severely underrepresented in, at least, financial and economic activities, with only 34% of women participating, as many of them are unpaid and/or underpaid workers.

5.1 *Exploring the Effects of Women-led Social Business Entities*

The Indian Government defines a woman-owned business as an enterprise that is owned by at least one woman or a set of women, and a minimum of 51% of the ownership of the enterprise rests with women. According to the latest census report of India, women constitute nearly 48% of the total population of India but in financial and economic activities at least they are least represented with a mere 34% of participation and many of them are either paid or underpaid employees. The social barriers can be broken by women through their entrepreneurial ventures while gaining financial independence, whereby they participate in sustainable development. Private sector-led women's venture has not only made provision for employment that is self-sustaining but has also been contributing significantly to offering solutions to some pressing social and ecological issues that are pressing. In a sense, when Governments, non-governmental organizations, or the private sector provide a conducive environment for female entrepreneurship, females can be given a chance to be Change agents within societies. Positive Impact on Economic Empowerment for Sustainable Human Development: For examining women entrepreneurs' case, Mohiuuddin [8] opined that more than 50 percent of the total population of Bangladesh is women. This cites that women's economic activity rates are highly impeccable. The study also depicted the need of women from both the extremes of urban and rural areas to set up small businesses in order to enhance the economy of the country (Fig. 1).

Fig. 1 Sustainable factors influencing women entrepreneurship

5.2 *Promoting Social Justice and Equality through Women-Led Enterprises*

Talking specifically about India in South Asia, at both the central and state levels, many government schemes provide support to help women generate income of their own through small-scale training courses. One of the prime sectors working in the department includes "The Small Industries Development Bank of India", which has specified schemes and provisions designed for women entrepreneurs.

The government allocates several other schemes to promote women in the field of entrepreneurship. These are offered by the government for MSMEs and provide concessions specifically for women. Gender ratio in these supported enterprises are imbalanced (refer the Fig. 2). One such scheme, discussed in depth, includes the 'Prime Minister's Rozgar Yojana', most particularly in terms of the benefit that preference is given to women. Several relaxations also have been provided for women that assist the women beneficiaries to participate in this initiative. Similar to that is the 'Cluster Development Programme by the Ministry of MSME'. In this scheme, it is stated that 30-80% of the final project cost owned by women entrepreneurs will be taken care of by the Ministry of MSME. This could even go up to 90% of the total project cost, depending on how attractive the central theme idea of the business idea is. A similar contribution made by the Ministry of MSME is extended within the "Credit Guarantee Fund Scheme for Micro and Small Enterprises", whereby for small and medium-sized businesses, loans cover nearly 75% of the project cost. This benefit is availed by nearly 80% of micro and small enterprises managed and/or owned by women. Most of Women led MSME enterprises are in West Bengal (refer the Fig. 3).

5.3 *Examples of Community Empowerment and Transformation*

Below are a few case studies discussed across India, who've empowered themselves to start with new entrepreneurial ideas and continue to inspire other women who're tired of working in the setup to join businesses.

Case Study 1: Neeta Adappa, Prakriti Herbals

Neeta Adappa, based in Bengaluru, was involved in the research department of a pharmaceutical company in the quality sector but eventually

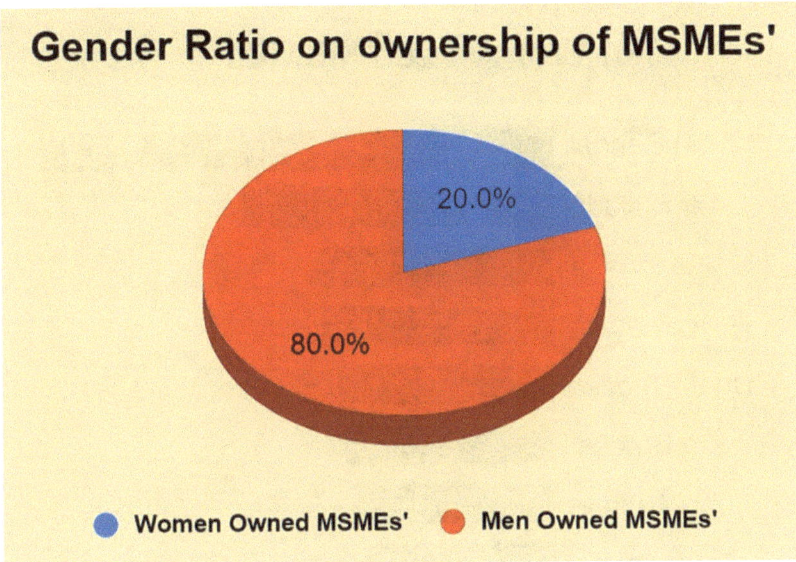

Fig. 2 Gender ratio of owned MSMEs, 7th Economic Census of India

became tired of her mundane schedule with no challenges. In 1995, when people were skeptical about entrepreneurs around, Neeta and her colleague Anisha Desai founded Prakriti Herbals. The project took off from Neeta's garage with an initial investment Rs 10,000. They started with a year of market research work about skin and hair care product formulations. The pilot survey was done on their relatives, friends, and family members. Eventually, they expanded their business and started producing on a commercial basis. They started receiving orders from premium hotels in the city. As of the present date, her brand is entrusted by premium five-star-rated hotels like the Goldman Sachs Spa, Park Hotel, Royal Orchid Hotels, etc., all across India.

Case Study 2: Japna Rishi, owner of Hungry Foal

A master's postgraduate in the department of food technology at Punjabi University, Japna from Patiala, was employed in the corporate sector for

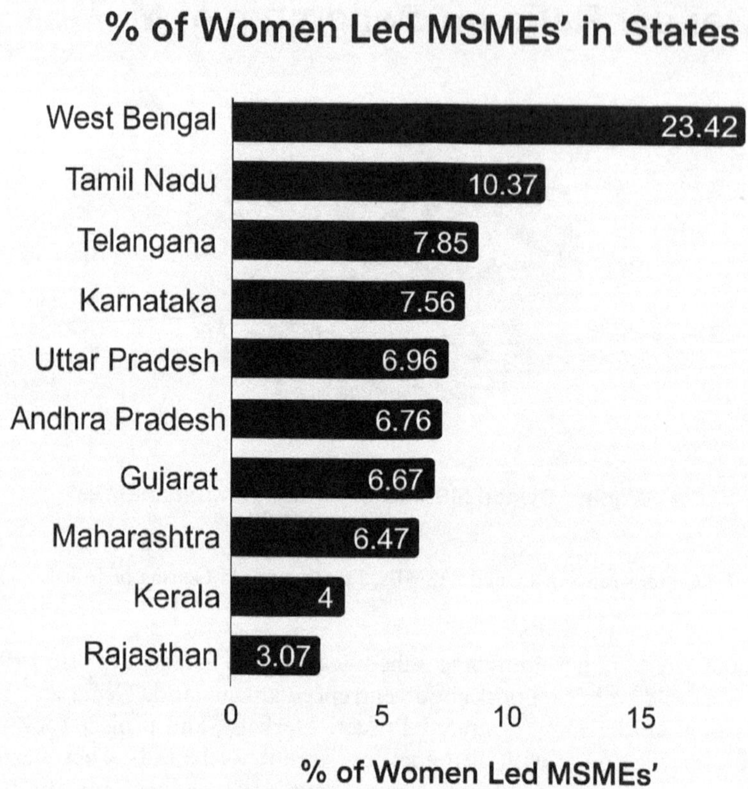

Fig. 3 Distribution of wMSMEs' across Indian states (*Source* MoMSME annual report 2021–22)

years before starting her venture. The ideation started in 2016 when she read in-depth about the alarming hunger state of young children in India. Japan and her husband Vivek Kaushik decided to take the bull by the horns and began Hungry Foal, a for-profit social venture, where they started selling Rs 5–10/unit nutritional snacks. The journey started from a 6ft. × 4ft. room in their house. They commenced with an annual revenue of around Rs 3 lakh, starting from scratch to now, clocking almost Rs 3.6 crore.

Case Study 3: Payal Mittal Agarwal, Tranquilitea

Payal Mittal Agarwal had a fascinating experience while in Slovenia with a woman, and this incident made her appreciate the excitement surrounding varieties of Indian tea. After her return from Slovenia, she began her entrepreneurial journey with a small-scale restaurant in her birthplace, Siliguri, along with a play school. Payal, while looking for options, discovered a tea enthusiast who was interested in opening tea centers across India. During a tea exhibition in China, she determined the objective of popularising the Indian tea business as she recognized it was very prevalent but not as popular as she would like it to be.

Case Study 4: Pritika Singh, Tvakh

A young postgraduate student in the field of biotechnology from Punjab's Thapar Institute of Engineering and Technology in the year 2013, Pritika wanted to evolve the chemically driven skincare products that were extremely toxic to the skin over time. After school, to dive deep into her field of interest, she enrolled in research and development teams related to cosmetics and the ingredients used to get to know about the formulations and intricacies of the industry. To her surprise, all that she availed was disappointment. To minimize the usage of harmful/toxic ingredients, especially in skincare products, she decided to launch her venture, which would have products in the line of natural hair and skin care products named Tvakh in 2016. Her first product was natural aloe-vera gel, which she prepared in her own kitchen. As the business gradually expanded, she received a manufacturing license, and with the investment of money, she bought a new machine for Rs. 1 lakh, expanding her space and product label.

5.4 *Key strategic takeaways from the case studies*

It's evident, women who've aspirations to start their businesses are looking for gaps in societies while working/studying in institutions at any level. With small savings, they are ready to take the leap of faith in starting their brands. Irrespective of the capital in their hand or the room size, they're starting their businesses with hope and have drawn a pathway for other aspirational female entrepreneurs to take the first step. They've empowered the economy and also helped build networks for collaborations at the global level, providing employment opportunities for other women in their locality, which helps them increase their family income. The government has helped these business projects to grow from small-scale to medium enterprises and beyond by providing them with funds and schemes. Such women serve as a source of inspiration for other budding female entrepreneurs who've ideas and wish to work for personal stability as well as the national economy.

5.5 *Case Studies: Transformative Impact of Women Entrepreneurs in Industry 5.0*

In the process of leveraging Industry 5.0 technologies, women entrepreneurs across South Asia are revolutionizing their respective industries. In India, VLCC was started by Vandana Luthra, who has integrated the use of AI-backed personalized wellness solutions powered by data analytics to give customers a better experience and penetrate the global market through digital transformation. Bibi Ayesha Lubna, located in Bangladesh, is leading sustainable textile production by integrating blockchain in the supply chain for transparency. She draws her business based on her ethical practices to labor and the waste generated in the environment. Similarly, Avika, which I founded in India, is an eco-friendly textile company selling sustainable fashion. She's scaled her business through e-commerce platforms and AI-driven marketing while supporting rural artisans through a digitally integrated supply chain. A few of these examples show how women entrepreneurs' use of technology and sustainable business models are helping to shape Industry 5.0.

6 Comparative Analysis: South Asia and Other Regions

In the 2021–22 report of Global Entrepreneurship Monitor (GEM) on Women Entrepreneurship, there is a variation of women's share in total entrepreneurs by region. Statistics also show that women have adopted the culture of entrepreneurship; in North America, new entrepreneurial entities are 42% women, in Europe 37%, and 27% overseas. The global proportion stands at 37%, while that of Asia is very small at 22%, including India. For Nepal, it is 18%, as for the first-time funded entrepreneurs, 4% belong to the early-stage startups, and 3% of established business owners are also expected to be affected, according to the results of a recent survey.

Table 1 Percentage of women entrepreneurs' satisfaction level in different countries

Countries/Nations/Continents	*Women entrepreneurship satisfaction (%)*
North America	42
Europe	37
Asia	22
China	8
India	12
Nepal	4
Pakistan	7

For Bangladesh, it is 16% and for other countries, it is as follows: for China, India, and Pakistan, early-stage entrepreneurs reported a satisfaction level of 8%, and 12% while the latter reported a satisfaction level of 7%. Nowadays, the countries from South Asia, predominantly India, Sri Lanka, Nepal, Bangladesh, and Pakistan, are still not very beneficial for women in starting and expanding their businesses (Table 1).

6.1 Takeaways from Other Countries

The 2021 Mastercard Index of Women Entrepreneurship (MIWE) generated a report showcasing the scope of women's entrepreneurship across the world. It showed that the United States ranked at the top of the list, with a score of 69, and proceeded with the support of female entrepreneurs. New Zealand and Canada, respectively, stood in second and third positions. India stands at 57th position out of 65 listening countries. The report was generated based on three parameters: financial accessibility of starting a new venture, knowledge and training availability, and the availability of support for the entrepreneurial journey. Females own only one-third of all small, medium, and large companies across the world. This rate ranges from 18% in South Asia to 50% in the LAC, which includes Latin America and the Caribbean.

Through the research and analytical data, we can visualize that the prospects of growth in women-led entrepreneurship are better in other continents and nations when drawing comparisons with South Asian countries. Yet, the disparity between opportunities given to men and women is still yet to be equalized. The key takeaways that can be implemented in India or its neighboring countries include government initiatives in the form of policies. One such example is the women's guarantee fund offered by the government of Rwanda to offer financial support to women entrepreneurs. Other such models include educating women in the field of entrepreneurship, similar to Germany's dual education system specially designed for women; organizations like *SCORE* and the *National Association of Women Business Owners (NAWBO) of the USA* provide networking and one-to-one opportunities for women interested in building businesses of their own. Israel understands the true value of technology-driven business models and educates women through digital literacy and technology-focused incubators. Iceland is amongst the top nations that promote gender parity and has strong legal bindings for women's participation in entrepreneurship. Sweden understands the needs of a female worker. It has a model that provides subsidized child-care units and programs along with family support policies to promote work-life balance for women (Fig. 4).

A study conducted by Emerald used data from 77 countries to calculate the Female Entrepreneurship Index (FEI) of 2015. The survey was conducted by the Global Entrepreneurship and Development Institute (GEDI) to consider the significance of women's entrepreneurship. Amongst the list of countries with prospects for women entrepreneurship, the USA held the first position with an overall score of 82 points. Australia was in second place with a score of 74. The rest of the world's average is 70, whereas the 3rd, 4th, and 5th positions were marked by the UK, Denmark, and the Netherlands, respectively. The total percentage is 61%, which means that the majority of the countries still have their ranking below 50. This, in a way, implies that in different sections around the world, women are not yet able to avail themselves of the resources. They require social and moral support to become effective business people. In general, there is evidence that the risk of doing business in these countries has been reduced and the ease of availability of resources has risen to around15% while the technological aspects have been made better, even though in the aggregate, the women entrepreneurs' engagement rate has increased to nearly 7%. Thus, it becomes imperative to understand why the increasing rate of women-engaged entrepreneurship is not in proportion with other facets of economic growth. As an added value to the body of knowledge, this study complements different parameters of the development of the economy as well as the gender parity index to determine the trend in advancing economic development on the global front. South

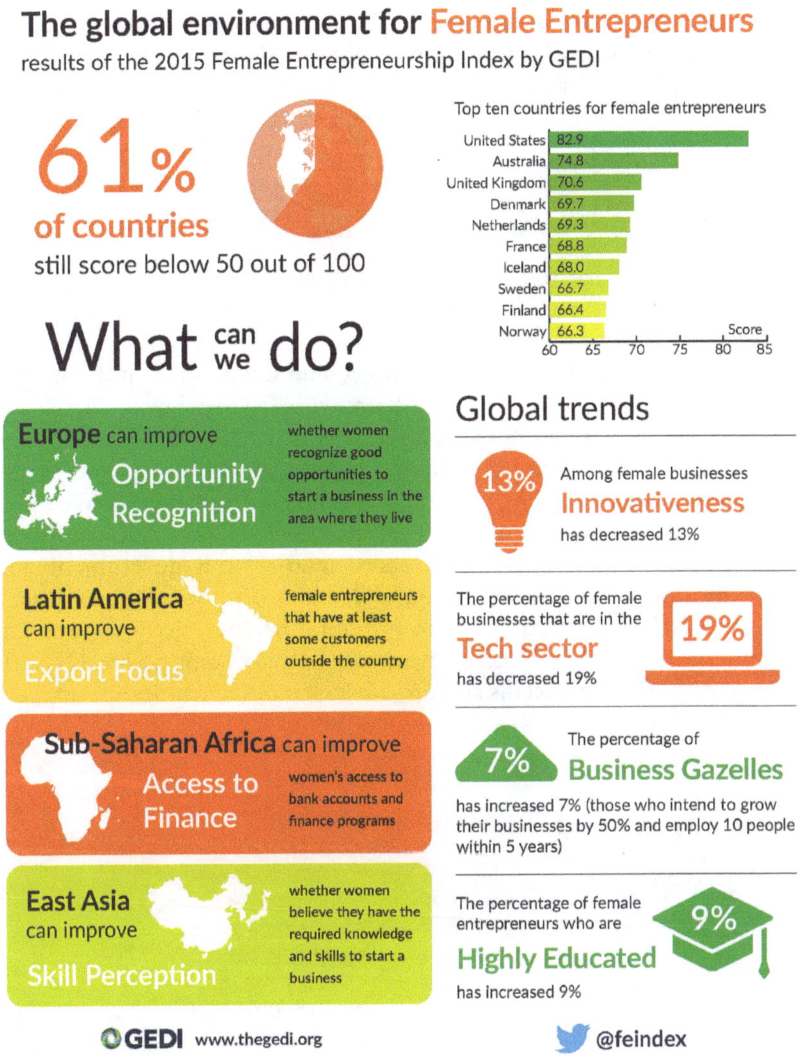

Fig. 4 Comparison of other countries for female entrepreneurship

Asian countries can seek lessons from other nations around the globe by providing them with more opportunities from the government fund, creating provisions for upskilling the scale business to expand, henceforth creating aspirations amongst other women in South Asia to explore more avenues in the field.

6.2 *The Role of Women-Led Social Enterprises in Global Contexts*

It is noteworthy that today almost 30% of all the firms are managed by women who started companies when they were relatively young and took part in the setup of more experienced businessmen. Unlike in the past, women were more likely than men to become solopreneurs in the global market with a ratio of 47 women solopreneurs for every man (Fig. 5).

The issues faced by female entrepreneurs in SAARC countries are diverse and, hence, require a more integrated approach. Specifically about developing nations, budding women entrepreneurs in South Asia must go through some form of formal education and vocational training. According to M Goyal and Parkash, both government and non-governmental organizations (NGOs) in many South Asian countries offer a low level of support to promote the education of women in entrepreneurship. Therefore, it is necessary to make some policy interventions to solve these problems and provide enhanced amenities and support

Fig. 5 Represents female entrepreneurs around the world

to women entrepreneurs (Panda and Dash 2014). Such challenges mean that education and skill improvement interventions for women entrepreneurs [9], that is, the importance of mentorship programs and developing network forums as well as training for women entrepreneurs cannot be overemphasized. This indicates that there is also a necessity for government intervention, funding opportunities, and familiarity with market conditions for the prosperity of women entrepreneurs [10]. The financial institutions and key policymakers must come up with policies and functioning to support Women Entrepreneurs even more as [9–13] they require more Government support and Finance facilities for women entrepreneurs for their success in the heart, there is a need for financial institutions to enhance the credit and financial services to women entrepreneurs.

7 Recommendations for Strengthening Women-Led Social Enterprises

7.1 Policy Recommendations

These six ecosystems that need to be redefined are:

- Entrepreneurship promotion, including the awareness and the knowledge of various entrepreneurship opportunities.
- Availability of cheap and easily accessible credit facilities;
- Education and socialization in technical and business competencies
- Entrepreneurs and peer networking; master coaching from professionals to help nurture talents and newcomers into the market.
- Existence of market linkages under domestic and international markets;
- Improved engagement with business, legal, digital as well as other higher support services for efficiency purposes and productivity.

Given this, some policy and strategic intervention to enhance women participation in Industry 5.0 is needed. Government and private sectors' need to set up dedicated women entrepreneurship funds, undergo gender sensitive industrial policies, and praise corporate partnerships to women entrepreneurship. Based on this, it is important to educate and increase the skill of girls through STEM education, introduce digital literacy programs to equip them with the required skills, and also set up mentorship networks linking successful entrepreneurs with new women's leaders. Furthermore, it helps the women led entrepreneurship through funding and microfinance, capacity building programs such as training and workshops, and cross border collaboration that allow the women entrepreneurs to create partnership across borders. By focusing on these things, women can become the engine for economic transformation in the Industry 5.0.

7.2 *Strategic Initiatives for Enhancing Impact*

A recent Standing Committee based on the information available in the 'Report on Credit Demand and Supply for Finance to MSMEs', it was only estimated that the MSME sector requires a credit of up to INR 20-25 trillion. According to data from the Global Entrepreneurship Monitor (GEM), women in India and the Republic of Korea seem least likely to attain business financing compared to their male counterparts in the market.

Women-owned business with less access to credit is a major issue in the MSMEs segment due to the absence, or lack, of collateral and physical security; common structural barriers of credit facilities include a lack of collateral to provide to financiers to establish creditworthiness and perceptual issues that may compel financiers to hesitate in offering credit to female entrepreneurs or women-led enterprises.

Since most women's businesses can be described as home-based, micro, and informal, they are constrained on experience in market areas as well as knowledge in marketing competency. More than ever, female entrepreneurs have to contend with mobility and logistics problems and time scarcity, especially in female cases due to UW, safety, and security concerns, to contain the business and obtain the necessary results for the enterprise's growth. They are also behind in the area of digital and technical skills because of low levels of literacy and the lack of mobiles and the Internet. MSCs SAFE.

7.3 *Building Resilience and Sustainability*

The framework assists in identifying the main sources of problems, most of which have led to the stagnation of female entrepreneurship in India. These show that the majority of MSMEs owned by women are more or less survival-oriented than growth-oriented. They need a secure source of income rather than the chances of wealth creation by participating in entrepreneurial activities. This needs to compel women to engage in subsistence entrepreneurship. Factors that we consider in making this choice for women include poor employment chances, the responsibility of providing care to their families at home, and limited movement and contact with other people. In essence, many women work from home and are paid on piece rates. These enterprises are also very vulnerable to external forces like virus attacks such as the current COVID-19. Bain22 indicates that the following is the market structure of the video-sharing application. The company also comes to the forefront to explain how COVID-19 affected almost 73 percent of women-led businesses in India, which is the revenue.

8 Transformative Impact of Women in Business

- Enhancing Global Competitiveness: The female business people enable their nations to compete internationally through the advancement of women's issues. Being the most powerful assets, they unlock creativity, innovation, and economic development which forms the basis of competition, especially in the global market.
- Job Creation and Economic Empowerment: There is a need for women entrepreneurs to employ themselves and other women and other marginalized persons in society. They are significant in creating new employment opportunities thus helping in lowering the unemployment rate and stability of the economy.
- Improving Social Status: Women entrepreneurs also advance their status and that of other women as they start and develop their businesses which in turn enhances society's acceptance of women in economic activities
- Elevating Living Standards for Families: Economic Independence, single, economically independent women business owners can come up with proper decisions that affect the welfare of their families.
- Empowerment in Family Decisions: Women with financial freedom can directly participate in decisions that shape the future of their children for instance the quality education and health care that the children need.
- Role Models for Rural Areas: Women entrepreneurs' role models within their communities especially in the rural setting where women are discouraged from taking up business ventures. Their success

stories motivate other women to come out of their cocoons and try their hands in the field of entrepreneurship.

- Resource Optimization: By ensuring that every available resource is fully utilized, women entrepreneurs enhance good business practices that create enthusiasm towards the establishment of their own businesses among women.
- Educating Girl Child: Creating an Ecosystem for Growth: Women role models also support the creation of environments that allow women to succeed in business. They ensure that the girl child education as they prepare for the future generation of women entrepreneurs who are capable of steering the companies and charting new frontiers.

9 Conclusion

India has been a patriarchal nation from its roots, especially women who are presumed to require financial aid from male members of the society. Women entrepreneurs face many obstacles through their entrepreneurial activities. Issues such as illiteracy, minorities, bureaucracy, production, male-centered society, low levels of managerial capacity, low levels of self-confidence etc., and cost, among other issues, are big setbacks. In different ways, pull and push factors which influence women entrepreneurs. Some of the leading businesswomen of India. The government takes several measures regarding the development of women entrepreneurs through their yearly plans. As for women they have the potential and resolution to put in place, maintain, and oversee their particular business in a very organized approach, support and motivation from the society ought to be addressed systematically.

Women entrepreneurs, as an intricate part of the national economy, can potentially be utilized to uphold India's economic growth. Realizing that this level of support will vary with the stage that the entrepreneurs are in as location, size, gender, sector, and geographic location of the client play a vital role. Likewise, certain instituted individual needs associated with ecosystems might be more than in the other States in the sense that they are more or less pronounced. The support, however, should be targeted mainly at opportunity-oriented female entrepreneurs. It is a selective approach, or in other words, it is targeted, allowing for the achievement of more meaningful results as an advocacy strategy to guarantee that such high-potential female entrepreneurs are creating more jobs.

References

1. Raman, R., Subramaniam, N., Nair, V. K., & Shivdas, A. (2022). Women entrepreneurship and sustainable development: Bibliometric analysis and emerging research trends. Sustainability, 14(15), 9160.
2. Sahoo, C. K. (2020). Women entrepreneurship in India: Problems and prospects. International Journal of Advanced Science and Technology, 29(5), 12847–12855.
3. Rajalakshmi, R. (2014). Women entrepreneurship and empowerment through education in India. IOSR Journal of Business and Management, 16(1), 30–33.
4. ESCAP. (2013). Fostering women's entrepreneurship in ASEAN: Transforming prospects, transforming societies. United Nations Economic and Social Commission for Asia and the Pacific.
5. Masih, S., & Sharma, S. H. (2022). Bridging profit and purpose through social entrepreneurship: The case of RangSutra Crafts India. Emerald Emerging Markets Case Studies, 12(2), 1–24.
6. Kanegae, H., et al. (2021). Social entrepreneurship and SDGs: Case studies in Asia. Journal of Cleaner Production, 280, 124–134.
7. Rev. Gest. Soc. Ambient. (2024). Articles on sustainability and women-led social enterprises. Revista de Gestão Social e Ambiental (RGSA), 18(1).
8. Mohiuuddin, M. (1998). Entrepreneurship development in Bangladesh: Issues and perspectives. Dhaka University Journal of Business Studies, 19(1), 125–145.
9. Goyal, M., & Parkash, J. (2011). Women entrepreneurship in India—Problems and prospects. International Journal of Multidisciplinary Research, 1(5), 195–207.
10. Panda, S. (2018). Constraints faced by women entrepreneurs in developing countries: A review and future research agenda. International Journal of Entrepreneurial Behavior & Research, 24(3), 478–493.
11. Ahammad, M. F., & Moudud-Ul-Huq, S. (2013). Women entrepreneurship development in Bangladesh: Constraints and prospects. Global Journal of Management and Business Research, 13(4), 47–56.
12. Maden, C. (2015). A gendered lens on entrepreneurship: Women entrepreneurs in Turkey. Gender in Management: An International Journal, 30(4), 312–331.
13. Ramadani, V., Dana, L. P., Ratten, V., & Tahiri, S. (2015). The context of women's entrepreneurship in developing and transitional economies: Family,

society, and culture. International Journal of Entrepreneurship and Small Business, 26(2), 169–185.
14. Al-Hossienie C.A. (2011). "Socio-Economic Impact of Women Entrepreneurship in Sylhet City, Bangladesh", Bangladesh Development Research Working Paper Series, Bangladesh [http://www.bangladeshstudies.org/files/WPS_no12.pdf]
15. Dr. Sadhna Aarya (2017). "Women Entrepreneurship- A study of Indian Scenario", [https://www.raijmr.com/ijrsml/wp-content/uploads/2017/12/IJRSML_2017_vol05_issue_10_Eng_08.pdf]
16. Anjum, M N (1995). 'Entrepreneurship Development in the northern districts of Bangladesh' October 1995, Rajshahi University, Rajshahi - 6205, Bangladesh
17. Boretos, G.P. (2009), "The future of the global economy", Technological Forecasting and Social Change, Vol. 76 No. 3, pp. 316-326.
18. Baporikar, N. (2007). entrepreneurship development & project management Himalaya publication house. 8. Damwad, (2007). Women Entrepreneurship – A Nordic Perspective, August 2007, Nordic Innovation Centre.
19. Gordon E. & Natarajan K. (2007). entrepreneurship development – Himalaya publication house, second revised edition.
20. Hena, M. H. (2006). 'Role of Women Entrepreneurs of Grameen Bank of Bangladesh: An Evaluation of Bogra Zone' (Thesis Report), November 2006, University of Rajshahi, Rajshahi - 6205, BangladeshKhan, M M H & Kraemer A. (2008). "Socio-economic factors explain differences in public healthrelated variables among women in Bangladesh: A cross-sectional study", BMC Public Health, Deutschland [http://www.biomedcentral.com/14712458/8/254]
21. Lall, Madhurima, & Sahai Shikha, (2008) Women in Family Business, presented at first Asian invitational conference on family business at Indian School of Business, Hyderabad.
22. Mahanty Sangram Keshari – fundamentals of entrepreneurship – prentice hall of India raheem a.: (2006), "role of shgs", yojana, vol. 50, no.
23. Renuka v. (2001) opportunities and challenges for women in business, India together, online report, civil society information exchange.

Human-Centered Infrastructure for Sustainable Smart Cities in Industry 5.0

Reeta Mishra, Padmesh Tripathi, and Nitendra Kumar

1 Introduction

The dawn of Industry 5.0 marks a profound and epochal shift in the trajectory of technological and societal advancement, moving decisively beyond the predominantly efficiency-driven paradigm that characterized its immediate predecessor, Industry 4.0. This nascent era is distinguished by a fundamental re-evaluation of the relationship between humanity and technology, championing a synergistic and symbiotic interplay where the unique cognitive capabilities, creative prowess, and nuanced decision-making of human beings are not supplanted but rather amplified and augmented by the sophisticated capabilities of advanced machinery and intelligent systems. At its very core lies the foundational principle of

R. Mishra
IILM University, Greater Noida, UP, India

P. Tripathi (✉)
Delhi Technical Campus, Greater Noida, UP, India
e-mail: padmesh01@rediffmail.com

N. Kumar
Amity Business School, Amity University, Noida, UP, India

© The Author(s), under exclusive license to Springer Nature Singapore Pte Ltd. 2025

P. Agarwal et al. (eds.), *Building a Human-Centred Infrastructure for Sustainable Industry 5.0 in Asia*,
https://doi.org/10.1007/978-981-95-0417-6_13

human–machine collaboration, a paradigm that envisions a future where the respective strengths of both humans and machines are not merely juxtaposed but are seamlessly integrated to achieve outcomes that would remain unattainable through the isolated application of either. Consider, for instance, the increasingly sophisticated applications within the healthcare sector in a rapidly modernizing urban center like Ghaziabad. Imagine a highly skilled neurosurgeon at a leading hospital, leveraging the unparalleled precision and stability of a state-of-the-art robotic surgical arm during an intricate and life-saving procedure. The surgeon's years of rigorous training, their intuitive understanding of complex human anatomy, and their capacity for real-time, nuanced judgment are not replaced by the robot but are instead translated into highly precise and minimally invasive movements executed by the robotic system. This real-time, collaborative partnership exemplifies the transformative potential of Industry 5.0 to not only enhance the technical capabilities within critical sectors but also to foster a more human-centered experience, prioritizing patient well-being and optimizing outcomes through the judicious and integrated application of advanced technology. This paper technique facilitates sophisticated technology and human collaboration by integrating a robust infrastructure that blends digital and physical elements. With a focus on skill development, human engagement, and well-being, Industry 5.0 promotes ergonomic workplaces and smooth human–machine collaboration. Infrastructure and human-centered solutions must work together harmoniously to create sustainable environments that encourage personalization, moral reflection, and teamwork, all of which improve the standard of living in smart cities [1].

Their influence on pandemic response, healthcare innovation, product development, the creation of nature-inclusive business models, and smart city development were the main topics of the paper. We examine the impact of these technologies on SDGs 4 (Quality Education), 9 (Industry, Innovation, and Infrastructure), 11 (Sustainable Cities and Communities), and 3 (Good Health and Well-Being). We offer a coordinated framework to improve the attainment of these objectives by incorporating these ideas into smart cities. We also present a SWOT analysis to assess this strategy. The purpose of this project is to help researchers, politicians, and businesspeople use technology to achieve the SDGs [2]. Furthermore, Industry 5.0 places an unprecedented emphasis on personalization, signaling a decisive departure from the standardized, mass-produced models that defined earlier industrial revolutions. This new era is characterized by the capacity to tailor products, services, and experiences to the highly specific and evolving needs and preferences of individual users, achieved through the sophisticated application of technologies such as artificial intelligence, advanced data analytics, and flexible manufacturing processes. Envision a resident of a burgeoning smart home within the expanding urban landscape of Ghaziabad, interacting with an intelligent, AI-driven home automation system. The paper aims to improve human well-being, sustainability, and resilience by incorporating human capabilities and cutting-edge technologies into manufacturing processes [3]. This system, through continuous learning and adaptation, anticipates the resident's daily routines, dynamically adjusts environmental parameters such as lighting, temperature, and even ambient music to their stated preferences and historical patterns, and proactively manages household tasks based on their individual schedule and anticipated needs. This granular level of personalization, powered by the intelligent analysis of vast datasets and sophisticated algorithms, significantly enhances user comfort, convenience, and overall quality of life within the urban environment. In the industrial sphere, particularly within Ghaziabad's burgeoning manufacturing sector, additive manufacturing technologies, commonly known as 3D printing, are enabling the creation of highly customized components and products tailored to the precise specifications of individual clients or niche applications. This capability not only caters to increasingly diverse and individualized demands but also promotes resource efficiency by minimizing material waste and enabling the on-demand production of bespoke solutions. The study places a strong emphasis on using AI and human-centered solutions to create sustainable smart cities [4]. The study integrates design and systems thinking and stresses a human-centric approach based on safety, inclusivity, and empowerment [5].

The principle of **resilience** constitutes another critical pillar of Industry 5.0, acknowledging the increasing interconnectedness and inherent vulnerabilities of our contemporary global systems. In an era marked by unforeseen disruptions, ranging from global health crises to the escalating impacts of climate change and the ever-present threat of cyberattacks, the ability of systems and processes to not only withstand such shocks but also to rapidly adapt and recover becomes paramount. Consider the strategic development of urban infrastructure within a future-oriented smart city in Ghaziabad, potentially leveraging the power of digital twin technology. A comprehensive digital twin, serving as a dynamic virtual replica of the city's essential infrastructure systems—encompassing its energy grid, transportation networks, water management systems, and communication networks—would allow urban planners and emergency responders to simulate a wide array of disruptive scenarios. This proactive simulation capability enables the development and refinement of robust contingency plans and optimized response strategies. In the event of a localized environmental crisis, such as severe flooding within a specific district of Ghaziabad, the digital twin could provide real-time insights into the affected areas, optimize the deployment of emergency services, dynamically reroute traffic flows, and efficiently allocate critical resources, thereby minimizing the overall impact on the city's inhabitants and facilitating a more rapid and effective recovery process. Similarly, within Ghaziabad's industrial ecosystem, the adoption of flexible and localized production capabilities, facilitated by advanced robotics, modular manufacturing systems, and additive manufacturing technologies, can significantly enhance the resilience of local businesses to global supply chain disruptions by enabling them to adapt production schedules, source materials locally when necessary, and even manufacture critical components on-demand.

Finally, **sustainability** stands as an undeniable and ethically imperative cornerstone of Industry 5.0, fundamentally integrating environmental and social responsibility into the very fabric of both industrial production and urban development. This commitment transcends mere incremental improvements in efficiency, demanding a holistic and systemic approach that considers the entire lifecycle of products, services, and infrastructure, striving towards the principles of a circular economy, minimizing negative environmental externalities, and promoting equitable social outcomes. Imagine the comprehensive implementation of a smart waste management system across the entirety of Ghaziabad, leveraging a network of interconnected IoT sensors embedded within waste receptacles. These sensors would dynamically monitor fill levels, optimize collection routes for waste management vehicles, thereby significantly reducing fuel consumption and associated greenhouse gas emissions, and provide valuable data on waste generation patterns. Furthermore, the intelligent analysis of this data, potentially through AI-powered algorithms, could identify trends and patterns in waste composition, enabling the implementation of targeted public awareness campaigns to promote more effective recycling practices and reduce the overall volume of waste generated. Within Ghaziabad's industrial sector, a growing emphasis on sustainable practices is evident in the increasing adoption of cleaner and more resource-efficient production processes, investments in renewable energy sources to power manufacturing facilities, and a conscious shift towards designing products with enhanced durability, reparability, and recyclability, contributing to a more environmentally responsible and economically viable industrial ecosystem within the region.

These fundamental principles of Industry 5.0—human–machine collaboration, personalization, resilience, and sustainability—are not abstract ideals but rather deeply intertwined and mutually reinforcing drivers in the development of **human-centered infrastructure** within the context of **sustainable smart cities**. The study offered a paradigm for creating supply chains and processes that are human-focused, sustainable, and resilient [6]. In sustainable smart cities, the study recommended enhanced data management, intelligent automation, human–machine collaboration, and superior cybersecurity [7].

Human-centered infrastructure fundamentally reorients the design and implementation of urban systems, placing the diverse needs, holistic well-being, and individual experiences of the people who interact with and are affected by it at the very forefront of consideration. According to the study, giving robots the ability to understand and react to human emotions improves human–robot collaboration. In industries including healthcare, manufacturing, and education, this promotes trust, enhances communication, and boosts productivity. Robots with emotional intelligence adjust to their users' requirements, facilitating easier communication and more efficient, sympathetic, and perceptive human–machine collaborations [8]. This approach moves decisively beyond purely utilitarian and efficiency-oriented design paradigms, consciously integrating crucial human factors such as universal accessibility for individuals of all abilities, genuine inclusivity for diverse populations and socio-economic backgrounds, the paramountcy of safety and security, the provision of comfort and convenience in daily urban life, and the deliberate creation of opportunities for meaningful social interaction and the fostering of strong community bonds. In the context of a future-oriented smart city like a technologically advanced and socially conscious Ghaziabad, this principle could manifest in the design of public transportation systems that adhere to the highest standards of universal accessibility, ensuring seamless and dignified mobility for individuals with disabilities, the elderly, and families with young children. Real-time information systems, intuitively accessible through user-friendly mobile applications and public information displays, could provide personalized route guidance, detailed accessibility information for various transportation options, and real-time updates on service disruptions, significantly enhancing the overall commuting experience for all residents, regardless of their individual needs or circumstances.

The very foundation of a truly human-centered and sustainable smart city rests upon a robust and **intelligent digital infrastructure** that is both seamlessly integrated and inherently user-friendly. Secure and interoperable data platforms are absolutely essential for the efficient and ethical collection, comprehensive analysis, and responsible sharing of the vast amounts of urban data generated by interconnected sensors, devices, and citizen interactions. Imagine the Ghaziabad Municipal Corporation operating on a unified and secure data platform that seamlessly integrates information streams from a multitude of sources, including real-time traffic sensor data, continuous environmental monitoring stations strategically located throughout the city, and invaluable feedback directly provided by citizens through dedicated online platforms and mobile applications. This rich and integrated dataset can then be analyzed using sophisticated artificial intelligence algorithms and advanced data analytics tools to identify critical patterns, predict potential challenges, and inform evidence-based decision-making across a wide range of urban domains, from optimizing traffic flow and resource allocation to enhancing public safety and improving the delivery of essential municipal services, ultimately leading to a more responsive, efficient, and citizen-centric urban environment. However, the immense power of such interconnected digital systems necessitates an unwavering commitment to robust cybersecurity measures to safeguard critical infrastructure from malicious cyber threats and to ensure the absolute privacy and security of sensitive citizen data, fostering public trust and ensuring the reliable and ethical operation of all smart city systems. Furthermore, the design of intuitive and accessible user interfaces and applications is paramount to ensure that all citizens, regardless of their level of digital literacy or technological proficiency, can readily access and meaningfully benefit from the wide array of smart city services and information resources.

Finally, the establishment of **participatory and collaborative governance frameworks** is absolutely indispensable for the successful creation and sustained operation of human-centered and sustainable smart cities. Actively and meaningfully involving citizens in the crucial processes of planning, designing, and rigorously evaluating infrastructure projects and urban policies is not merely a matter of procedural fairness but is fundamentally essential to ensure that these initiatives genuinely reflect and effectively address the diverse needs, preferences, and aspirations of the entire community. Imagine the Ghaziabad Development Authority proactively utilizing innovative online platforms, conducting inclusive community workshops, and organizing public consultations to actively solicit feedback and gather valuable insights from residents on proposed infrastructure developments, such as the creation of new green and public spaces or the strategic implementation of smart and sustainable mobility solutions. This deeply participatory approach fosters a profound sense of civic ownership, enhances the legitimacy of urban development initiatives, and ensures that the evolving urban landscape truly aligns with the collective vision and priorities of its inhabitants. Furthermore, the cultivation of strong and effective multi-stakeholder partnerships, bringing together diverse actors including government agencies at various levels, private sector enterprises with relevant expertise, leading academic and research institutions, and crucially, active and representative citizen groups, is absolutely critical for fostering a culture of innovation, leveraging diverse perspectives and resources, and ensuring the successful and sustainable implementation of complex human-centered smart city initiatives. Underlying all of these efforts must be a strong ethical framework and a commitment to responsible innovation, guiding the development and deployment of all smart city technologies with principles of fairness, transparency, accountability, and a deep respect for human rights and societal values. The convergence of Industry 5.0's transformative principles and enabling technologies with the overarching goals of sustainable smart cities, viewed through the essential lens of human-centered infrastructure development, holds the extraordinary potential to fundamentally reshape urban living in dynamic and rapidly evolving urban centers like Ghaziabad. By consistently prioritizing human well-being, actively fostering environmental sustainability, strategically promoting inclusive economic prosperity, and steadfastly strengthening social equity, these deeply integrated approaches can pave the way for the creation of more livable, resilient, and truly inclusive urban environments for all residents, ushering in a new and transformative era of urban development where technology serves not as an end in itself, but as a powerful and ethical catalyst for human flourishing and the long-term well-being of our planet.

2 Understanding the Core Concepts

2.1 *Industry 5.0: The Human-Centric Revolution*

The next industrial revolution will be based on the following fundamental principles: sustainability, resilience, personalization, and human–machine collaboration. This article explores the technologies used by Industry 5.0, including digital twins, blockchain, big data analytics, the Internet of Things, collaborative robots, and upcoming 6G systems. Three main pillars were identified by Industry 5.0: human-centric, resilient, and sustainable. They are expected to influence all three business strategies. Disaster Recovery Management Plans, Cloud Environment, Smart Education, Supply Chain Management, Smart Hospital, and Production Management are among the innovative uses of Industry 5.0. Sustainability, resilience, customisation, and rationing are the main tenets of the upcoming industrial revolution [9].

The study concentrated on blockchain-based security technologies, which are revolutionizing cybersecurity by offering transparent, decentralized, and impenetrable data protection frameworks. Blockchain improves confidence, guarantees data integrity, and fortifies authentication procedures by removing central points of failure. Its distributed ledger technology and cryptography methods make cyberattacks less successful and more challenging. Blockchain is changing cybersecurity, from protecting digital identities to averting data breaches. The robustness, transparency, and dependability of contemporary digital infrastructures in a variety of industries might be greatly improved by this technology [10]. The study offers a Reference Architecture Model for mass personalization that helps comprehend how Industry 5.0 builds on Industry 4.0 for greater sustainability and resilience by taking a human-centered approach. According to the report, Human Capital 5.0 drives cooperation with machines and technology, resulting in more sustainable and valuable products [11].

1. **Human–Machine Collaboration**: Focus on cooperation between humans and machines to enhance productivity and creativity.
2. **Personalization**: Tailoring products and services to individual needs and preferences.
3. **Resilience**: Building systems that can withstand disruptions and adapt to changes.

4. **Sustainability**: Emphasizing environmentally friendly practices and resource conservation. **Technological Enablers:Advanced Robotics**: Robots that work alongside humans in various industries. **AI (Artificial Intelligence)**: Technology that simulates human intelligence for decision-making and problem-solving. **IoT (Internet of Things)**: Network of interconnected devices that collect and exchange data. **Digital Twins**: Virtual replicas of physical systems to monitor and optimize performance. **Additive Manufacturing**: Also known as 3D printing, it creates objects layer by layer, allowing for customization. **Shifting Focus**: The emphasis is transitioning from purely automating tasks for efficiency to enhancing human well-being and creating value in society.

2.2 *Sustainable Smart Cities: Balancing Progress and Planet*

The study focused to create data-driven, smart, sustainable cities that balance the three pillars of sustainability, institutional changes are necessary [12]. An overview of sustainable smart cities worldwide is given in this study, with particular attention to their salient characteristics, obstacles, and case studies. Smart technology, environmental sustainability, equity, inclusion, and public involvement are all integrated into sustainable smart cities. The digital gap, data privacy, governance, and cooperation are some of the issues that sustainable smart cities must deal with [13].

2.2.1 *Pillars of Sustainability*

1. **Environmental Dimensions**: Protecting ecosystems and reducing pollution.
2. **Economic Dimensions**: Promoting economic growth without compromising the environment.
3. **Social Dimensions**: Ensuring equity and improving quality of life for all citizens.

2.2.2 *Smart City Technologies for Sustainability*

1. **Renewable Energy Integration**: Incorporating solar, wind, and other renewable sources into the energy grid.

2. **Smart Grids**: Intelligent electricity networks that optimize energy use and supply.
3. **Waste Management**: Technologies that enhance recycling and reduce landfill waste.
4. **Water Conservation**: Efficient systems for water usage and management.
5. **Sustainable Transportation**: Promoting public transit, biking, and electric vehicles to reduce carbon footprint.

Challenges and Opportunities: Cities face hurdles in implementing sustainable practices but also have the potential to innovate and improve urban living through new technologies and policies.

2.3 Human-Centered Infrastructure: Prioritizing People in Design and Implementation

This article offers a human-centered design methodology for next-generation transportation infrastructure that combines human-driven and connected/automated vehicles [14]. The study examines the history of the idea for creating such a comprehensive system in the context of urban and transportation planning, and it goes over a number of common methods for applying design theories to different urban settings. A history of multidisciplinary theories and a table of development patterns of context-based solutions for balancing people, spaces, and transportation are used to explain the paper's conclusions. Theoretical and practical understanding of methods for combining people, places, and transportation in urban renewal initiatives is increased by these findings. Furthermore, they could assist academics and practitioners in reexamining current urban initiatives and creating sustainable transportation plans that give people's responsibilities and public space top priority [15].

Principles of Human-Centered Design:

1. **Empathy**: Understanding the needs and experiences of users.
2. **User Needs**: Designing with the end-user in mind to improve functionality and satisfaction.
3. **Accessibility**: Ensuring that infrastructure is usable by everyone, including those with disabilities.

4. **Inclusivity**: Fostering designs that reflect diverse communities and promote participation.

Key Areas of Infrastructure: **Physical**: Infrastructure such as transportation systems, energy supply, water management, and waste disposal

1. **Digital**: Systems that support connectivity, data collection, and cybersecurity.
2. **Social**: Services and spaces that enhance education, healthcare, and community interaction. **The Role of Citizen Engagement**: Involving the community in infrastructure development ensures that projects meet the actual needs of the people and enhances public trust and collaboration.

3 The Interplay: Human-Centered Infrastructure Driving Sustainable Smart Cities in Industry 5.0

The study's focus was on human-centric smart manufacturing, which uses new technologies, human adaptability, and machine accuracy to build robust and sustainable production systems [16]. In order to promote sustainable development in Industry 5.0, the study seeks to focus industrial processes around human well-being [17].

3.1 Enhancing Quality of Life and Well-being

1. **Smart Healthcare and Personalized Wellness Infrastructure**: Implementing technology-driven healthcare solutions that cater to individual health needs.
2. **Accessible and Inclusive Smart Mobility Solutions**: Developing transportation options that are easy to use for everyone, including people with disabilities.
3. **Creation of Livable and Engaging Public Spaces**: Designing parks and community areas that encourage social interactions and activities.
4. **Smart Education and Skill Development for the Future Workforce**: Investing in educational technologies to equip people with skills for emerging job markets.

3.2 *Fostering Environmental Sustainability*

The study's objectives Interventions that focus on public education, message framing, feedback, decision making, the media, incentives and disincentives, and social marketing demonstrate how well-developed psychological research is on encouraging ecologically sustainable behaviors. A sustainable environment is actively promoted by other professions and disciplines, as well as by ethics and religion. For psychology to have a tangible impact and to draw on our present knowledge, it should be more directly, methodically, and transparently involved [18].

1. **Human-Centric Design for Energy Efficiency in Buildings and Infrastructure**: Creating buildings that are designed to minimize energy use while being comfortable and functional for occupants.
2. **Smart and Participatory Approaches to Waste Reduction and Circular Economy**: Encouraging community involvement in waste management and promoting recycling and reuse.
3. **Promoting Sustainable Behaviors through Smart City Applications**: Using technology to encourage citizens to adopt environmentally-friendly habits.
4. **Utilizing Digital Twins for Environmental Monitoring and Management**: Implementing digital replicas of physical environments to track and manage ecological conditions.

3.3 *Promoting Economic Prosperity and Resilience*

1. **Creating New Job Opportunities in Human–Machine Collaborative Industries**: Fostering industries where humans and machines work together to enhance productivity.
2. **Supporting Local Businesses and Entrepreneurship through Smart City Platforms**: Providing tools and resources to help local entrepreneurs thrive.
3. **Building Resilient Infrastructure to Withstand Climate Change and Other Disruptions**: Developing robust infrastructure that can endure natural disasters and climate impacts.
4. **Enhancing Resource Efficiency and Reducing Operational Costs**: Streamlining processes to save resources and decrease expenses for businesses and municipalities.

3.4 Strengthening Social Equity and Inclusion

1. **Designing Accessible and Affordable Smart City Services for All**: Making city services available and affordable for every citizen, regardless of their background.
2. **Addressing the Digital Divide through Inclusive Connectivity Infrastructure**: Ensuring everyone has access to the internet and technology, reducing barriers for underrepresented groups.
3. **Empowering Citizens through Data Transparency and Participation in Decision-Making**: Allowing citizens to access information and participate in local governance to foster accountability.
4. **Fostering Social Cohesion and Community Building through Smart City Initiatives**: Promoting programs that encourage collaboration and relationships among community members.

4 Key Elements of Human-Centered Sustainable Smart City Infrastructure in Industry 5.0

4.1 Smart and Adaptive Physical Infrastructure

1. **Flexible and Modular Design Principles**: This involves creating structures that can be easily adapted or modified, allowing for quick changes to meet evolving needs.
2. **Integration of Green Infrastructure and Nature-Based Solutions**: Emphasizes the use of natural elements (like parks or green roofs) in urban planning to enhance environmental sustainability and improve quality of life.
3. **Sensor-Enabled Monitoring and Predictive Maintenance**: Utilizes sensors to monitor the condition of infrastructure in real-time, allowing for proactive maintenance and minimizing disruptions.
4. **Focus on Circularity and Sustainable Materials**: Encourages the use of materials that can be reused or recycled, reducing waste and promoting sustainability in construction and urban development.

4.2 *Intelligent and User-Friendly Digital Infrastructure*

1. **Secure and Interoperable Data Platforms**: Establishes platforms that are both secure and capable of working with different systems, ensuring smooth data exchange and collaboration.
2. **Human–Machine Interfaces for Seamless Interaction**: Involves designing user interfaces that make it easy for people to interact with technology, enhancing user experience.
3. **AI-Powered Personalized Services and Recommendations**: Leverages artificial intelligence to offer customized services and suggestions to users based on their preferences and behavior.
4. **Robust Cybersecurity and Data Privacy Measures**: Prioritizes protecting user data and ensuring privacy through strong security practices, essential for maintaining public trust.

4.3 *Participatory and Collaborative Governance Frameworks*

1. **Citizen Engagement Platforms and Feedback Mechanisms**: Creates tools and channels for citizens to share their opinions and feedback, fostering a two-way communication with authorities.
2. **Multi-Stakeholder Partnerships and Co-Creation Initiatives**: Encourages collaboration between governments, businesses, and communities to jointly develop solutions for urban issues.
3. **Ethical Considerations and Responsible Innovation in Smart City Development:** Ensures that ethical standards are met in the implementation of smart technologies, considering their social implications.
4. **Transparent and Accountable Governance Structures**: Implements structures that promote transparency in decision-making and accountability of public officials, increasing trust in governance.

5 Challenges and Opportunities in Implementing Human-Centered Sustainable Smart City Infrastructure

Technological Complexity and Integration Issues: Managing the interplay of various technologies can be intricate, leading to difficulties in effectively implementing smart urban solutions.
Data Privacy and Security Concerns: The increased use of data in urban environments raises significant concerns regarding the protection of personal information and cybersecurity.
Ensuring Inclusivity and Addressing Digital Divides: It's crucial to ensure that technological advancements are accessible to all communities, especially marginalized groups that may lack access to digital tools.
Securing Funding and Investment for Sustainable Infrastructure: Attracting sufficient financial resources is essential for developing and maintaining sustainable urban infrastructure.
Overcoming Institutional Barriers and Fostering Collaboration: Existing bureaucratic hurdles can impede progress, making it vital to encourage cooperation among different stakeholders, including government, businesses, and communities.
Ethical Implications of AI and Automation in Urban Environments: The use of AI and automation raises ethical questions about employment, accountability, and how these technologies affect societal norms.

5.1 Opportunities

The study's objectives To handle the benefits and risks of smart city IoT deployments, human-centered IoT systems that are owned and run like public infrastructure are required [19]. The study illustrates the application of the INCOSE Smart Cities framework to assess and enhance human-centered smart city initiatives [20]. The study shows that technology-driven smart city implementations are less successful in tackling urban issues than human-centered smart cities, where residents are the primary agents of change through participation and empowerment [21].

Enhanced Quality of Life and Citizen Well-being: Improved urban technology can lead to better services, healthcare, and overall living conditions for residents.
Driving Innovation and Economic Growth: New technologies can spur economic development by fostering entrepreneurship and creating jobs.
Achieving Environmental Sustainability Goals: Smart urban solutions can help cities reduce their carbon footprint and promote more efficient use of resources.
Fostering Social Cohesion and Equity: Urban initiatives that focus on inclusivity can strengthen community bonds and ensure equitable access to resources.
Creating More Resilient and Livable Urban Environments: Investments in infrastructure and technology can make cities more adaptable to challenges like climate change and population growth.
Establishing Global Leadership in Sustainable Urban Development: Cities that successfully implement these strategies can become models for sustainable practices worldwide, enhancing their global standing.

6 Case Studies and Best Practices

6.1 Examples of Cities Implementing Human-Centered Smart Infrastructure

This code refers to specific cities that have adopted infrastructure designed with a focus on enhancing the quality of life for their residents. These examples may include the implementation of smart transportation systems, energy-efficient buildings, and public spaces that encourage community interaction, prioritizing the needs and well-being of citizens over mere technological advancement.

6.2 Successful Integration of Industry 5.0 Technologies in Urban Contexts

This code highlights how urban areas are successfully incorporating advanced technologies from Industry 5.0, which emphasizes human-centric solutions and collaboration between humans and machines. Examples include the use of robotics and AI to improve urban services, enhance manufacturing with worker input, and promote sustainable practices that benefit both communities and the environment.

6.3 *Innovative Approaches to Citizen Engagement and Co-Creation*

This code discusses new methods for involving citizens in the decision-making processes concerning urban development. This could involve participatory planning sessions, digital platforms for feedback, or collaborative projects where residents actively participate in creating and designing public initiatives, ensuring that their voices and needs are considered in urban planning.

6.4 *Models for Sustainable Infrastructure Development and Financing*

This code refers to frameworks or strategies used for developing infrastructure in a way that is financially viable and environmentally sustainable. It includes innovative financing mechanisms, such as public–private partnerships or green bonds, and emphasizes long-term planning that balances economic growth with ecological stewardship, ensuring infrastructure can be maintained without depleting resources.

7 Conclusion

In the context of Industry 5.0, where human skills synergize with advanced technology, the development of sustainable smart cities hinges critically on the adoption of human-centered infrastructure, which prioritizes the experiences and needs of urban dwellers; this necessitates the integration of key principles such as sustainability, inclusivity, effective technology deployment, and active community involvement, as these form the bedrock of successful smart city development. Embracing this approach promises numerous benefits, including an enhanced quality of life for residents, stimulated economic development, and the preservation of the environment; however, it also presents challenges related to equitable technology access, safeguarding individual privacy, and the imperative for supportive and adaptive policies. Future progress in this domain will necessitate collaborative research and innovation across various sectors to explore novel approaches that further optimize smart city initiatives, ultimately envisioning a future where technological advancements are seamlessly aligned with fundamental human values and a deep commitment to environmental stewardship, thereby creating urban environments that are not only intelligent and efficient but also inherently equitable, supportive, and thriving for all residents within a sustainable ecosystem.

References

1. Daoud, A. O., Kineber, A. F., Ali, A. H., & Elseknidy, M. (2025). Empowering Sustainable Infrastructure and Sustainable Development Goals Through Industry 5.0 Implementation. *Sustainable Development.*
2. Adel, A., & Alani, N. H. (2024). Human-Centric Collaboration and Industry 5.0 Framework in Smart Cities and Communities: Fostering Sustainable Development Goals 3, 4, 9, and 11 in Society 5.0. *Smart Cities*, *7*(4), 1723.
3. Verma, D. (2024). Industry 5.0: A Human-Centric and Sustainable Approach to Industrial Development. *Int. J. Soc. Relev. Concern*, *12*(5).
4. Ramírez-Gordillo, T., Mora, H., Maciá-Lillo, A., Amador, S., & Gil, D. (2023, April). Human-centric solutions and AI in the smart city context: the industry 5.0 perspective. In *The International Research & Innovation Forum* (pp. 193–203). Cham: Springer International Publishing.
5. Dehbozorgi, M. H., Postell, J., Ward, D., Leardi, C., Sullivan, B. P., & Rossi, M. (2024). Human in the loop: revolutionizing industry 5.0 with design thinking and systems thinking. *Proceedings of the Design Society*, *4*, 245-254.
6. Ivanov, D. (2023). The Industry 5.0 framework: viability-based integration of the resilience, sustainability, and human-centricity perspectives. *International Journal of Production Research*, *61*(5), 1683–1695.
7. Adel, A. (2023). Unlocking the future: fostering human–machine collaboration and driving intelligent automation through industry 5.0 in smart cities. *Smart Cities*, *6*(5), 2742–2782.
8. Mishra, R., Tripathi, P., & Kumar, N. (2024). Application of Emotional Intelligence in Improvement of Human-Robot Collaboration. In *Human-Machine Collaboration and Emotional Intelligence in Industry 5.0* (pp. 251–267). IGI Global.
9. Singh, J., & Verma, K. K. (2024). Industry 4.0 to Industry 5.0: A Paradigm Shift towards Sustainable and Human Centric Production. *COMMERCE RESEARCH REVIEW*, *1*(2), 68–75
10. Mishra, R., Kumar, K., Mehta, S. N., & Chadhuary, N. (2024, March). Exploring the Effects of Block Chain-Based Security Systems on Cyber Security. In *2024 2nd International Conference on Disruptive Technologies (ICDT)* (pp. 687–692). IEEE.

11. Aheleroff, S., Huang, H., Xu, X., & Zhong, R. Y. (2022). Toward sustainability and resilience with Industry 4.0 and Industry 5.0. *Frontiers in Manufacturing Technology*, *2*, 951643.
12. Bibri, S. E. (2021). A novel model for data-driven smart sustainable cities of the future: the institutional transformations required for balancing and advancing the three goals of sustainability. *Energy Informatics*, *4*(1), 4.
13. AlZu'bi, S., Hendawi, S., Elbes, M., Kanan, T., & Mughaid, A. (2023, August). Towards a Sustainable Future: Exploring Key Features, Challenges, and Global Examples of Building Smart Cities. In *2023 International Conference on Information Technology (ICIT)* (pp. 284–291). IEEE.
14. Feng, Y., Chen, Y., Zhang, J., Tian, C., Ren, R., Han, T., & Proctor, R. W. (2024). Human-centred design of next generation transportation infrastructure with connected and automated vehicles: a system-of-systems perspective. *Theoretical Issues in Ergonomics Science*, *25*(3), 287-315.
15. Yang, L., Majumdar, A., van Dam, K. H., & Zhang, L. (2022, December). Theories and practices for reconciling transport, public space, and people–a review. In *Proceedings of the Institution of Civil Engineers-Municipal Engineer* (Vol. 175, No. 4, pp. 187–203). Thomas Telford Ltd.
16. Zhang, C., Wang, Z., Zhou, G., Chang, F., Ma, D., Jing, Y., ... & Zhao, D. (2023). Towards new-generation human-centric smart manufacturing in Industry 5.0: A systematic review. *Advanced Engineering Informatics*, *57*, 102121.
17. Leng, J., Sha, W., Wang, B., Zheng, P., Zhuang, C., Liu, Q., ... & Wang, L. (2022). Industry 5.0: Prospect and retrospect. *Journal of Manufacturing Systems*, *65*, 279–295.
18. Kazdin, A. E. (2009). Psychological science's contributions to a sustainable environment: Extending our reach to a grand challenge of society. *American Psychologist*, *64*(5), 339.
19. Bergés, M., & Samaras, C. (2019). A path forward for smart cities and IoT devices. *IEEE Internet of Things Magazine*, *2*(2), 2-4.
20. CSEP, J. L. R. E., Dugar, J., & III, J. W. S. (2024, July). Human-centered Smart Cities: An evaluation of a small community using the Smart Cities Initiative framework. In *INCOSE International Symposium* (Vol. 34, No. 1, pp. 1211–1226).
21. Oliveira, Á., & Campolargo, M. (2015, January). From smart cities to human smart cities. In *2015 48th Hawaii international conference on system sciences* (pp. 2336–2344). IEEE.

FSC
www.fsc.org
MIX
Papier | Fördert gute Waldnutzung
FSC® C083411

Kolibri 360 GmbH
Ferdinand-Jühlke-Straße 7
99095 Erfurt, Deutschland
produktsicherheit@kolibri360.de